Culture and Development
No. 5

General Editor
Kapila Vatsyayan

Life-style and Ecology

UNESCO Chair in the field of Cultural Development

Indira Gandhi National Centre for the Arts

Life-style and Ecology

Edited by
Baidyanath Saraswati

Indira Gandhi National Centre for the Arts
New Delhi

D.K. Printworld (P) Ltd.
New Delhi

Cataloging in Publication Data — DK

Life-style and ecology / edited by
Baidyanath Saraswati.
(Culture and development series; no. 5).
Includes bibliographical references.

1. Human ecology — India. I. Saraswati, Baidyanath, 1932- II. Series : Culture and development series; no. 5.

ISBN 81-246-0103-8

First Published in India in 1998

Publishers
Indira Gandhi National Centre for the Arts
Central Vista Mess, Janpath, New Delhi - 110001

D.K. Printworld (P) Ltd.
Regd. office ; '*Sri Kunj*', F-52, Bali Nagar, New Delhi - 110015

Printed in India

Foreword

Kapila Vatsyayan

ONE of the main programmes of the Indira Gandhi National Centre for the Arts is the Lifestyle Studies, which aim at exploring all fields of cultural knowledge with a view to understanding the structure and function of various communities in their totality. So far societies have been studied in linear, unidimensional form, by such disciplines as anthropology, sociology, economics, politics, science, history, art-history, development planning, etc. The Centre is evolving a model of studies based on the premise that life is not fragmented into separate dimensions, neither can a model replicate in full a total picture of the cultural life of the diverse groups and communities. It addresses itself to fundamental questions regarding Man's relationship with the Cosmic Order, his worldview on the manifestation of Space for various purposes through various mediums, his perception of Time through the ages and across cultures, his experience of Nature with reference to the Five Elements (Earth, Water, Fire, Air and Sky), and his symbiotic relationship with Nature.

Pilot studies are being initiated on the interrelationship of nature, ecology, social structure, worldview, cosmology, daily routine, lifecycle, annual calendar, knowledge, skills, traditional technologies and artistic manifestations. Through specific community studies the interdependence in the arts, mutual influence amongst regions and interrelationship of the 'tribal', rural and urban, the literary and oral traditions are investigated. These studies often culminate in a monograph, audio-visual documentation and/or cartographical presentation of specific aspects of arts and crafts. The field studies also provide information to evolve computerizable modules for conducting further studies.

I am happy to introduce the first thematic monograph in this series of Pilot Studies.

Contents

Introduction

Nature as Culture

Baidyanath Saraswati

THE essays here collected are the result of the IGNCA Pilot Studies of Lifestyles carried out in four different locations, namely, the high Himalayas of the Garhwal region, the rich forests of Western Ghats in South India, the enchanting archipelago of Lakshadweep in the Arabian Sea, and the coastal village of the fisherfolk located above Cape Comorin. The authors of the essays are knowledgeable experts — ecologist, anthropologist and folklorist of repute. In what follows we may briefly highlight the essence of each of these contributions.

The contribution by the ecologist Madhava Gadgil is an excellent overview of the field of ecology and traditional resource management systems. Investigating the several different worldviews in relation to ecologically prudent resource use practices, the author has arrived at the conclusion that scientific prescriptions often resemble or parallel 'pre-scientific' prescriptions based on traditional ecological knowledge and simple rules of thumb. An important point which has been stressed here is that with all its power, modern science seems unable to halt and reverse the depletion of resources and the degradation of the environment. The reason for this, he says, may be that scientific resource management, and Western reductionist science in general, developed in the service of the utilitarian, exploitative "dominion over nature" worldview of colonialists and developers.

The anthrolopist R.S. Negi dwells on the symbiotic relationship between man, animal and nature in the Garhwal Himalaya. Rich in ethnographic details, the paper highlights the sociocultural aspects of the Muslim Gujar pastoralists. Their concept of time and space, defined as ecological and structural, has a special significance for pastoral lifestyles which follow horizontal seasonal migration between two ecozones and transhumant mode of subsistence based on buffalo herd. Addressing the strategies of life-support and herd raising, the author finds that the Gujars are ideally adapted to the requirements of the pastoral ecosystem. He also touches on their knowledge of the various diseases that the buffaloes suffer from, and gives a good account of Gujar cosmology and belief system. On the recent changes from pastoral nomadism to sedentarisation and rehabilitation, his analysis indicates that Gujars today use their experiential knowledge for over-exploitation of the forest resources, allowing no opportunity for regeneration. This, he says, eventually goes against their own interest.

The ecologist M.D. Subash Chandran presents a case study of an ancient sacred grove in the Western Ghats. Introducing the concept of sacredness of trees, primarily by examples from different parts of the world, he turns to the Indian scenario where Hindus maintain sacred forests all over. Giving scriptural and historical references of sacred groves and trees, the author shows continuity of the sacred tradition through the ages. In particular, the sacred *kans* forest rich in biological diversity is identified as the property of the village Gods. This central belief has played an important role in the conservation of biodiversity and helped regeneration and restoration of the degraded forests around. Decline of the *kans* begins with the decline of faith. Also the State domination over the forest and subsequent exploitation by forest-based industries, followed by negative change in Indian attitude toward nature, have caused disappearance of sacred groves. Finally, what seems evident is the fact that the groves, once an integral part of the village landscape and ecosystem, are no more sacred.

The anthropologist Makhan Jha has taken fishing and coconut as the dual entry point for studying the cultural perception of the Muslim islanders of Lakshadweep. Describing and illustrating their lifestyle, he arrives at the conclusion that the island culture and its ecology are inseparable in their structure and function. He brings sophistication to the study of the islanders' knowledge of the sea, flora and fauna, space and time, and cosmos by referring to the people's historical background as well as the existing ecological setup. It has been pointed out that some of their archaic pre-Islamic traditions, folklore, folksong, belief in spirit, myth and mysterious dreams are shaped and determined by ocean ecology. But it is feared that since the natural eco-system today is greatly influenced by man-made structure, the old cultural values and traditions may become extinct soon.

The folklorist John Samuel has studied Christian Mukkuvar, a marine fishing community in Kannyakumari district of Tamil Nadu. The first part is devoted to Mukkuvar's conversion to Christianity. The impact of Christianity on their life and culture is said to be both positive and negative. The author turns to account their cultural perception of soil, flora and fauna, seasons, ocean currents, winds, cycles of the sea, the atmosphere (sky), the fire, the sun, the moon, and the divine fish, in order to initiate an analysis of the Mukkuvar worldview. This also helps understand their tools and techniques of fishing. A glimpse of their cycle, and associated beliefs and rituals provide the distinctive features that make a Mukkuvar culture what it is. While considering the implication of oral tradition and its modification at each generation, as witnessed today, the author has been prudent enough to draw our attention back to the Mukkuvar's intrinsic uniqueness.

In conclusion, the contributions to this volume provide us with a new perspective in ecology and culture. We wish to stress the point that the examples presented here are sufficient to give the savour of distinction between traditional sacred science and modern reductionist science. Anthropology, the modern science of man and culture, has given us two incompatible maxims: *cultura ex cultura* and *cultura ex natura*. Culturalists grant cultural phenomena as autonomous and efficient agent of themselves. Naturalists, on the other hand, attribute cultural forms to nature, that is, cultural forms are said to have evolved from nature. In other words, culture is a step beyond nature. Both these perceptions have given rise to what might be called the "ladder mentality". The ladder symbolizes a climb through simple to complex, from instinct to intelligence, from non-living to living, from less conscious to more conscious, from inorganic elements to plants, to animals to humans, from savagery to barbarism to civilization. In each case, the ladder refers to a progressive development. In contrast, the present studies have shown that there is an existential connection between nature and culture. Man cannot live without nature, for he cannot live without spirit either. For instance, despite their conversion to non-Hindu religion, the Himalayan pastoral nomads, the Lakshadweep islanders and the Mukkuvar fisherfolk follow the spirit of the natural world, not in imitation of olden times but in continuation of the primal vision. There is enough evidence to say that the initiatic lifestyles of traditional cultures all over the world are built around nature. It is this mystery of inseparability of nature and culture which has to be understood in regard to the lived experience of traditional societies.

1

Traditional Resource Management Systems

Madhav Gadgil

Human influence on natural systems has often been portrayed as destructive. It is only relatively recently that ecologists have started to appreciate how traditional peoples use their resources without destroying them. For many marine ecologists, Johannes' *Words of the Lagoon* (1981) brought this point home. Several studies have documented systems of traditional knowledge (Ruddle and Johannes, 1985; McNeely and Pitt, 1985; Freeman and Carbyn, 1988). Others showed that community-based resource management systems worked because of the presence of appropriate common property *institutions*, not merely because of a superabundance of resources (McCay and Acheson, 1987; Berkes, ed., 1989). Particularly rich case studies came from agroecosystems, showing how traditional peoples interacted or co-evolved with (Norgaard, 1984) their environment, modifying nature but actively maintaining it in a diverse and productive state (Gliessman *et al.*, 1981; Irvine, 1989).

Different human societies have elaborated a striking diversity of ways of working with nature. Many of these are ecologically adaptive, but this is not to say that all of them make ecological sense. Some certainly do not, and some may have become ecologically maladaptive. The point, however, is that the diversity of traditional resource use practices represents a pool of human experience spanning many millennia and many cultures. The conservation of this rapidly diminishing pool of experience, a kind of cultural diversity, is as pressing as the conservation of biological diversity (Gadgil, 1987).

The irony is that, as scientists are beginning to appreciate folk ecology and its implications, a monolithic vision of modern management is engulfing these traditional systems. This is an underlying theme of the present paper, which proceeds through a number of interrelated themes. First, different world-views are examined in relation to the evolution of ecologically prudent resource use practices. Second, the paper examines traditional views of the world as an interacting community of beings. This leads to a discussion of belief systems and prescriptions for restricted resource use and a synthesis of some resource management 'rules of thumb' that emerge from that experience.

The paper then reviews similarities between old and new conservation prescriptions and explores the questions of why modern scientific resource management has been so ineffectual in bringing about ecologically sustainable use and how the science of ecology may fit into a new synthesis of old and new environmental wisdom. In keeping with the holistic approach developed in the paper, an eclectic diversity of examples, not just from the marine environment but also from terrestrial and freshwater environments, is used.

Ecological Prudence

It is generally known that the way in which various societies approach the utilization of their natural resource base depends on their perception and experience of how it responds to patterns of resource use. For example, if the resource base is perceived as fluctuating in a capricious fashion regardless of how it is used, a society would tend to impose few restraints on its use. Some hunting-gathering and herding societies are likely to behave in this fashion. Societies that perceive their resource base as infinite, and in fact ever-expanding by virtue of technological advances, are even less likely to observe any resource use restraints. Agrarian societies colonizing new lands, as during European settlement of new overseas territories, or the early industrial societies confident of the ability of technology to take care of any problems of resource exhaustion that may arise, adopt this approach.

It is when the resource base is perceived as well-demarcated, finite and sensitive to the resource-use pattern that societies are most likely to stress restrained, sustainable patterns of resource-use. Many horticultural societies, or those combining fishing with horticulture, have developed sustainable resource-use practices, and it is possible to examine the conditions under which ecological prudence has presumably evolved. These societies are characterized by plant cultivation without the use of the plough or iron implements. Particular methods of cultivation tie them to a specific, rather restricted locality for extended periods of time. Given a simple technological base and an inability to engage in large-scale land clearance, these horticulturists live in small communities of a few hundred individuals, cultivating small plots of land surrounded by extensive tracts of land under natural vegetation. Consequently hunting, fishing and gathering of a whole variety of resources from a finite territory is critical to their subsistence. Such communities are linked together in societies of very modest size, around 100 and 6,000 for simple and advanced horticultural societies, respectively (Lenski and Lenski, 1978).

Prudent resource use is likely to be of survival value for such societies, for they are often in acute territorial conflict with neighbouring societies. At the same time, any serious resource shortages, even if short-lived and seasonal, are apt to seriously weaken the ability of these societies to withstand assaults on their territories by their neighbours. Such societies may therefore be in danger of cultural, if not genetic, extermination if they exhaust their resource base. This may have favoured the evolution of cultural traditions of prudent use (Gadgil, 1987).

"Community of Beings" vs. "Dominion over Nature"

Many horticultural societies seem to have elaborated a world-view which provides the underpinning for a whole range of practices of restrained resource-use. They often either have no conception at all of a single supreme creator, or believe that such a creator has little concern with human affairs. Instead they impute sacred qualities to a number of landscape elements, plants and animals in their own immediate surroundings. Indeed, their world is perceived as a community of beings: rocks, rivers, trees, birds and beasts with whom humans are linked in a variety of ways. Rivers may be seen as mothers, altruistically bestowing waters that are valued; trees as demons that need to be placated by offerings so that they will reciprocate by not harming people; antelopes as brethren for whose killing one must apologize.

It appears that horticultural societies are characterized by a number of conditions conducive to the evolution of a "community of beings" world-view: small community size, the presence of extended kin groups, repeated social interactions, and a geographically well-defined resource base. However, many other non-industrial societies also show many or most of these characteristics. In fact, many rural societies of the contemporary world do this as well.

It is not surprising, therefore, that a "community of beings" world-view is not restricted to horticulturists. In general, these beliefs go back to the pantheistic tradition dominant before the rise of monotheistic religions. Such pantheistic traditions still exist in some modern hunter-gatherer groups (Tanner, 1979). They existed in pre-Christian Europe, survived for a time in the Christian mysticism of St. Francis (White, 1967), and their remnants may still be found today, for example in rural Irish society (Nuala Ni Dhomhnaill, personal communication). Similarly, under Islam pantheism is in the traditions of many cultures, including many in Africa (Omari, 1990) and North Asia (Martynov, 1988). It is seen also among the native peoples of Australia and the Americas (Williams and Hunn, eds., 1982).

By contrast, there is no identification with nature in the "dominion over nature" world-view. The roots of this world-view, however named, have been hotly debated (Capra, 1982). It may be argued that this world-view derives from the Judaeo-Christian tradition and early European science, as well as from the values and perspectives that emerge from the Industrial Revolution.

If the "community of beings" world-view can be characterized as an "I — thou" relationship between humans and nature, the "dominion over nature" world-view is characterized as an "I — it" relationship. Nature is viewed as clockwork and is considered to exist separately from humans (Worster, 1977). It can be studied by taking it apart and by asking systematic, testable questions. It can be brought under control and made to yield human benefits. Economic growth is seen as a consequence of somehow freeing these limitless resources. Productive activity, therefore, is seen as a process of overcoming environmental constraints.

Resource management science in the employ of the "dominion over nature" world-view has given us the MSY concept to maximize fish yields and has paved the way for the giant trawlers, seiners and drift-netters of today. It has also given us such management techniques as clear-cutting large tracts of land and predator control. Utilitarian approaches such as these have clashed not only with the "community of beings" world-view but also with the naturalist-ecological tradition in the West (Worster, 1977).

Regier *et al.* (1989) use the term "conventional exploitative development" to refer to the utilitarian ideology which has dominated resource management science in the West. They have pointed out that more ecologically sensible alternatives are available, and further, that these alternatives are beginning to take a foothold in some parts of the West (Regier *et al.*, 1989). Some of these alternatives are consistent with traditional ecological views.

Traditional Ecosystem Views

Many traditional societies view physical as well as biological components of the environment and the human population as being linked together in a web of relationships. This is akin to the modern ecosystem view of the natural world. By ecosystem view we mean a holistic view that takes into account all ecosystem components and their interactions, including those involving human societies.

The beginnings of the ecosystem concept in Western science go back to von Humboldt's writings of 1807, but traditional ecosystem ideas may extend as far back as the ancient Sumerians, according to one review of the historical development of the concept (Major, 1969). One particular ecosystem concept, that of a watershed managed as a unit with interacting components of water, land, plants and animals, crops up in several ancient cultures. There are written records going back nine centuries to show that Swiss communes controlled watersheds and used watershed resources in an integrated fashion (M.F. Price, personal communication). In Japan the use of the watershed ecosystem idea goes back at least to the 1600s (R. Hunt, personal communication). There are records showing that in the Ottoman Empire Sultan Mehmed II instituted watershed conservation measures (prohibition of overgrazing, prohibition of tree-cutting, river bank stabilization, and the revegetation of the catchment area) in the river basin supporting Constantinople (later Istanbul) when he captured that city in 1453 (Gurpinar, 1978). Table 1.1 summarizes a diversity of traditional ecosystem views and practices from a variety of different cultures and geographical areas. Amerindians of the west coast of North America 'managed' their salmon fisheries and a number of other marine resources, depending on the area, through a variety of traditional practices, rituals and taboos signifying respect. The key to this management system was the territorial control of resources. By the early 20th century, however, these native systems were overpowered by commercial salmon fishing interests and open-access conditions created in place of communal management (Rogers, 1979).

Although there was much variation in resources use practices from area to area, the general picture is that of a nested system of rights. For example, the entire Nass River watershed in northern British Columbia was claimed as traditional land by the Nishga tribe. Each Nishga community used one part of the watershed. Some fisheries were conducted communally, but specific salmon fishing sites were controlled by individuals on behalf of 'house' groups or the local divisions of clans. Thus there was a hierarchy of control of resource use rights, from the watershed level down to specific fishing sites (Berkes, 1985).

Table 1.1

A Summary of Some Traditional Ecosystem Views

System	*Country / region*	*Reference*
Watershed management of salmon rivers and associated hunting and gathering areas by tribal groups and kin groups	Amerindians of coastal British Columbia, Canada	Williams and Hunn, eds. (1982)
Delta and lagoon system management for fish culture (*tambak* in Java), and the integrated cultivation of rice and fish	South and Southeast Asia, especially Indonesia	Lasserre and Ruddle (1983)
Vanua (in Fiji), which refers to land-water area and its water, soil, plants, animals and human occupants seen as an interrelated whole	Parts of Oceania, including Fiji, Solomon islands	Baines (1984) Hviding (1989)
The caste system, in which different endogamous groups hold exclusive rights and responsibilities for the use and management of specific resources	Indian subcontinent	Gadgil (1985a, 1985b)
The integrated resource management system (*dina*), in which farming, grazing and fishing territories are shared by different social groups through reciprocal arrangements for access	Mali, Africa	Moorehead (1989) Fay (1989)

In Southeast Asia the use of brackish water fish-ponds (*tambaks*) dates back as far as the 15th century (Lasserre and Ruddle, 1983). Since delta and lagoon systems often extend inland, fish cultivation in *tambaks* can be integrated with rice culture. These rice irrigation systems (*subaks*) are not merely autonomous local-level management units. In Bali, for example, *subaks* are part of a water temple system, and the entire regional terrace ecosystem is managed as a unit (Lansing, 1987). Thus, the integration of *tambak* and *subak* systems for combined rice and fish cultivation, as practised in some areas, is a sophisticated application of the relatively recent ecological idea of the coupling of land and water systems (Hasler, ed. 1974).

The terms *vanua* in Fiji and *puava* in the Solomon Islands refer to the intimate association of individuals with land, reef, lagoon, and all that grows on or in them (Baines, 1984). *Vanua* refers to a land-sea continuum, but it has social-cultural as well as biological-physical dimensions. As Hviding (1989) puts it, *puava* is "a defined, named area of land and in most cases sea. A *puava* in the widest sense includes all areas and resources associated with a *butubutu* (descent group) through ancestral rights, from the top of mainland mountains to the open sea outside the barrier reef".

The caste system of the Indian subcontinent may also be seen as a traditional ecosystem approach. Caste groups may be considered a human-ecological analogue of 'species' specializing on different resources. Caste society, which crystallized around the 5th century, promoted sustainable resource use by restricting access to many specialized resources of a given locality to members of just one endogamous group (some 40,000 of them in total). Both rights to and responsibilities for the use of a specific resource vested in one group. This improved the feasibility of the long-term conservation of that resource.

Further, just as the resources of a specific area are linked together, members of different endogamous groups were also linked together in a network of reciprocal exchange and mutual obligations. The overall picture is one of an ecosystem in which different human groups assumed specialized but interconnected 'niches', interconnected not only functionally but also culturally through time-honoured practices and reciprocal obligations (Gadgil, 1985b; Gadgil and Malhotra, 1983).

The *dina* system of Mali also provides for integrated resource management through resource specialization by different groups. The system was formalized in the 19th century by codifying the then existing resource management systems into grazing, fishing and farming territories. Resource specialists were ethnic or tribal groups and much fewer in number than in India. In the inland delta of the Niger river, for example, the Bozo people specialized in shallow water fishing whereas the Somono people specialized in net fishing. The farmers consisted of four ethnic groups, and among the herders the Fulani people were the dominant group (Moorehead, 1989). Detailed rules of access governed productive activities and provided for reciprocal rights for the various groups. Fishing, for example, was regulated by "masters of the water", who supervised the use of allowable techniques, set opening dates for different fisheries, could extend fishing rights to outsiders (for a tithe) and conducted ceremonies for water deities (Moorehead, 1989; Fay, 1989).

There is relatively little historical information about how these various ecosystem approaches developed. Geertz (1963), however, has traced some 400 years of the history of paddy rice culture in Indonesia. He found that as the system developed from less intensive modes of agriculture, productivity was increased through the building of dikes, terraces and irrigation canals. Water was managed for weed control and nutrient retention. At the same time, the developing irrigation technology necessitated the parallel development of appropriate common property institutions for collective action. The users established ways of collective decision-making and resource management, since the maintenance of the irrigation work and the security of food production depended upon the cooperation of all participants. Thus Norgaard (1984) comments, "contrary to the view of growth as a process of overcoming environmental constraints, the coevolutionary perspective emphasizes an increasingly important, and frequently more complex, interaction between man and his environment".

Such a view, whether in *subak* maintenance or in the management of Pacific salmon stocks, is ecologically more sensible than the conventional developers' view of achieving dominion over nature. Closely linked, two-way feedback interactions and reciprocal responses of the social system and the natural system, or coevolution, is an appropriate paradigm under which resource management activities can be structured. In general, traditional resource management fundamentally differs from the utilitarian approach in emphasizing interaction and co-existence rather than control, and by incorporating personal — spiritual components instead of an impersonal I — it relationship with nature.

Restraints on Resource Use

These various traditional ecosystem approaches require a belief system which includes a number of prescriptions for restrained resource use. It is of course possible that such apparent restraint may have nothing to do with long-term conservation of the resource base. A harvester interested in the calculus of immediate return may still not use a resource if the net gain obtainable from it is below a certain threshold, or lower than the net gain obtainable from alternative resources. We must therefore examine each supposed instance of restraint to assess whether it could involve such a discontinuation of resource use, for instance, because the cost of harvest has increased excessively (Johannes, 1978; Smith, 1983; Borgerhoff-Mulder, 1988).

The range of practices pertaining to restrained resource use by human groups may be classified under ten broad categories:

(i) There may be a quantitative restriction by harvesters on the amount of harvest of a given resource stock of a species or from a given locality. The imposition of such quotas implies that harvesting is halted at resource densities greater than those at which individuals would find the net gains too low to continue. As a corollary, these quotas are likely to enhance total yields on a long-term basis, at the sacrifice of some immediate return. These are therefore likely to be genuine instances of restraint.

(ii) Harvesting a certain resource may be abandoned when resource densities decline. In parts of New Guinea, for example, the hunting of birds of paradise is temporarily abandoned if their populations decline (Eaton, 1985). Such a response is expected from harvesters attempting to maximize short-term net gain, since a fall in resource density would progressively increase the cost of harvesting. It is possible, though perhaps less probable, that harvesting may be abandoned well before this level is reached, in the interest of long-term yields. Such management has been documented by Feit (1986) for Canadian subarctic hunter-trapper-fishermen.

(iii) Harvesting from a certain habitat patch may be abandoned if yields from that patch are reduced. Thus in the Torres Strait, fishing may be stopped in regions where fish yields are known to have declined (Nietschmann, 1985). This again is the response expected from a forager attempting to maximize immediate net returns, and could be related to long-term resource conservation only if concrete quantitative evidence is available that harvesting is abandoned before returns reach a value low enough to justify abandoning it.

(iv) Harvesting of a certain species may be abandoned in a certain season. Illustrative here is the taboo in many Indian villages on hunting certain animals in the four months from July to October (Gadgil, 1985a). In the Torres Strait, hunting and fishing are carried out in phases with appropriate tides, winds, seasons and sea conditions, which renders them highly sporadic over time (Nietschmann, 1985). It is possible that this is a consequence of returns that are too low to justify harvesting for immediate gains in a particular season. Conversely, if in fact net returns in that season are expected to be relatively high, it is likely to be a conservation measure.

(v) Harvesting from a certain habitat patch may be abandoned in certain seasons or years. In James Bay certain fishing grounds are regularly rotated or fallowed

(Berkes, 1977), and the same is done with goose hunting areas, creating, in effect, a shifting sanctuary system (Berkes and Freeman 1986). Again, this could possibly be a response to an excessively low level of net gain from that habitat patch in that season or at those times. This should be verified by comparing it with net gains in other seasons, and if possible by a quantitative assessment.

(vi) The harvest of certain life history stages by age, sex, size or reproductive status may be prohibited. For example, in the village of Kokre-Bellur in the southern Indian state of Karnataka, birds breeding at a heronry may be left unmolested, though they may be hunted elsewhere and in other seasons (Gadgil, 1985b). Similarly, Cree Amerindian waterfowl hunters in the James Bay coastal wetlands avoid critical goose feeding areas and do not hunt during the breeding season (Berkes, 1982). If such protected stages appear to be critical to population replenishment, and if they are likely to yield net gains as high as or higher than the unprotected stages, it is reasonable to assume that this measure is designed specifically to conserve the resource. On the other hand, if these stages are likely to yield lower net returns in comparison with the unprotected stages, then they might be left out of the harvest simply in the interest of maximizing immediate net gains.

(vii) The harvest of certain species may be prohibited. Some species are never harvested because of the relative difficulty of procuring them or the risk of injury during hunting, or they may carry parasites that can affect humans. If these conditions do not operate, then conservation can indeed serve the long-term interests of numan resource use if the species thus protected enhances the availability of other species that are harvested. This is likely for some widely protected species such as trees belonging to the genus *Ficus*, but less likely for a wide variety of species protected as totemic by given tribal groups (Gadgil, 1989).

(viii) Certain habitat patches may either never be harvested or may be subject to very low levels of harvests through strict regulation. It is extremely difficult to arrive at workable prescriptions on quantitative quotas, closed seasons or protected life history stages that would decidedly guard against resource decimation. Providing refugia (sacred groves, sacred ponds, etc.) may then be the most easily perceived and most efficient way of guarding against resource depletion (Gadgil and Vartak, 1976).

(ix) Certain age-sex classes or social groups may be banned from employing certain harvesting methods or from utilizing certain species or habitat patches. Thus in New Guinea adult males are banned from hunting rodents, and on Fanafuti atoll in the Pacific, turtle meat was taboo to all except the king (Rappaport, 1984; Zann, 1985). This could contribute towards long-term resource conservation by moderating the total amount harvested. It could also assist in long-term conservation by restricting access to a limited number of individuals who may more readily use the resource in a prudent fashion. It is of course quite possible that such restrictions merely benefit certain segments of the community in positions of power without serving the interests of long-term conservation.

Some Rules of Thumb

It is increasingly realized that precise prescriptions for the prudent use of living resources are difficult and that detailed quantitative ones might be impossible to arrive at in the present state of our knowledge (Clark, 1985). This is particularly so if the entire prey population is continually subject to harvesting. By contrast, some simpler general prescriptions for averting resource collapse may be feasible and yet have a significant effect in enabling sustainable use. These are five: (i) Provide total protection to some habitat patches, representing different ecosystems, so that resource populations are always maintained above some threshold level; (ii) provide total protection to some selected species so that community level interactions are minimally disrupted; (iii) protect such life history stages as appear critical to the maintenance of the resource population; (iv) provide total protection to resource populations at certain times; and (v) organize resource use in such a way that only a relatively small group of people controls access to a particular resource.

Modern ecological and evolutionary theory does indeed suggest that such prescriptions are likely to assist in avoiding resource collapse, although they would by no means ensure harvest at maximum sustainable yield levels. In his classic experiments on prey — predator cycles of protozoans, Gause showed that prey extinction could be effectively avoided only by providing the prey a refugium, an area of the experimental arena inaccessible to the predator, where the prey could maintain a minimal population and from which other areas could be colonized (Gause, 1969). Sacred groves, sacred ponds, and stretches of sea coast or coral reefs from which all fishing is prohibited are such refugia.

Modern ecological theory also stresses the significance of some species that serve as 'keystone resources' or mobile links in maintaining the overall functioning of the community (Terborgh, 1986). The tree genus *Ficus*, to which belong species such as the banyan and the *peepal*, widely protected in Asia and Africa, is one such keystone resource genus. Contemporary ecological theory also points to the fact that certain stages in a population are of higher "reproductive value" and therefore more significant for permitting continued population growth. Pregnant does and nesting birds, again often protected by humans, are such stages. Finally, there is a rapidly growing body of literature to show that sustainable resource-use develops when a particular group has both control over and responsibility for a particular resource (Berkes, ed. 1989). Recent work on the evolution of cooperative behaviour emphasizes that restraint is more likely to evolve in groups of smaller numbers of individuals in repeated social interactions (Joshi, 1987; Berkes and Kence, 1987).

It thus appears plausible that over the course of human history there have been human groups whose interests were strongly linked to the prudent use of their resource bases, and that such groups did evolve appropriate conservation practices. These practices were apparently based on simple rules of thumb that tended to ensure the long-term sustainability of the resource base. These rules would necessarily have been approximate. They would have been arrived at through a process of trial and error, with the continued acceptance of practices which appeared to keep the resource base secure, coupled with the rejection of those practices which appeared to destroy it. Practices observed by other social groups may also have been adopted if they appeared to lead to the persistence of a whole range of practices, some beneficial from the point of view of resource conservation, but also others that were neutral, and perhaps some that once were beneficial or neutral but became harmful due to changed circumstances.

Some hunter-gatherer, horticultural and simple fishing societies institutionalized a number of such measures of resource conservation through their religious belief systems. The nomadic herder as well as technologically more advanced agrarian and early industrial societies became progressively less concerned with the well-being of their resource base, and consequently abandoned a number of these practices. The mainstream monotheistic traditions of the more recent Middle Eastern religions rejected them with great vehemence as pagan practices; however, the religions of the East — Buddhism, Jainism, Taoism and Hinduism — absorbed several of these practices, partly as religious beliefs, partly as accepted customs.

Scientific Prescriptions

The modern scientific tradition arising in the advanced agrarian societies of Christian

Europe began with a strong faith in man being apart from nature and fully entitled to the unrestrained exploitation of natural resources (White, 1967). The relatively late development of the science of ecology and resource management may be related to this. Resource management science did not begin until the second half of the 19th century, when the finite nature of the world's resource base first began to be evident to European civilization with the closing of the many frontiers along which European expansion had been in progress during the previous three centuries. Only then did scientific prescriptions for restrained resource use make a slow appearance. However, these new prescriptions for preservation in many ways merely paralleled the pre-scientific prescriptions typical of earlier modes.

(i) Just as there were quantitative restrictions on the amount of fuelwood extracted by a family from a community woodlot, or on the number of animals to be grazed on a fodder reserve, there are now quantitative prescriptions as to the amount of timber to be removed during the course of selection cutting from a designated patch of forest, or regarding the number of tigers that may be shot by a licence holder in a given year.

(ii) Just as Torres Strait islanders stop fishing a particular species when its population density falls below a certain level, the International Whaling Commission has banned the hunting of certain species of whale whose populations have been severely depleted.

(iii) Just as certain coastal fishing areas are fallowed by traditional societies when yields become very low, there have been prescriptions to 'rest' certain forest areas, for instance, in India after the excessive harvests of the Second World War.

(iv) Just as there is a traditional ban on hunting in certain seasons, there are closed seasons for mechanized fishing and for timber extraction.

(v) Just as certain life history stages are traditionally given protection, for instance breeding birds at heronries in many villages in peninsular India, the younger, growing stock in a forest is supposed to be spared all extractive pressure.

(vi) Just as certain methods of harvest, e.g. poisoning of streams, may be traditionally forbidden, there are regulations forbidding fishing with destructive or overly efficient gear.

(vii) Just as certain habitat patches, for instance sacred groves or sacred ponds, may be fully protected from any harvest, there are prescriptions for keeping certain forest areas such as national parks totally free from human interference, for watershed conservation, maintenance of biological diversity and other ecological functions.

(viii) Just as certain species are totally protected from hunting or felling, e.g., monkeys or *Ficus* trees in Indian villages, complete national or international protection may be extended to certain endangered species such as the California condor or the whooping crane.

(ix) Just as north-west Pacific coast Amerindian societies controlled access to the most productive marine resources, contemporary techniques for salmon management in Alaska and elsewhere include access and entry limitations.

Perhaps most important of all, just as many societies developed systems for integrated resource management, the ecosystem approach now provides a guide towards more sustainable resource use.

Conclusion

Scientific prescriptions thus often resemble or parallel 'pre-scientific' prescriptions based on traditional ecological knowledge and simple rules of thumb. Indeed, considering the track records, one could argue that the scientific prescriptions of industrial society show little evidence of progress over simple rule-of-thumb prescriptions. Similarly, one could argue that government enforcement of these scientific prescriptions represents little progress compared with the earlier enforcement of procedures based on religion or social convention.

To many it is a paradox that with all its power, modern science seems unable to halt and reverse the depletion of resources and the degradation of the environment. Part of the reason for this paradox may be that scientific resource management, and Western reductionist science in general, developed in the service of the utilitarian, exploitative "dominion over nature" world-view of colonialists and developers. It is best geared to the efficient utilization of resources as if they were boundless. This is a legacy of the *laissez-faire* doctrine of Adam Smith and still persists in the neoclassical economic theory of today (Daly and Cobb, 1989).

Thus modern resource management science is well suited by design for conventional exploitative development but not for sustainable use (Regier *et al.*, 1989). The task then is to rethink and reconstruct a new resource management science that is better adapted to serve the needs of ecological sustainability and the people who use resources. To do this, there is a need to conserve both biological and cultural diversity, which are tied together (Gadgil, 1987; Norgaard, 1987); there also is a need to conserve the diversity of traditional resource management practices and systems.

During the past century the diversity of resource management systems has been replaced by a monolithic scientific management vision — one that often has not led to sustainable outcomes. Such a trend is clearly maladaptive, but the indigenous, adaptive systems have in the mean time suffered as well. Each of the traditional ecosystem approaches summarized in this paper has been impacted by colonialists or developers. Contrary to conventional wisdom, these systems did not collapse primarily because of population pressure. For example, Johannes (1978) has shown for the Pacific islands case, and Rogers (1979) for Alaska, that traditional systems collapsed because of outside interference and the forced institution of open-access conditions at a time when local populations were actually *declining*. Population pressure is real, of course, but in many cases it comes *after* local systems collapse and local resource users lose control, not before.

The rejection of a monolithic scientific resource management vision does not mean the rejection of all Western science. There are excellent examples of how modern and traditional management can be brought together successfully, as in Japanese inshore fisheries (Ruddle, 1989). Rather, as Regier (1975) suggested, the task is to develop a flexible approach by conserving what is useful in Western science and nurturing some of its more radical components. Ecology as a science concerned with the whole (rather than its parts) is one of the components. It stands at the fringe of Western scientific traditions because, together with a select few disciplines such as systems science, quantum physics, gestalt psychology, operations research, ecology is holistic. As such, ecological thinking is sympathetic to the mode of thinking of the ancient traditions of East Asian, African and Amerindian cultures. Especially important in this regard, ecology is concerned with diversity and adaptiveness.

All these put ecology in a unique position to be the cornerstone of a new science of resource management that synthesizes the best of old and new wisdom towards a more sustainable future. But ecology would first have to extricate itself from the older, utilitarian "control over nature" tradition of resource management. For ecology's involvement with that tradition is very real (Worster, 1977). The challenge posed by Theodore Roszak (1972) is still relevant, albeit in a somewhat different context: "The question remains open: Which will ecology be, the last of the old science or the first of the new?"

References

Almstedt, R.L., 1968. 'Diegueno Tree: An Ecological Approach to a Linguistic Problem'. *International Journal of American Linguistics*, 34, pp. 9-15

Baines, G.B.K., 1984. 'Traditional Resource Management in the Melanesian South Pacific: A Development Dilemna'. In Firket Berkes, ed., *Common Property Resources, Ecology and Community-Based Sustainable Development*, Belhaven Press, London

Bartlett, H.H., 1940. 'History of the Generic Concept of Botany'. *Bulletin of the Torrey Botanical Club*, 67, pp. 349-62

Berkes, F., 1982. 'Water-Fowl Management and Northern Native Peoples with Reference to Cree Hunters of James Bay. *Musk-Ox*, 30, pp. 23-35

———, 1977. 'Fishery Resource Use in a Subarctic Indian Community'. *Human Ecology*, 5. pp. 289-307

———, 1985. 'Fishermen and "The Tragedy of the Commons"'. *Environmental Conservation*, 12, pp. 199-206

Berkes, F. and A. Kence, 1987. 'Fisheries and the Prisoner's Dilemna Game: Conditions for the Evolution of Cooperation among Users of Common Property Resources'. *Middle Eastern Technical University Journal of Pure and Applied Sciences*, 20, p. 209.

Berkes, F., ed., 1989. *Common Property Resources, Ecology and Community-Based Sustainable Development*, Belhaven Press, London

Berkes, F. and M.M.R. Freeman, 1986. *Canadian Inland Seas*, Elsevier, Amsterdam

Berlin, B., 1972. 'Speculations on the Growth of Ethnobotanical Nomenclature'. *Language and Society*, 1, pp. 51-86

———, 1973a. First Ethnobotanical Expedition of the University of California to the Upper Maranon River, Amazonas'. *Peru Report* No. 1, Language Behavior Research Laboratory, Berkeley

———, 1973b. 'Folk Biology. In C. Sturtevant, ed., *Handbook of North American Indians*, Smithsonian Institution, Washington, D.C., in press

Berlin, B., D.E. Breedlove and P.H. Raven, 1966. 'Folk Taxonomies and Biological Classification', *Science*, 154, pp. 273-75

———, 1968. 'Covert Categories and Folk Taxonomies'. *American Anthropologist*, 70, pp. 290-99

———, 1973a. 'General Principles of Nomenclature in Folk Biology'. *American Anthropologist*, 75, pp. 214-42

———, 1973b. '*Pinciples of Tzeltal Plant Classification: An Introduction to the Botanical Ethnography of a Mayan Speaking People of Highland Chiapas*, Seminar, New York

Berlin, B., D.E. Breedlove, R.M. Laughlin and P.H. Raven, (in press). 'Lexical Retention and Cultural Significance in Tzeltal-Tzotsil Ethnobotany'. In, M.S. Edmonson, ed., *Meaning in the Mayan Languages*, Mouton, The Hague

Borgerhoff-Mulder, 1988. 'Behavioural Ecology in Traditional Societies'. *Trends in Ecology and Evolution*, 3, pp. 260

Brendt, R.M., 1962. *Excess and Restraint*, University of Chicago Press, Chicago

Buck, C.D., 1949. *A Dictionary of Selected Synonyms in the Principal Indo-European Languages*, University of Chicago Press, Chicago

Bulmer, R., 1970. 'Which Came First, the Chicken or the Egghead?', In Popuillon and P. Mavausa, ed., *Exhanges et Communication : Melanges offerts a Claude Levi-Strausse a l'occasion de son 60eme Anniversaire*, Mouton, The Hague

Bulmer, R. and M. Tyler, 1968. 'Karam Classification of Frogs'. *Journal of Polynesian Society*, 77, pp. 333-85

Capra, F., 1982. *The Turning Point*, Bantam, New York

Clark, C.W., 1985. *Bioeconomic Modelling and Fisheries Management*, Wiley, New York

Daly, H.E. and J.B. Cobb Jr., 1989. *For the Common Good*, Beacon, Boston

Demory, B., 1972. 'The Word "Tree" in the Hokan Language Family. Department of Anthropology, California State University, Long Beach

Dennler, J.G., 1939. 'Los nombres indigenas en Guarani de los mamiferos de la Argentina y paises limitrofes y su importancia para la systematica'. *Physis*, 16, pp. 225-44

Diamond, J.M., 1966. 'Classification System of a Primitive People'. *Science*, 151, pp. 1102-4

Eaton, P., 1985. 'Customary Land Tenure and Conservation in Papua New Guinea'. In J.A. McNeely and D. Pitt, eds., *Culture and Conservation: The Human Dimension in Environmental Planning*, Croom Helm, Dublin

Fay, C., 1989. *Cahiers des Sciences Humaines*, 25, pp. 213

Feit, H.A., 1986. *Native People and Renewable Resource Management*, Alberta Society of Professional Biologists, Edmonton, pp. 49-65

Freeman, M.M.R. and L.N. Carbyn, eds., 1988. *Traditional Knowledge and Renewable Resource Management in Northern Regions*, University of Alberta, Edmonton

Friedrich, P., 1970. *Proto-Indo-European Trees*, University of Chicago Press, Chicago.

Gadgil, M., 1985a. 'Social Restraints on Resource Utilization: The Indian Experience'. In J.A. McNeely and D. Pitt, eds., *Culture and Conservation: The Human Dimension in Environmental Planning*, Croom Helm, Dublin

———, 1985b. 'Cultural Evolution of Ecological Prudence'. *Landscape Planning*, 12, pp. 285-99

———, 1987. 'Diversity: Cultural and Biological'. *Trends in Ecology and Evolution*, 2, pp. 369

———, 1989. 'The Indian Heritage of a Conservation Ethic'. In B. Allchin, F.R. Allchin and Thapar, eds., *Conservation of the Indian Heritage*, Cosmo Publications, New Delhi

Gadgil, M. and K.C. Malhotra, 1983. 'Adaptive Significance of the Indian Caste System: An Ecological Perspective'. *Annals of Human Biology*, 10, pp. 465-78

Gadgil, M. and V.D. Vartak, 1976. 'Sacred Groves of Western Ghats of India'. *Economic Botany*, 30, pp.

Gajddusek, D.C. and V. Zigas, 1957. *New Engl. J. Med.*, 257, pp. 974

Gatschet, A.S., 1890. 'The Klamath Indians of Southwestern Oregon'. *Contributions to North American Ethnology*, Vol. II, Pt. II, US Geographical and Geological Survey, Rocky Mountain Region, Washington, D.C.

———, 1899. '"Real," "True", or "Genuine" in Indian Languages'. *American Anthropologist*, 1, pp. 155-61

Gause, G.K., 1969. *The Struggle for Existence*, Hafner, New York

Geeertz, C., 1963. *Agricultural Involution*, University of California Press, Berkeley

Gliessman, S.R., E.R. Gancia and A.M. Amador, 1981. *Agroecosystems*, 7, p. 173

Greene, E.L., 1909. *Landmarks of Botanical History*, Smithsonian Miscellaneous Collection, Washington, D.C.

Gurpinar, T., 1978. *Yabani Bitkilerimiz*, Redhouse, Istanbul

Harrington, J.P., W.W. Robbins and B. Freire-Marreco, 1916. 'Ethnobotany of the Tewa Indians. *Bureau of American Ethnology Bulletin*, 55

Hasler, A.D., ed., 1974. *Coupling of Land and Water Systems*, Springer Verlag, New York

Hunn, E.S., 1973. 'Tzeltal Folk Zoology: The Classification of Discontinuities in Nature'. Ph.D. thesis, University of California, Berkeley

———, 1970. *Cognitive Processes in Folk Ornithology: The Identification of Gulls*, Language Behavior Research Laboratory, Berkeley

Hviding, E., 1989. *Traditional Marine Resource Management in the Pacific*, Unesco,

Jakarta

Irvine, D., 1989. *Advances in Economic Botany*, 7, p. 223

Johannes, R.E., 1978. 'Traditional Conservation Methods in Oceania and Their Demise'. *Annual Review of Ecology and Systematics*, 9, pp. 349-64

———, 1981. *Words of the Lagoon*, University of California Press, Berkeley

Joshi, N.V., 1987. 'Evolution of Cooperation By Reciprocation within Structured Demes'. *Journal of Genetics*, pp. 66-9

Kay, P., 1971. 'On Taxonomy and Semantic Contrast'. *Language*, 47, pp. 866-87

Lansing J.S., 1987, *American Anthropologist*, 89, 326.

Lasserre, P. and K. Ruddle, 1983. 'Traditional Knowledge and Management of Marine Coastal Systems'. *Report of the Ad Hoc Steering Group*, Unesco, Paris

Lenski, G. and J. Lenski, 1978. *Human Societies*, McGraw Hill, New York

Major , J., 1969. *The Ecosystem Concept in Natural Resource Management*, Academic Press, New York, pp. 9-19

Martynov, A., 1988. *Arctic Anthropology*, 25, p. 12

Mayer, E., 1963. *Animal Species and Evolution*, Harvard University Press, Cambridge

———, 1941. *List of New Guinea Birds*, American Museum of Natural History, New York

McCay, B.J. and J.M. Acheson, eds.. 1987. *Human Ecology of the Commons: Introduction to the Question of the Commons*, University of Arizona Press, Tucson

McNeely, J.A. and D. Pitt, eds., 1985. *Culture and Conservation: The Human Dimension in Environmental Planning*, Croom Helm, Dublin

Moorehead, R., 1989. Changes Taking Place in Common Property Resource Management in the Inland Niger Delta of Mali'. In F. Berkes, ed., *Common Property Resources: Ecology and Community-Based Sustainable Development*, Belhaven Press, London, pp 256-72

Nietschmann, B., 1985. 'Torres Strait Islander Sea Resource Management and Sea Rights'. In K. Ruddle and R.E. Johannes, eds., *The Traditional Knowledge and Management of Coastal Systems in Asia and the Pacific*, Unesco, Jakarta

Norgaard, R.B., 1987. *Ecological Modelling*, 38, p. 107

———, 1987. *Economic Development and Cultural Change*, 32, p. 525

Omari, C.K., 1990. In *Ethics of Environment and Development*, Belhaven Press, London

Rappaport, R.A., 1984, *Pigs for the Ancestors*, Yale University Press, New Haven.

Raven, P.H., B. Berlin, and D.E. Breedlove, 1971. 'The Origins of Taxonomy'. *Science*, 174, pp. 1210-13

Regier, H.A., 1975. *A Balanced Science of Renewable Resources*, University of Washington Press, Seattle

Regier, H.A., R.V. Mason and F. Berkes, 1989. 'Reforming the Use of Natural Resources'. In F. Berkes, ed., *Common Property Resources: Ecology and Community-Based Sustainable Development*, Belhaven Press, London

Rogers, G.W. 1979. 'Alaska's Limited Entry Program: Another View'. *Journal of the Fisheries Research Board of Canada*, 36, pp. 738-88

Roszak, T., 1972, *Where the Wasteland Ends*, Doubleday, Garden City

Ruddle, K., 1989. 'Solving the Common-Property Dilemma: Village Fisheries Rights in Japanese Coastal Waters. In F. Berkes, ed., *Common Property Resources: Ecology and Community-Based Sustainable Development*, Belhaven Press, London

Ruddle, K. and R.E. Johannes, eds., 1985. *The Traditional Knowledge and Management of Coastal Systems in Asia and the Pacific*, Unesco, Jakarta

Smith, E.A., 1983 'Anthropological Applications of Optimal Foraging Theory: A Critical Review'. *Current Anthropology*, 24, p. 625

Stross, B., 1969. 'Language Acquisition by Tenejapa Tzeltal Children'. Ph.D. thesis, University of California, Berkeley

Tanner, A., 1979. *Bringing Home Animals : Religious Ideology and Mode of Production of the Mistassini Cree Hunters*, Hurst, London

Terborgh, J., 1986. 'Keystone Plant Resources in the Tropical Forest'. In M.E. Soule, ed., *Conservation Biology — The Science of Scarcity and Diversity*, Sinauer Associates, Inc., Publishers, Sunderland

Trager, G.L., 1939. '"Cottonwood" "Tree": A Southwestern Linguistic Trait'. *International Journal of American Linguistics*, 9, pp. 177-18

Ullman, S., 1966. 'Semantic Universals'. In J.H. Greenberg, ed., *Universals of Language*, MIT, Cambridge

White, L., 1967. 'The Historical Roots of Our Ecologic Crisis'. *Science*, 155, pp. 1203-07

Williams, N.M. and E.S. Hunn, eds., 1982. *Resource Managers: North American and Australian Hunter Gatherers*, AAAS Selected Symposium 67, Washington, D.C.

Worster, D., 1977. *Nature's Economy*, Cambridge University Press, Cambridge

Wyman, L.C. and S.K. Harris, 1941. 'Navajo Indian Medical Ethnobotany'. *University of New Mexico Bulletin*, 366, Anthropological Series 3.5

Zann, L.P., 1985. Traditional Management and Conservation of Fisheries in Kiribati and Tuvalu Atolls'. In K. Ruddle and R.E. Johannes, eds., *The Traditional Knowledge and Coastal Systems in Asia and the Pacific*, Unesco, Jakarta

2

Symbiotic Relationships Between Man, Animal and Nature

A Study of the Gujar of Garhwal

R.S. Negi

Our genus *Homo* has been on earth for some two million years. Of this time span, almost 99.5 per cent is a history of subsistence on hunting of animals and gathering of plant food. It was total dependence on nature for life support. This kind of subsistence strategy necessitated living in small bands and moving from place to place in pursuit of game, as well as exploring new areas for vegetative food resources. As such, the nomadic hunting-gathering way of life is the primal adaptation of hominids for food procurement, which set the course for human bio-cultural evolution in a harmonious relationship with nature. During the course of this primal adaptation early hominids and their descendants must have, by trial and error, learnt about the characteristic features, specially behaviour pattern and habits, of the animals which constituted their food supply and their food reserve. They also must have learnt about the edible qualities and desirability of almost all available plant resources. As a result of this knowledge base built over hundreds of generations, a major shift was bound to come in the subsistence strategy.

About 10,000 years ago the transition from hunting and foraging for food to the domestication of plants and animals took place. It was a shift from food quest or food procurement to food production. It was by no means a smooth transition and may have been spread over many centuries. At first people may have had to supplement the food they produced with food they procured by hunting and foraging, but gradually the dependence on wild food resources may have lessened as domesticated plants and animals increased in quantity and improved in quality. Spatial mobility, a basic requisite of the nomadic way of life, may also have given way to the process of sedentarisation, which is a necessary condition for the domestication of plants or cultivation. However, the domestication of animals or animal husbandry has different requirements. Spatial mobility, which may have temporarily been given up, became the basic requisite for animal herding.

The shift from food quest to food production occurred with the onset of the Neolithic period, and one of the first regions to undergo this transition was south-west Asia, as is shown by polynological and archaeo-zoological studies of the remains of domesticated plants and animals in Israel, Jordan, Syria, Turkey, Iraq and Iran, all from before 5000 BC.

The first animals to be domesticated, before 6000 BC, were probably sheep and goats from the arid highlands of Persia and Anatolia, to be followed by cattle (*Bos*) in the lowlands of Mesopotamia. Gradually diverse animals would have come under human control in other regions also. In the Indian subcontinent there is evidence from Mohenjo-Daro and Harappa indicating the domestication of sheep, cattle (even buffaloes) from the animal remains that have been found and studied (Clason, 1977).

Historically, pastoralism is considered an offshoot of mixed agricultural and herding subsistence patterns, in adaptation to grasslands and marginal areas not suitable for growing cereal plants. Pastoralism was probably the consequence of new problems in managing domesticated plant and animal resources (Darlington, 1969).

After about 4,000 years of mixed farming and animal husbandry, two different kinds of people emerged: the peasant, who was completely sedentarised on permanent sites suitable for agricultural pursuits, and the herdsman or pastoralist, who was almost entirely dependent on livestock raising. People in remote parts of the world have maintained nomadic pastoralism as a way of life, but as a cultural system it has Old World origins. The livestock on which pastoralism is based include sheep, goats, bovines (cattle, yaks), equines (horses, asses). Buffaloes (*Bubalis bubalis domesticus*) seem to have come under human control at a later period about 2000 BC in the Indus Valley and 1000 BC in China.

Pastoralism as a cultural system has existed longest in the Middle East, from the Mediterranean to the Indus Valley, and also extending to the Himalayas. Over the past fifty years or so a great deal of information has been assembled about the beginning of domestication of animals, but we do not yet have the answer to how and why this happened. It is certain that there will have been different causative factors in different regions as well as for different animals. One observation of general validity needs mention. As a hunter our ancestor must have ensured that the animals whom he considered his food reserve and whom he followed closely would propagate and grow into large herds in order to maintain adequate food supply in the following seasons. It was a kind of unconscious herd management and suggestive the of first step towards domestication. Adult females capable of reproduction may not have been hunted and may have been taken under human care.

Pastoralism is an economic activity involving the care of herds of domesticated livestock. Man and herd live in a symbiotic community, making social and psychological adjustments to each other, together adapting to the natural environment in which the herds have their special ecological niche, the pasture. Since pastoralists and their herds depend upon the bounty of nature (the animals graze the grass and browse the foliage), it follows that nature must be allowed time to regenerate and provide for the following season. As such, mobility from pasture to pasture is a characteristic feature of pastoralism. Pastoral people are traditionally mobile, as they have to follow or lead their herds in a never-ending quest for pasture and water. Their movement is seasonal, often from drier and warmer regions in the summer months to moister and cooler mountains and back again in the winter months. This kind of movement is known as transhumance. Anthropological usage of the term links it with a subsistence pattern combining agriculture and animal husbandry. In this mixed subsistence strategy, generally the herder and the herd move seasonally between a permanent settlement and known pastures (Evans-Pritchard, 1940), or else only livestock moves between mountains and plains without any agriculture (Gulliver, 1955).

By about 3000 BC pastoral communities were firmly established in Central Asia, South West Asia and North-East Africa, later spreading to contiguous areas of the major nuclear regions, and distinct from farming villages. The pastoral people may have relied on horticulture to supplement their subsistence but rarely practised agriculture.

Transhumance is a highly developed form of pastoralism and has varying forms in different parts of the world. In the Himalayas, where transhumance is almost universal, it takes the form of cyclic movement of people and their livestock between previously earmarked sites which become more or less permanent seasonal encampments or bases. These seasonal cyclic movements allow time for the regeneration of resources, which alone can sustain this kind of life-style. The seasonal cyclic movements and utilisation of resources in a rotational manner has placed transhumant people in a situation where they are nomadic on the one hand and transitionally or marginally sedentary on the other. The Garhwal Himalayas, where this pilot study has been undertaken, support a number of transhumant populations, chief among whom are the Bhotia, the highland shepherds and the Gujar. The Bhotia raise sheep and goats and combine trade with cultivation, while the highland shepherds raise sheep and goats and are agropastoral. The Gujar raise mainly buffaloes and till recently were completely pastoral nomads. We shall here view the Gujar life ways in order to have an insight into pastoral nomads' perception of the relationship between the herder, the herd and the resources, that is, man, animal and nature.

Land and People

Garhwal, one of the administrative divisions of the Uttar Pradesh hills, comprises five districts, Chamoli, Pauri, Tehri, Uttarkashi and Dehradun. It has an area of 29,089 sq km and lies between 77° 35' E and 80° 6.0' E longitude and 29° 32' N and 31° 27' N latitude. The Garhwal region has rugged mountainous terrain. It has some of the highest peaks and passes and deep gorges cut by swift-flowing rivers, thus providing great contrast's between in high ranges and deep valleys. Physiographically there are three well recognised divisions from south to north (Nityanand and Kumar, 1989):

(i) The outer or sub-Himalayas or the Siwaliks, with varying elevation of 330m to 1100m.

(ii) The lesser or middle Himalayas, also known as Himachal. With an approximate width of 75 km, Himachal is a massive mountainous tract with elevations between 1100m and 3300m.

(iii) The greater or inner Himalayas, also known as Himadri. It has an average width of 50 km and main relief average between 4800m and 6000m. The Himadri is the most majestic range of the Himalayas and has two peaks which rise above 7500m (Nanda Devi, 7816m and Kamet, 7756m).

RIVERS

The Garhwal Himalaya's are drained entirely by the Ganga and its tributaries, and the drainage can be divided into the following systems (ibid.):

(i) The Bhagirathi system.
(ii) The Alakananda system.

(iii) The Ganga system. The name Ganga is attained by the river only at Deoprayag by the confluence of the Bhagirathi and the Alakananda.
(iv) The Yamuna system.
(v) The Western Ramganga system.

However, it is topical to make mention of the Bhilangana which falls into the Bhagirathi at Tehri, and the Tons, which, although more than twice the volume of the Yamuna, loses its name at Kalsi, where it falls in confluence with that river.

CLIMATE

There is considerable variability in the climatic conditions of the Garhwal Himalayas. The determinant of this variation is chiefly the immense variation in altitude, but the direction of ridges, wind conditions, degree and aspects of slopes, intensity of forest cover and proximity of water bodies and glaciers also influence the climate from locality to locality. However, according to Nitya Nand and Kumar (ibid.), it is convenient to base the regionalisation of climate on altitude. The following Table, adapted by them from S.D. Kaushic, shows the climate zones of Garhwal.

Table 2.1
Climate Zones of Garhwal

	Climate zone	*Altitude in metres*	*Mean annualmtemperature in degrees centigrade*
1.	Sub-Tropical	Below 300 — 900	18.9 — 21.1
2.	Warm Temperature	900 — 1800	13.9 — 18.9
3.	Cool Temperature	1800 — 2400	10.3 — 13.9
4.	Cold Zone	2400 — 3000	04.4 — 10.3
5.	Alpine Zone	3000 — 4200	03.0 — 04.5
6.	Glacial Zone	Above 4200	Ten months below zero

VEGETATION

The area is also rich in natural vegetation, which includes meadow, marshes and swamps, with their characteristic plants such as angiosperms, herbs and shrubs, with some gymnospermic plant variety. Most of the area is covered by forest and the remaining is cultivated. The Siwalik area mostly embraces evergreens, semi-evergreens, deciduous forest and grassland. The forests are predominatly of *sal* (*Sorea robusta*), *khair* (*Acasia catechu*), *sisham* (*Dalbergia sissoo*), teak (*Tectona grandis*), alanthus (*Cassia flstula*), *bans* (*Dendrocalumus strictus*), *kanzu* (*Holoptelea intigrifolia*), etc. (Appendix I). The vegetation is influenced by slope aspect, soil, altitude and water availability, and can be broadly classified into alpine, temperate, sub-tropical and tropical.

Alpine Vegetation

According to Puri (1960), four distinct types can be recognised in the alpine vegetation of the Himalayas:

(i) Alpine stony desert (3600 — 4200m), a little below the perpetual snow.

(ii) Alpine scrub (3000 — 3600m).

(iii) Alpine meadows, generally above 3500m.

(iv) Alpine forest, about the tree line.

Flowering herbs and shrubs are the usual occurrence at altitudes above 3000m. They blossom during summer and autumn.

Above the tree line (3500m and above) are pastures known as *bugyals*. The main component of these meadows are grass-like *Phelum alpinum* and *Poa alpina*, with a multitude of colourful herbs like anemones, gentians, patentiallas and Primulas. Alpine forests are classified into two types, alpine fir-birch forests and birch-rhododendron forests.

Temperate Vegetation

This type is characterised by oaks and conifers over extensive areas, oaks on the southern slopes and conifers on the northern slopes.

The temperate forest zone above 1500m provides favourable conditions for human habitation, and consequently forest growth has been greatly disturbed. Felling, lopping, fire and grazing have reduced some of the high-altitude forest areas to open scrub or grassy meadows.

Sub-tropical and Tropical Vegetation

Among the lower altitude deciduous species, *Shorea robusta* (*sal*) is most conspicuous.

On the slopes of the Siwaliks, *sal* forests are predominant. In the riverine tracts, acacia catechu-tamoric, with little or no *adhatoda vasica*, occurs.

Large tracts of forest occur in western Garhwal, west of the Mandakini river and in the Siwaliks in the south Yamuna basin. Three forest divisions — Tons, Yamuna and Chakrata — are in the Yamuna valley. The northern part of the valley is well wooded. Some of the finest forests are in this area. The total area under forest is 2,289 sq km. Sub-tropical vegetation is negligible in the valley (Nitya Nand and Kumar, 1989).

WILDLIFE

Owing to the diversity of cover and natural food, the Garhwal Himalayas have a wide variety of fauna. Amongst the prominent animals are the Asian elephant (*Elphas maximum*), tiger (*Panthra tigris*), leopard cat (*Fellis beggalensis*) and *cheetal* or spotted deer (*Axis axis*) (Appendix I). The westernmost population of the elephant is found in the Siwaliks and the tarai. Apart from these, the area boasts a number of bird species, most of which are the *kalij* pheasant (*Lophura leueomelana*), Himalayan yellow-throated martin (*Marces flavigula*), red junglefowl (*Gallus gallus*) and pied hornbill (*Anthraceros melabaricus*) (Appendix II).

THE GUJAR

The Gujar derive their name from the Sanskrit term "Gurjara". Historically they were once a dominant people in western India and gave the territory occupied by them the name Gujarat or Gujrat. However, for unknown reasons, the Gujar migrated from western India and spread all over the north-western part of the Indian subcontinent and to some extent central India. Cunningham (1871) described their distribution to be "... in great numbers in every part of north-west India, from the Peninsular Gujrat. They are specially numerous along the banks of the upper Jamuna near Jagadri and Buriya, and in the Saharanpur district, which during the last century was actually called Gujrat. To the east they occupy the petty state of Sampatpur in Bundelkhand, and one of the northern districts of Gwalior which is still called Gujorgarh". The Gujar were mostly Hindu, but sizeable sections of them were converted to Islam in the Mughal period, especially during the reign of Aurangzeb. At present there are both Hindu and Muslim Gujar populations in northern India: but whereas the Hindu Gujar are mostly in the plains of Punjab, Haryana and western Uttar Pradesh, the Muslim Gujar inhabit the Himalayan region of Jammu and Kashmir, Himachal Pradesh, and Garhwal and Kumaon divisions of Uttar Pradesh. There is yet another remarkable difference between the Hindu and Muslim Gujar populations: the former are entirely settled agriculturists while the latter are semi-agriculturist pastoralists in some areas and completely pastoralists in others.

There is a great controversy regarding the origin of the Gujar. According to the one view they were pastoral nomads of Central Asia and came into India during the 5th or 6th century AD. But according to another view they are of Indian origin and were inhabitants of the region extending around Mount Abu in western Rajasthan, Malwa and Gujarat. They are said to have migrated around the 16th century AD in a north-westerly direction into Punjab Kandi, in primary and secondary waves. The primary wave of migrants comprised pastoralist nomads who moved into the hilly unproductive marginal area bordering the Siwaliks, where there were pastures for their herds of baffaloes (Manku 1986). It is not very important for us here to resolve the controversy regarding the origin of the Gujar. What is important and interesting is that according to both the views the Gujar were pastoralists. As pastoralists of Central Asian origin they would have entered India with their stock of sheep and goats, later taking to buffalo raising, which they were doing already according to the theory of their being of Indian origin. The contemporary Gujar, especially that section which has embraced Islam, are, however, known to raise sheep and goats as well as buffaloes. The former are known as Bakkarwal and the latter as Gujar or Dudh-Gujar. The Bakkarwal have their nomadic area in the territory of Jammu and Kashmir whereas the buffalo-raising Gujar are in Jammu, and sections of them have also moved in a south-easterly direction from Jammu and western Punjab to Himachal Pradesh and the hills of Uttar Pradesh. This movement has been caused by the depletion of grazing resources in Jammu and Punjab regions and also due to increase in both human and animal populations.

Although it is certain that in the Garhwal Himalayas the Gujar have migrated from the Jammu region through Himachal Pradesh, it is difficult to establish at what point of time they entered this territory. Atkinson and his contemporaries do not make any mention of the Gujar while describing the people of the Garhwal Himalyas in the gazetteer of the Himalayan districts of the north-western province of India. Walton (1910) also is silent about them in the gazeteer of Garhwal. However, it is generally believed that the Gujar migrated to Garhwal some 150 to 100 years ago and till very recently were fully pastoralists, following transhumance between two distinct ecozones without much diversification of subsistence strategy.

At present the Gujar have their winter camps in the lower regions of Garhwal and the Siwaliks, which have gained the status of their semi-permanent habitat over the course of four to five generations. Beyond that, most of them trace their ancestry to Himachal Pradesh, Punjab or the Jammu region. In fact, some elderly Gujar in the age range of 80 — 90 years can remember their grandfathers migrating to the Garhwal region from Himachal Pradesh (then part of Punjab) or Jammu.

(1) The Siwalik Forest Division, west of the Delhi-Dehradun highway and outside the Rajaji National Park, lying between 20^0 25'N and 30^0 25'N latitude and 72^0 35'E to 78^0 15'E longitude and (2) the Rajaji National Park area, east of the highway and including Rajaji, Motichur and Chila, lying between 29^0 50'N and 30^0 15'N latitude and 77^0 55'E to 78^0 30'E longitude. Sanctuaries, Division/Rangewise areas of the Siwalik Forest Division and the Rajaji National Park as well as the distribution of Gujar families are given in Tables 2.2 to 2.6.

Table 2.2

Siwalik Forest Division Land Area

	Forest Range	*Area in Hectares*
1.	Asarori	4,444.50
2.	Timli	9,006.50
3.	Badkala	19,998.72
4.	Malhan	7,590.20
5.	Mohand	13,230.74
	Total	55,170.66

Table 2.3

Rangewise Distribution of the Gujar and Their Buffaloes in the Siwalik Forest Division

Sl. No.	*Name of the Range*	*No. of Families*	*Population*	*No. of Buffaloes*
1.	Asarori	4	34	50
2.	Timli 21	24	5	184
3.	Malhan	10	56	95
4.	Badkala	40	368	247
5.	Mohand	89	1.163	1,259
	Total	164	1,866	1,785

Source: Siwalik Forest Division, Dehradun

Table 2.4
Rajaji National Park Area

Sl. No.	*Forest Division*	*Range*	*Area in Hectares*
1.	Siwalik Forest Division	Dhaulkhand	13,299.70
		Chilawali	11,531.39
		Haridwar	8,585.50
			25,656.59
2.	Eastern Forest Division	Motichur	8,042.20
		Kansro	7,932.70
			15,974.90
3.	Western Forest Division	Ramgarh	70,703.00
4.	Lansdowne Forest Division	Chila	14,829.80
		Gohri	10,177.90
			25,007.70
	Grand Total		**82,042.19**

Source: Rajaji National Park Directorate, Dehradun

Table 2.5
Distribution of Gujar Families in Rajaji National Park in Various Forest Divisions

Siwalik Forest Division	266
Eastern Forest Division	57
Western Forest Division	8
Lansdowne Forest Division	181
Total	512 Deras

Source: Siwalik Forest Division, Dehradun

Table 2.6
Distribution of Gujars and Their Livestock in Five Families Each of Three Different Regions of Study

Sl. No.	*Locality*	*Population*			*Buffaloes*			*Total Herd*	*Income (approx.) in Rupees*
		Male	*Female*	*Total*	*Milching*	*Dry*	*Total*		
1.	Haldugodam	5	2	7	8	5	13	22	3,960
2.	-	3	7	10	8	5	13	22	5,640
3.	-	6	4	10	8	5	13	26	3,780
4.	-	4	4	8	3	4	7	18	2,160
5.	-	6	3	9	12	8	20	41	4,880
6.	Kuluwala	3	5	8	10	15	25	42	3,700
7.	-	4	5	9	15	20	35	42	4,500
8.	-	10	7	17	30	25	55	73	6,000
9.	-	2	4	6	8	12	20	32	3,000
10.	-	4	4	8	30	25	55	79	5,500
11.	Mohand	14	15	29	15	10	25	46	5,460
12.	-	2	4	6	5	7	12	19	1,980
13.	-	3	7	10	20	10	30	48	8,100
14.	-	5	8	13	3	3	6	18	1,740
15.	-	7	8	15	14	10	24	32	5,470
	Total	78	87	165	189	164	353	560	65,870

Socio-Cultural Perspectives

The primary functional unit in the Gujar social system is the *dera* (household or homestead). It is synonymous with the family and is the most dominant institution in the pastoral Gujar society. The major subsistence, socio-economic, political, religious and reproductive activities are centred around a *dera*. It is usually composed of husband, wife, their sons and their wives, unmarried daughters and grandchildren. It is a joint extended family and usually three generations live under the same roof and eat from the same hearth. The joint family, however, tends to break into nuclear families when the sons marry and set up their own units, which may still share the same roof but have separate hearths and herds. Such nuclear units, with the passage of time, become joint families, again to break up. The reason behind this process is the permit system, which allows the Gujar to live in the Siwalik forest and follow their transhumant mode of subsistence. The head of each family holds a permit on the basis of the number of buffaloes owned by him and is known as a *numberdar* (permit holder with a specified number of buffaloes). The *numberdar* can set up his *dera* in an allotted locality within a specified forest range or coup. His sons, after marriage, may have separate hearths and may be given buffaloes from the parental herd, but they cannot set up separate deras unless they are given permits by the Forest Department and become *numberdars* themselves. Thus an extra-social factor has a determining role in a social phenomenon. It is also responsible for the sprawling nature of the Gujar *dera*, which is spread over a considerable area within which more than one *chappar* (hut/living space) may be constructed. The parents may share the hearth with one of their sons, even a married one. The Gujar also have the tradition of taking *ghar jawain* (a son-in-law who lives with and becomes a member of the family).

The Gujar are polygynous as Islam allows more than one wife (up to four) at one time. But actual cases of polygyny are not frequent, although marrying more than one wife, one after another, due to death or divorce is frequent. Where a man has more than one wife at one time, the wives may set up separate hearths with their children and the husband may join one of them. However, residential arrangements are dependent upon the fact of ownership of the herd. Separate residences are possible only if the units get buffaloes as their share from the family herd. In fact the herd acts as a cohesive factor in a situation where there are multiple marriages and frequent divorces.

The Gujar family is patrilineal and patrilocal. The father, the head of the house, is a strong figure and owns the entire herd as the permit is issued in his name. After the death of the father the property (mainly the herd) and liabilities are equally divided amongst the sons, but the responsibility for running the household devolves upon the eldest son, who inherits and wears the headgear of the father as a mark of authority. He is also given at least one buffalo more than the rest of the brothers but also gets a larger share of the father's debts. Where there are no sons the property is inherited by the widow, who has authority over the household. A *ghar jawain* inherits the property of his father-in-law through his wife.

MARRIAGE

The Gujar are divided into various *gotras*, (clans) which are the same as among the Hindu Gujar. Some of the clan names of the Gujar inhabiting the Siwaliks and the lower Himalayas are Kasana, Khatana, Chechi, Chauhan, Theckari, Dhinda, Pathan, Poshwal(d),

Vania/Bania, Maisi, Lodha and Kaalas. They follow *gotra* exogamy, although there may be exceptions as in cases of elopement. Parallel cousin marriages may take place. Cross-cousin marriages take place frequently, and the sanction is embodied in the kinship terminology, as husband's father, wife's father and mother's brother are all addressed by same term, *mamu* (Appendix III).

The different forms of Gujar marriage reflect their mode of subsistence as well as the place of buffaloes in marital alliances.

Marriage by Exchange (Badla)

The most preferred form of marriage among the Gujar is marriage by exchange, in which a son and daughter of one family are married to a daughter and son of another family. In such cases the paying of bride-price and dowry is avoided and the herds remain intact.

Marriage by Purchase (Mamla)

Generally bride-price is quite high among the Gujar. Fifteen years ago, among the Gujar of Kashmir it used to be as high as Rs. 10,000; but among the Gujar of the lower Himalayas and the Siwaliks it may now go up to Rs. 30,000 or Rs. 40,000. The bride-price can also be paid in kind by giving 5 or 6 buffaloes. As most of the Gujar cannot afford to pay such a high bride-price, there is a substantial number of unmarried males beyond the age of 25 years in the population as compared with females, who all get married before they attain that age.

Marriage by Service

A young Gujar man may take to serving in a family in which there is a marriageable daughter. He may enter into a contract to serve the family for one or two years, and at the end of the period, if found suitable, may be married to the daughter. This form of marriage is taken recourse to by poor Gujar males who do not have a sister to be given away in marriage.

Ghar Jawain

A wealthy Gujar with a marriageable daughter may bring in a suitable young man to his household and marry him to the daughter. The couple takes residence in the *dera* of the girl's father.

Marriage by Elopement (Udhala)

In the past there were very few cases of marriage by elopement, but their frequency is rising now. This can be attributed to high bride-price.

Widow Remarriage

The remarriage of widows is allowed by the Gujar, but in such cases the intending husband may have to compensate the family of the dead man. Junior levirate is quite common among the Gujar.

As in other pastoral societies the animal plays an important role in the marriage of the Gujar. Buffaloes are transferred between families as bride-price as well as dowry. In cases of marriage by service, if the couple subsequently sets up a separate household the father of the girl generally gives them some of his buffaloes. However, due to recent changes in the economic life of the Gujar, more and more money transactions are taking place instead of the transfer of buffaloes.

Generally the Gujar marry their children at a young age, specially girls. However, the *gauna* takes place only when a girl attains puberty.

The Gujar have their own language, Gojri. Their vocabulary has an assemblage of Punjabi, Dogri, Lahanda and Himachali words. According to Grierson (1916), the Gujar of the lower Himalayas speak forms of Rajasthani (Mewati or Eastern Rajasthani), which is also the fountainhead of Himachali dialects. After the migration to Garhwal some Garhwali words have also found their way into Gojri. The Gujar can also speak and understand Hindi, a language which they use to communicate with outsiders for business transactions (Appendix III).

MATERIAL CULTURE

Material culture is the tangible aspect of the life-style of a people. It includes the equipment and artefacts by which a people produce goods and services to meet their basic needs of food, water and shelter. In the case of the Gujar, a pastoral people following transhumance between the Siwaliks and high-altitude pastures, the material culture is centred around their subsistence strategy. As they do not practise horticulture or agriculture, there is a complete absence of agricultural technology. They have just simple digging sticks (*bashalli*). The entire gamut of the material culture of the Gujar can be grouped into:

1. Homestead (different elements).
2. Dress and ornaments.
3. Implements for collecting fodder.
4. Articles connected with milk storage and the processing of milk products.
5. Household utensils for food storage, processing and consumption.

ECONOMY

The Gujar economy is based on the keeping of buffaloes. There has been a shift in orientation from subsistence to commerce. Most of the milk and milk products are sold in the market through a middleman, the *bania*. Usually each Gujar family has an appointed *bania* to whom the entire produce is taken. The *banias* to have now arranged for the collection of the milk from the Gujar *deras* themselves. The Gujar do not get cash from the sale proceeds and rarely a fair price for the milk. The arrangement over the years has been that the *bania* offers monetary support for the purchase of provisions, *khal-chokar* and equipment and provides logistic support for the annual migratory journeys. All these expenses are supposed to be adjusted against the sale proceeds of the milk. Cash requirements for marriages and other social obligations are met by taking loans from the *bania*. The result of all this is that almost every Gujar family is heavily indebted to a *bania* and these debts are difficult to redeem as the Gujar are totally dependent on the *bania* for keeping accounts. On average a Gujar family has 20 to 25 litres of milk for sale per day, which, according to the market price, should fetch Rs. 150.00 to Rs. 200.00. But the Gujar never gets that price. The *bania* adjusts Rs. 2 — 3 per litre against his account. It has been estimated that the monthly income of the Gujar is about Rs. 4500 per family and Rs. 420 per capita, yet they remain perpetually indebted. This feature of indebtedness is one of the hurdles in the way of their rehabilitation. Unless the Gujar clear their debts they are not in a position to change the mode of subsistence and move from their present environs.

The sole means for the generation of income is the sale of milk and milk products. But expenses are mounting. The grazing fee has been raised by the Forest Department to:

01 — 10 buffaloes	Rs. 20
11 — 20 buffaloes	Rs. 25
21 — 30 buffaloes	Rs. 30
above 30 buffaloes	Rs. 40

The expenditure on *khal-chokar, pural* and salt for the animals is also rising. The cost of transport to move household goods and equipment during migratory journeys is also much more now. However, it has been observed that if the Gujar get a fair price for their milk, they would be able to save after meeting all their expenditure.

At present the average herd size of the Gujar per family is estimated to be 37.33, of which lactating buffaloes number 15.13, which comes to 1.09 per capita (Table 2.7). With such animal wealth the Gujar would be much better off economically than most of the neighbouring population if he were freed from the exploitative clutches of the middleman.

Table 2.7

Distribution of Livestock on the Basis of Data from Five Families in Each Region

Sl. No.	*No. of Families*	*Area*	*Per Family Buffaloes*		*Per Capita Buffaloes*		*Herd size*	*Income*	
			Milking	*Dry*	*Milking*	*Dry*		*Per Family*	*Per Capita*
1.	5	Haldu Godam	7.8	5.4	0.88	0.61	25.8	464.09	
2.	5	Kuluwala	18.6	19.4	1.93	2.02	53.6	4391.33	472.91
3.	5	Mohand	19.0	8.0	0.78	0.54	32.6	311.64	
		Total	**15.13**	**10.93**	**1.19**	**1.05**	**37.33**	**416.21**	

RELIGION

The pastoral Gujar of the Siwaliks like those inhabiting other parts of the Himalayan region, are Muslim by faith and claim to belong to the Sunni sect. They observe Ramzan and Moharram and celebrate Idul Fitr, Idul Zuha, Shaberat, etc., according to the tenets of Islam. A Gujar would like to offer Friday *namaz* in a mosque. They would also like to perform *haj*, but ordinarily a Gujar cannot raise the money required. There are few hajis among them. Some of the Gujar, specially those belonging to the Bania clan, celebrate Diwali a day after the Hindu Diwali. In the past the Gujar also celebrated Lohdi and Baishakhi, which signal the waning of harsh cold weather and herald the joyous spring so important for a pastoral community. However, now these celebrations remain only in people's memories, specially in that Islamic fundamentalism is slowly creeping into the lives of the community due to the frequent visits and religious preaching of *maulvis* from the neighbouring region of Saharanpur.

The seasonal migration to high altitudes plays a determining role in the education of Gujar children. They engage *maulvis* for the purpose, and education remains confined to religious teaching. Apart from the dominating influence of *maulvis*, Islamic institutions like Madarsa Islamia Lateefya Ahya-Ul-Islam are becoming popular amongst the Gujar. These also impart only religious (Islamic) teaching. One such school is running in Mohand.

Concepts of Space and Time

Concepts of space and time have special significance for pastoralist people like the Gujar, who follow seasonal migration between two distinct ecozones. "Most, perhaps all, concepts of time and space are determined by the physical ambience . . . ." (Evans-Pritchard, 1969).

Let us first consider the concept of time. There is a clear-cut dichotomy in time reckoning among the Gujar, and the two divisions can be termed ecological time and structural time, a scheme devised by Evans-Pritchard in his seminal work. The ecological time frame is in the form of both annual cycle and daily routine. The Gujar year has two major and almost equal divisions, defined by their mobility between two different ecozones. One, the winter months, from mid-September to mid-March, when they inhabit the winter camps in the Siwaliks and the lower regions of Garhwal; and the other from mid-March to mid-September, when they migrate to the high-altitude *bugyals*. These two divisions include the up and down journey time, which may be 15 — 20 days each way. The two major divisions are further divisible into two each, and the four divisions so arrived at coincide with the four major seasons, that is, winter (October — February), spring (March — April), summer (April — June) and rains (June — September). Time reckoning in the four seasons is important, because that is an index to the state of availability of the two main resources for the herd, that is, pasture and water.

During the winter months (the first major division of the year) the Gujar, while in the Siwaliks and the lower parts of Garhwal, graze their herds in the forest areas allotted to them in groups of families. As the grass in the forest is not plentiful it is supplemented by the tender leaves of trees. As the winter months pass there is a depletion of grass as well as leaves on the one hand and drying up of water sources on the other. This makes it necessary to first make minor movements in the lower regions, which can be termed horizontal migration, followed by the major vertical movement through the middle-altitude valleys to the high-altitude pastures. Migration to the high-altitude *bugyals* does not only ensure pasture and water for the herd but also allows the regeneration of resources in the lower regions during the rainy season. When the herds are brought back to the lower regions around mid-October, fresh regenerated grass, tender leaves of trees and recharged water sources are available to them. At the high altitudes also the pastures have time for regeneration during winter and spring in the absence of grazing activity. The Gujar also claim that their buffaloes are conditioned to the changing weather conditions, and therefore when there is a rise in temperature in the lower regions towards the end of spring, the animals start getting restive. It is even claimed that as the animals know the routes, some of then may even start to move towards the hills on their own. Whereas the annual time cycle is closely related to the needs and welfare of the animals, the daily time cycle is associated with the routine of both humans and animals. The twenty-four hours of the day are reckoned in four divisions:

1. *Bada pahar* (morning — pre-dawn to sunrise)
2. *Dopahar* (day — sunrise — afternoon)
3. *Sham* (evening — afternoon — sunset)
4. *Navasa* (night — after dusk)

The Gujar day begins at dawn, when the *loi tara* (morning star) is positioned above the *dera*. The *loi tara* is located next to *girgiti*, a constellation of six stars.

By *dhyada chadna* (sunrise) the Gujar household is agog with activity. The animals are given feed and soon are taken to the forest for grazing and feeding on leaves.

Before noon, that is *dopahar*, the animals are brought back to the *dera* for milking and are then led to water and again to the forest.

In the evening or *sham*, the animals are brought back to the *dera* and herded into an enclosure for the night.

The structural time of the Gujar is the usual division of a year into twelve months, a month into weeks and a week into seven days. The Gujar being followers of Islam, follow the Hijri calendar, but ecological time reckoning is according to the Gojri calendar (Table 2.8), a derivation of Vikram Samvat. Time reckoning in the annual cycle of subsistence activities is according to the Gojri calendar, whereas the Hijri calendar is followed for religious pursuits. All days of the week have Gojri (Hindu) names, but Friday is known by its Islamic name (Table 2.9).

Likewise, there is a recognisable dichotomy in the Gujar concept of space, which can again be defined as ecological and structural. Ecological space is defined ar various levels, beginning at the level of living space. The hut (*zhonpri*), followed by the homestead (*dera*); a group of *deras* (*tol*); Forest Compartment; Forest Range; Forest Division; and the seasonal encampment areas in different ecozones.

Table 2.8

Names of months

Gojri Calendar	*Islamic Calendar*	
Chaitar	Moharram	March — April
Baisakh	Safar	April — May
Jeth	Reviyolabbal	May — June
Arh	Raviyosani	June — July
Sann	Jamadiyolabbal	July — August
Bhado	Jamadiyosani	August — September
Asu	Razar	September — October
Kaliyado	Sahban	October — November
Mangeru	Ramzan	November — December
Pau	Shavval	December — January
Mago	Zokayada	January — February
Phagunn	Zilhijja	February — March

Table 2.9

Days of the Week

Tar/Atwar	*Sunday*	*The Gujar recognise two important*
Swar Pir	Monday	*dates in a year.* These are nauroz
Mangal	Tuesday	(21 March) and Het (21 September).
Badhar	Wesnesday	Nauroz heralds the migration to
Jammerat/Virwar	Thursday	high-altitude pastures and Het
Jumma	Friday	signals the journey back to the
Hafta/War	Saturday	winter camp.

Since the Gujar are transhumant they have two seasonal encampment locales, one in the forests of the Siwaliks and the lower regions of Garhwal and the other in the high-altitude pastures (*bugyals*) of the Garhwal Himalayas and Himachal Pradesh. But unlike other pastoral communities the world over, the Gujar have no *locus standi* in the spaces on which they are totally dependent for life support. They do not own land anywhere, either in the forest area or elsewhere. In the Garhwal region they entered about over a century back. Initially they may have followed their mode of subsistence freely, but after the colonial power formulated a revenue-earning forest policy the Gujar also came under it and a grazing fee of Rs. 2 and a lopping fee of Rs. 1 per buffalo were levied in the Siwalik forest as per Government Order No. 884-C dated 13.5.1921. Prior to this there was already a fee of 8 annas per buffalo on account of wood or grass for the construction of sheds, which was amalgamated with the new rates (Bhasin, 1979). As per C.O. No. 1119 XIV-332 dated 223.11.1937 also, the Gujar were granted the right to graze their buffaloes in the Dehradun forests on a year-to-year basis (Dang, 1991).

In the high-altitude pastures also the entry of the Gujar is on a year-to-year basis on permits issued by the Forest Departments of Uttar Pradesh and Himachal Pradesh for their respective areas against payment of fees per buffalo. It is interesting to note that both in the low forests and in high-altitude pasture, the right granted to the Gujar is on an annual basis and for grazing their buffaloes. The Gujar thus cannot have a permanent settlement in either location. Both remain just encampment areas.

In the Siwaliks, the winter encampment area, the Gujar *deras* are semi-permanent in nature. Previously they were temporary in that they were dismantled when the Gujar migrated to the high-altitude pastures. The timber was either taken away by the Forest Department and auctioned or simply stolen by nearby villagers. The sites, however, remained permanent, as families returned to them with the onset of winter and rebuilt their *deras* afresh, for which they got timber and thatching grass free or at nominal cost from the Forest Department. Gujar *deras* are invariably located at the perinneal water-holes on the hill slopes or at the seepage springs along the courses of small streams or rivulets (*sot*), thus known after them, e.g., Munal Sot, Amla Sot, Papri Sot, Mang Sot, and so forth. Such locations, although they facilitate the availability of water for humans and for watering and laving the animals, nevertheless do create environmental problems. The matter is dealt with elsewhere.

The Gujar homestead is both an organic and a spatial concept. Although the Gujar are organised in groups of families known as *tol*, inhabiting particular localities on allotment by the Forest Department, the homesteads are far apart from one another. Once a number of families are issued permits by the Forest Department for a particular locality in the forest, the Gujar partition the locality into family (*dera*) territories where the sole right of grazing and lopping is bestowed on the *dera*. The area of these territories can be 2 — 5 sq km. This way ample forest space is available to each *dera*.

A homestead is a composite space and is comprised of several structures:

(i) *Chhappar* (hut), the main living space of the family. It is a large squarish structure between 15' x 15' and 25' x 25' depending upon the economic status and size of the family. It has a conical shape, 15' — 16' high at the centre post; the walls are about 12' high. The *chappar* has a large entrance at the front and smaller door in one of the side walls. This smaller door serves as an escape route in case wild elephants attack the *dera*. The inner space is partitioned by a wall called *androthi* to demarcate about one-third of the rear space for the *rasoi* (kitchen). The *androthi* is usually 5' — 6' high and is not built from side wall to side wall, in order to leave space on both sides to enter the kitchen area. The front area is used as sitting as well as sleeping space on one side and for storing the household equipment, animal feed, etc., on the other. In the centre, just in front of the entrance, is a dug-in roundish fireplace where fire is kept burning throughout the night in order to ward off wild elephants and other predators. In some cases a separate *rasoi* may also be constructed.

(ii) *Baithak* (sitting place). This is smaller structure than the *chappar* but similar in shape. The walls of the *baithak* do not reach up to the roof and are only about 5' — 6' high. The *baithak* is used to receive guests and also for social occasions.

(iii) *Nikki chhan* (small byre). This is small covered structure to house calves.

(iv) The *twala* (feeding platform for the animals) is a sizeable raised platform made of logs or stone and mud on which the buffaloes are given food. The *twala* normally is open to the sky.

(v) A Store shed for *khal-chokar* and fodder may be constructed by well-to-do households.

In the high-altitude pastures the Gujar homestead has only two compartments, the *chappar* for humans and the *nikki chhan* for calves. The *chappar* is on a smaller scale but usually of the same design as in the Siwaliks. There is no need of a *twala*, as in the pastures the grass is much more nutritious and the buffaloes are not required to be given any feed of *khal-chokar*. The building materials, timber and thatching grass, are available from the forest.

Life Support Strategy

The Gujar subsistence pattern, characterised by a near-total dependence on buffaloes, is so remarkable that their relationship with the animal may be regarded as parasitic, the Gujar being parasites of buffaloes. But through a close examination it is seen that the Gujar life-style includes the care and welfare of their herds. They build sheds for adult buffaloes and special enclosures for calves to protect them from predators as well as the elements; they take the animals for grazing and watering; they feed them with fodder, leaves, oilcake and bran; they shave them periodically to ensure protection against lice; they move with them from one locality to another in search of pasture and water; and so on. In a sense the buffalo also becomes dependent on the herder. As the herd and the herder actually sustain life by their reciprocal services to each other, their relationship can only be termed symbiotic; and man and animal form a single community of the closest kind.

In the Gohri range of lower Garhwal, the Gujar move horizontally to at least three encampments during their winter sojourn in order to ensure adequate fodder for their herds, before undertaking the vertical move to the high-altitude pastures. The first move of the Gohri range Gujar is within the Kunao beat along different *sots* (small rivulets). The buffaloes are fed with the leaves of the *bankuli* (*Anogeissus latifolia*) and the *haldu* (*Adina cordifolia*). When lopping of these trees is no longer possible they move towards the bank of the Ganga and to the Haldugodam beat of the Barkot range across the river. In Haldugodam it is mostly the leaves of the *sain* (*Terminalia tomentosa*) and the *sal* (*Shorea robusta*), even through lopping of *sal* trees is prohibited by the Lopping Rules. In the Haldugodam beat fodder is also supplemented by *pural* (paddy stock). It is from Haldugodam that the Gujar finally move to the high-altitude pastures.

Horizontal movements, which are always on a small scale in terms of spatial spread, depend on the availability of fodder, the major portion of which is constituted of leaves obtained by lopping. In the Siwaliks (the winter camp), leaves of the following trees are usually lopped by the Gujar:

1.	*Bakli*	*Angeissus latifolia*
2.	*Sain*	*Terminalia tomentosa*
3.	*Padal*	*Stereospernmum suavelolens*
4.	*Bhimal*	*Grewia oppositifolia*
5.	*Faldu*	*Mitregyna parviflora*

6.	*Harad*	*Terminalia chebula*
7.	*Baheda*	*Terminalis balerica*
8.	*Papdi*	*Bauhinia malabarica*
9.	*Kharwa*	*Ficus hispida*
10.	*Pipal*	*Ficus religiosa*
11.	*Kachnar*	*Bauhinia variegata*
12.	*Pilkham*	*Ficus infectoria*
13.	*Gujar*	*Ficus glomerata*
14.	*Baurang*	*Hymenodictyon excelsum*
15.	*Sanjna*	*Moringa oleifera*
16.	*Jhingan*	*Lannea coromadilica*
17.	*Kharpat/titmira*	*Garuga pinnata*
18.	*Khaman*	*Grewia elastica*
19.	*Kaim/aimraae*	*Ulmus wallichaiana*
20.	*Ganj*	*Croton rox*
21.	*Lisoda*	*Cordia obliqua*
22.	*Sandan*	*Ougenia oegeinesis*
23.	*Maida lakdi/chandna*	*Wend lanelia excerte*
24.	*Khadik*	*Celtes tetrandra*
25.	*Maljhan*	*Bauhinia vahlii*
26.	*Kairwal*	*Bauhinia purpurea*
27.	*Kusum*	*Schleichera oleosa*
28.	*Jarpal/khaina*	*Ficus semicordata*
29.	*Aru/ailanthus*	*Ailanthus excelasa Roxl*
30.	*Khair*	*Acacia catechu*
31.	*Semal*	*Bombax ceeiba*
32.	*Haldu*	*Adina cordifolia*

In addition to fodder, the buffaloes are fed 1.5 kg *khal-choker* (oilcake and bran in the ratio of 1:2) purchased from the *bania*. The calves are given only 500 gm of the feed. Usually the feed is purchased from those traders to whom the milk is sold but it can also be purchased from others. The daily quantum of *khal-choker* naturally depends on the economic status of a family.

Pural is purchased from Rishikesh or the villages in the area. Some is also available from the Gujar households who were allotted land in the 1970s and are cultivators. Feeding of *pural* is from February to April, till the seasonal migration to the high-altitude *bugyals* takes place.

Usually in the Siwaliks, mobility is within the vicinities of *deras* and may not exceed a radious of 5 km. But in some localities such as the Gohri Range, movement, even in the winters, to the Barkot Range for instance, is comparatively extensive mainly for the following reasons:

1. Shortage of fodder.
2. Comparatively more heat due to sun-facing slopes.
3. Drying up of water sources.
4. Restlessness of the buffaloes due to heat.

It is obvious that considerations of fodder, water and general welfare of the herds are uppermost in the life of the Gujar, which prompt these movements. Sometimes in some forest localities there is a sudden increase in the number of flies and other insects which trouble the herds. In such cases also there are frequent movements.

SEASONAL MIGRATION

The seasonal movement of herds to high-altitude pastures is the adaptive strategy followed by the Gujar in the interest of the welfare of the herds and food production for the herders. Livestock husbandry and mobility are closely associated because the livestock must be fed throughout the year to maintain its productivity. With the approach of the summer months, when grass and other fodder as well as water become scarce in the lower regions of Garhwal, the Gujar take their herds to high-altitude pastures where nutritious grass is regenerated after the melting of snows. The nutritious grasses have an invigorating effect on the animals, improve their health and increase productivity both quantitatively and qualitatively. It is also noticed that the animals start becoming restive as soon as the temperature starts rising in the Siwaliks and are conditioned to move to cooler zones in the summer months. There is thus an interdependence between the Gujar and their herds and a dependence of both herder and herd on pasture and water, both in the Siwaliks and in the higher regions. To a certain extent this relationship is symbiotic.

The Gujar inhabiting the Siwaliks migrate to the pastures of Tons, Yamuna and Tehri Forest Division of Garhwal Himalaya as well as Choupal Rodu and Simla Forest Divisions of Himachal Pradesh. The *deras*, which are located in the Siwaliks on the basis of kinship, move to high altitudes maintaining the same neighbourhood relationship during the migratory journeys through the middle-altitude region along river valleys. There may, however, be variation in spatial separation according to the nature of the terrain and the availability of resources. The migration is between predetermined sites through traditionally set routes and according to a more or less fixed time table. The outward and inward journeys take 15 to 20 days each. Thus the actual encampments in summer and winter are for five or five-and-a-half months each. Some of the traditional migratory routes are:

(1) Siwalik region: Sagdiwala — Sahaspur — Yamunapul — Juddo — Nainbag — Damta — Kunwa — Naugaon — Haddoli — Purola — Jurmola — Miyagad — Naitwad — Sidri-Kurti — Taluka — Harkidoon (Uttarkashi)

(2) Siwaliks — Sadwala — Sahaspur — Yamunapul — Juddo — Nainbag — Damta — Kunwa — Naugaon — Haddoli — Purola — Jurmola — Miyagad — Naitwad — Rupin/Supin — Kedarkantha (Uttarkashi)

(3) Rishikesh — Chorpani — Narendra Nagar — Agrakhal — Khadi — Chamba — Tehri — Ghandoli — Ghuttu — Panwali (Tehri)

(4) Siwalik camping site — Mulhan — Konthar — Sahaspur — Jamunapul — Sayya — Kalsi — Chakrata/Panch Bhaiya (Dehradun)

(5) Siwalik — Khafnawar — Asan — Jamunapul — Achhari — Quano — Sainj — Jinus — Rona — Vatera — Nirul — Chanpal — Chhakri — Khirki, etc. (Himachal Pradesh).

Until a few years ago the Gujar used to migrate to the pastures of Badrinath, Kedarnath, Tunganath and a few other places in Chamoli District, but nowadays the Chamoli administration does not sanction them grazing permits because of opposition from local people as well as pastoral communities like the Bhotiya, the Kharkiya and the Khadwals. In 1974, due to similar opposition from the people of the Rupin and Supin Ranges in the Tons valley, the Forest Secretary of Uttar Pradesh sent a wireless message that no Gujar or their buffaloes should be allowed to go to the Rupin and Supin ranges of the Tons Forest Division or the Rawain Range of the Yamuna Division. Permits, if any had been issued, were to be cancelled. Instead, the Gujar going to these ranges should be allowed to continue where they were during winter. It was supposed that by such a measure the Gujar would ultimately be compelled to change their attitude towards migration and would stay back in the Siwaliks. However, the Gujar were averse to this forced change and a delegation met the State and Central Government authorities and implored them to restore their right to follow seasonal migration to high-altitude pastures. The U.P. Government, after reconsideration of the case, ordered telegraphically (Originator No. 1385/4.3.1975 dated 16 April 1975) that summer movement for that year was permitted but that from the next year the Gujar would have to stay back in the Siwaliks. However, despite that order, the Gujar continue their seasonal migration to Rupin, Supin and

Rawain Ranges. For them it is a life-support matter.

Earlier the Gujar *dera* would migrate with all its belongings and livestock to the high-altitude *bugyals*. But recently a change has set in due to forest policies and opposition from the local populations. Fewer and fewer *deras* migrate to high altitudes. At the same time, the *deras* do not moving as a whole: some members with some buffaloes remain behind in the winter habitat. This has resulted in partial sedentarisation with more and more horizontal transhumance. This has increases the pressure on the scarce resources in the Siwaliks.

MIGRATION THROUGH THE MIDDLE ALTITUDES

The mode of migratory journeys has undergone some change over the years. Until about half a century ago the journey each way used to take a longer time as there were no modern means of communication and transportation to the remote approach points to the *bugyals*. Household material and camping equipment had all to be carried by pack animals such as hores, ponies and bullocks. With the road network in the interior of the Himalayas the Gujar can now use public motorised transport to carry their equipment as well as other necessary provisions up to the points from where the trek up mountainous trails to the *bugyals* begins. For example in the Tons Valley, public transport extends to Sankri, some 200 km from Dehradun. The Gujar migrating to Fateh Parbat, Kedarkantha, Harki Doon, Posthar, etc., can use it to transport their equipment and advance parties up to Mori, Naitwad or Sankri in just one day, as against about ten days taken previously.

The herd and some of the herders follow the old foot trail but the movement is a bit faster. Besides, the herds pass through a number of villages through the middle altitudes where fodder and water are available. Earlier the movement was during the day and the herds were halted in agricultural fields where substantial quantities of dung was left when the herd moved. Thus the villagers got manure without any expenditure. There were other transactions also, such as the purchase of fodder (*pural*) by the Gujar and occasional purchase of *jhotas* (male buffaloes) by the villagers for breeding purposes. The relationship between the Gujar and the local populations was cordial and the Gujar were welcome in the vicinity of the villages. However, there has been some change in the attitude of the local populations which is related to resource availability as well as reasons political. The Gujar are no longer welcome in the vicinity of villages, although economic transactions are still carried through. The result is that movement is now mostly during the night and the camps are at secluded places away from the villages, at times on the highway itself. The availability of fodder and water remains the sole determinant camping in the choice of sites. The objective is to reach the *bugyals* the shortest possible time so that the herds can graze the healthy and nutritious grasses. The return journey does not entail that much hardship so far as availability of fodder is concerned, because the animals after grazing in the *bugyals* for about six months are in a much more healthy condition and can sustain the rigours of the journey without much strain.

HIGH-ALTITUDE CAMPING

In the high-altitude *bugyals* the encampment locales are predetermined *tol*-wise. The *tol panchayat* has a role in the allocation of grazing areas to the individual *deras*. When the migration begins, some members of the *tol* representing individual *deras* arrive at the pasture in advance to reconstruct or repair the *deras* which had been left in the previous season.

In the *bugyals*, Gujar *deras* are situated near springs. In the high-altitudes too a conflict situation is arising. Previously the high-altitude agropastoral people raised only goats and sheep, which used to go to pastures at higher elevations where cattle cannot easily climb. Now they keep cattle, which are led to pasture at lower elevations where previously the Gujar used to graze their herds. Consequently the Gujar are compelled to take their buffaloes to high pastures. The presence of Gujar herds in the higher *bugyals* thus creates a multiple conflict situation. First, the highland shepherds do not want the Gujar to migrate to the *bugyals* as these are considered within the jurisdiction of their villages; and second, the presence of two kinds of animals in the *bugyals* results in competition for resources. Sheep do not touch the grass browsed by cattle and therefore are taken higher and higher beyond the reach of the buffaloes. This entails physical hardship for the shepherds, which they resent. There are thus frequent feuds between the Gujar and the shepherds. This is a complex situation as the Gujar have the backing of the official permits issued by the Forest Department and the shepherds have the backing of traditional rights as the inhabitants of the region. Fortunately, thus far no serious situation has arisen and every feud is amicably settled in the spirit of the old amity between the people; but there is little doubt that the situation is fast changing.

SIGNALLING THE CHANGE

The Gujar would like to continue their transhumant mode of subsistence. They are dependent on the buffalo and therefore have the welfare of the animal uppermost in their minds. Over the years their herds have been conditioned to move to cooler climatic areas in summer where nutritious grass is available, which not only improves their health but also increases milk yield. Thus there is an interdependence between the herd and the herder and a dependence of both of them on nature, in this case the regenerated pastures. In the past the Gujar saw to it that the entire pasture was not grazed, that is there was no overgrazing and that scope remained for regeneration during the winter months. This kind of resource management promoted a relationship which to some extent can be termed symbiotic. But such a relationship can exist only up to a point, beyond which an imbalance is bound to occur due to clearly recognizable factors such as increase in the animal population and consequent increased grazing pressure on the pastures. The Gujar are aware that the optimum level has been reached and that imbalance has set in. Though man and animal are still in a sybiotic relationship, their relationship with nature has turned parasitic instead, which is indicated by overgrazing and resource depletion. Change due to competition between sheep and buffaloes for pasture is also contributing to the imbalance. It would thus appear that the Gujar mode of subsistence, transhumant pastoralism based on the buffalo herd, is gradually becoming unsustainable.

Herd Raising

GENERAL PRINCIPLES

Herding or pastoralism was initially an adaptation to semi-arid and marginal areas where pasturage was available. Such areas were not suitable for cultivation and thus could not support large populations. Besides, for regeneration of the grass it was necessary that there was no animal or human presence on the pastures for at least part of the year, and thus no permanent settlements were sustainable in such areas. Pastoral communities, comparatively small and mobile, are ideally adapted to the requirements of the pasture ecosystem. The first animals to be domesticated around 7000 BC were probably sheep followed by goats. These animals subsist on grass and are mobile, so their domestication necessarily meant following them from pasture to pasture. It may have been a pattern similar to that followed by hunters and gatherers, with the difference that hunters follow the herd to kill while pastoralists deliberately cultivate the herd so that it increases in size. Both the hunter and the herder must synchronise their lives with the needs of the herd, but whereas hunters simply follow the animals wherever they go, herders lead their herds to areas where natural resources are available.

Pastoralism therefore involves mobility and a series of encampments varying seasonally, as the resources of different areas are used up and must be allowed time to regenerate. Typically there is a winter encampment and a summer one, between which pastoralists move back and forth. Concomitant with this kind of subsistence strategy or life-style are certain actions based on some basic principles which are the characteristic feature of herd raising, care and management.

1. Objective

Orientation

Subsistence Dependency — Economic/Commercial Motivation

One or other kind of orientation may lead to different care and management strategies.

(i) raising for subsistence as a source of food production and constituting essential life support of the herd;

(ii) maximising products such as milk, meat, wool, etc., for trading.

2. Gaining access to pastures, water and to some extent salt licks. This will necessitate gaining information about the localities where these resources are available; the right to move to such localities; and the right to use the routes leading to such localities.

3. Herd size and composition

(i) Minimum/maximum size according to the objective as well as efficient management depending on natural and manpower resources.

(ii) Qualitative status of the herd, which may involve breeding towards improvement for productivity.

(iii) Sorting out management problems with the growth of the herd, such as feeding time, watering time, quick depletion of natural resources, scarcity of fodder, and so on.

4. Diversification of the stock. Usually herders raise diverse kinds of animals besides the animals which constitute the base of their pastoralism.This diversification may be for supplementing the food supply or towards logistic support for food production.

5. Disease and curative system and health status of the herd.

6. Allocation and partitioning of resources according to herd size and composition. Political organisation may also come into play in guiding this and ensuring submission to authority.

7. Relationships, with neighbouring populations in the encampment areas and on migratory routes.

GUJAR LIVESTOCK HERDING

All these factors are applicable to Gujar pastoralism, as has already been stated. However, a few points need a little elaboration. First of all, the raising of buffalo herds by the Gujar, its origin, continuance and pastoralism.

It has already been pointed out that the buffalo came under human control at a relatively late stage, that is about 2500 BC, in the Indus Valley. The animal is still found in the wild in the Nepal Tarai and the submountain region of north-east India, where it has no history of domestication for constituting the sole basis of subsistence. In other parts of world such as south China, Indonesia, Mexico, etc., the buffalo is used as a draught animal in agriculture. It is only in India that pastoralism is based on raising buffalo herds.

The Gujar, it is claimed, were a pastoral people who migrated into the Indian subcontinent from Central Asia in the 5th or 6th century AD, when they probably raised sheep and goats. The shift to buffalo raising could have taken place due to ecological pressures and the fact that the animal was already domesticated in north-western India. Later the Gujar are known to have migrated to northern India, specially the marginal areas of Punjab and Jammu, where pasturage was available for their buffaloes. At what point of time and why the Gujar shifted to buffalo raising is difficult to say, but its continuance to present times is an observable phenomenon.

THE TODA PARALLEL

There is one more community, the Toda of the Nilgiris in southern India, which has also adopted the pastoral mode of subsistence based on raising buffaloes. Like the Gujar, the Toda have a near-total dependence on the buffalo for food production, but they are settled in one locality. The Toda supplement their subsistence by practising horticulture and agriculture. There is yet one more significant difference between Gujar and Toda pastoralism. For the Gujar the buffalo is an animal which is their life support both in terms of subsistence and also for cash generation, whereas for the Toda the buffalo is a sacred animal: it does provide life support, but it also has a place in their ritualistic practices. Milk produced by the buffalo has ritual significance and constitutes the only offering to the deity. The Toda also construct a separate house, denominated as the temple, to house the sacred buffalo and the priest who looks after the sacred animal. The milk of the sacred buffalo is taboo to women. The Gujar, on the other hand, do not have any rituals connected with the buffalo or its produce.

Herd Size and Maintenance of Reproductive Base

There is a general apprehension among the Gujar about the increasing number of dry buffaloes and low productivity of milk. Almost 50 per cent of the stock, and at times even more than that, of almost every family remains dry. This has caused a panic situation in a people who have a near-total dependence on their herds. The objective therefore would be

1. Optimum yield from minimum herd size.
2. More grazing and fodder resources for lactating females in their prime.
3. Culling of male animals at a younger age, as large number are not needed for reproduction.
4. Weeding out of unproductive or dry females past their reproductive potential in the interest of better resource management.

The strategy adopted by the Gujar is to take great care of female calves to maintain a herd's reproductive base, whereas male calves are allowed to wane and die, not being allowed to suckle milk and not being taken care of. Quite often male calves are fed upon buttermilk so that they die. In an average herd of 25 — 30 female buffaloes, one or two male adults are considered adequate for reproduction.

Adult females past their lactating and reproductive spans are also neglected and are not given any fodder or feed. Such animals are not looked after and are left out to fend for themselves and to die uncared for. By taking recourse to this culling process the Gujar try to manage grazing resources and save on fodder and feed and ensure the reproductive base of the herd.

The Gujar give individual attention to lactating female animals and their female calves. In the event of the death of a calf the buffalo may withhold the flow of milk, which can only be restored by faking. The dead calf is skinned and the skin is filled with husk so that the buffalo takes it to be the calf and releases the flow of milk.

The Gujar let old and weak animals die in the forest. But in case an animal dies in the *dera* it is dragged out and left out in the open. Dead animals are skinned by Khatik, government (Forest Department) contractors who deal in the hides. The Gujar owner of the dead animal does not get a share of the tender money as all of it goes into the government account.

The case of dung is similar. The Forest Department calls for tenders for the collection of dung accumulated in the Gujar *deras*, but the Gujar do not get any share of the tender money.

HERD SIZE AND GENETIC RECORD

Gujar herds are bred and raised in individual households. This is more or less a result of conscious selection for breeding, since the processes of animal reproduction are similar to those of humans. The Gujar are well aware of them, but, there is a negative aspect which will be evident from observations from the field.

Munalsot, a sizeable river, almost dries by the time winter sets in. A trickle may run down here and there but it is mostly *rauknad*. Some 2 km up the *sot* from Chila is a lone *dera* of Lal Hussain. There are two dwelling units, one of Lal Hussain himself and the other that of his daughter and son-in-law, Yusuf. Yusuf entered Lal Hussain's household about two years ago as a servant, offering his services as an aspirant for Lal Hussain's daughter's hand in marriage. Lal Hussain was satisfied with him and Yusuf was accepted as *ghar jawain*.

Lal Hussain is 85 years old. It is amazing that the Gujar generally have a correct knowledge of their ages. Even women folk know their ages and those of their children correctly. Lal Hussain remembers that when he was 12 years old his grandfather was still living, at the age of 65. He says that his stock has all been bred and raised in his *dera*. There has not been any addition from outside. All his stock descends from the buffaloes his grandfather came with, more than 60 years ago, from Himachal Pradesh. However, he says, he is now facing some problems in breeding as more and more buffaloes remain infertile after a few calvings. The milk yield has also come down.

Although no genetic record as such is available, Lal Hussain (as well as other Gujar) has a record in his memory of the number of times a buffalo has calved and the generation of its descendants. Normally a buffalo generation is of 3 — 4 years, that is, the first calving is after a buffalo has attained the age of 3 — 4 years, and it is 14 — 15 months until the subsequent calving. If the maximum age of a buffalo is assumed to be 15 years, the reproductive span may be 10 — 12 years, during which period it may undergo 7 — 8 calvings on the average. Lal Hussain in his lifetime has seen about twenty generations of his herd bred in his *dera* from the original stock owned by his grandfather.

Traditionally the Gujar raise the stock bred in their own *deras*, and it is a common observance that fertility performance as well as productivity are not as good as they used to be. Both of these attributes may be influenced by a number of factors:

(i) Genetic make-up of the animals.
(ii) Nutrition, which in turn is dependent on the quality of grass and fodder.
(iii) Health status of the animals, that is, freedom from disease.

Although nutritional and health status are important, in this case the most obvious reason for the poor fertility performance and low productivity of Gujar stock seems to be the genetic make-up of the stock. It appears that the stock bred and raised by the Gujar is highly inbred. There is no evidence of replenishing herds by adding animals purchased from outside. There also have not been any efforts to improve or hybridise stock by importing bulls of better breed. It seems that the general practice is that each *dera* keeps one or two bulls from its own stock for breeding purposes. This close breeding may have resulted in some kind of degeneration which would explain the relatively high incidence of fallowness among stock. There is a reduction in calvings on the one hand and a lowering of milk yield on other. Since Gujar pastoralism is both for subsistence and market-oriented they would be anxious to maintain a certain quantitative level to bring in sufficient income to feed their families and supplement the stock feed.

The Gujar can possibly solve the problem by importing better bulls from outside their own stocks to improve the breed and reinvigorate their stock. Whether the Gujar will take that measure is uncertain since they would be eager to preserve the purity of the breed of the stock which they have inherited from their ancestors (*purkha*).

What we observe here is close inbreeding which occurs in small animal populations such as the Gujar stocks. Mating pairs share recent common ancestors which means frequent homozygous pairing of recessive genes which often have harmful effects. Their expression may be through by increased incidence of disease and higher mortality rates. There may also be other effects such as decreased fertility performance and lower productivity, as is the case with Gujar stocks.

DIVERSIFICATION OF STOCK

It has already been mentioned that the Gujar raise a few cattle and horses or ponies, since bullocks and horses or ponies are used as pack animals. Cow's milk is also considered useful for children, pregnant women and the sick. But the Gujar also raise goats for milk as well as meat. This has a degenerating effect on the forest, as the plants and saplings browsed by the goats wither away. There is a feeling among forest officials and environmentalists that the Gujar are doing this deliberately.

ALLOCATION OF RESOURCES

The allocation of resources (territory) is based on a twofold system in which both the State and the Gujar political organisation are involved. It has already been stated that the Gujar do not own any land anywhere and their habitation in the forests of the Siwaliks is on the basis of permits. The Forest Department of the government which has the responsibility of forest management, first allots a particular range or coup to a *tol* of Gujar *deras*. After that the *tol panchayat* consisting of the leader (*bada numberdar*) and the *heads* of individual *deras* (numberdars) apportion the territory among the individual *deras*. The rights of a *dera* to its space are strictly protected and any encroachment by other *deras* is punishable by the *tol panchayat*.

Till recently the simple organisation was effectively and smoothly managing the affairs of the Gujar residing within the forest but due to recent conflicts, dealt with elsewhere, an external agency (NGO), in the name of fighting for the rights of the Gujar in the forest, has been able to influence some of the *tol* leaders and has thus assumed the leadership role among a section of Gujars for ulterior motives.

POPULATION STRUCTURE

As a transhumant population the Gujar have to face the hazards of journeying and camping under extreme climatic conditions. This has an influence on the structure of the population in terms of fertility, mortality, age and sex structure (Negi, 1982), which in turn influences herd management. A detailed analysis of changes in the population structure will be attempted elsewhere.

HUMAN AND ANIMAL ROUTINE

Gujar daily routine is closely integrated with herd management. The day starts very early for adult males and females. Lighting the hearth is the job of young women in the family, who prepare tea and serve all. The next task is the churning of curdled milk. Fodder is given to the animals and the stalls are cleared of dung. Around 7 a.m. almost all the adults take the herd to the forest for grazing. Often young children also accompany the herd. Division of labour depends on the available labour in a *dera*. If the family is large, the aged remain in the *dera* and clean the stalls, fetch water, cook food and mix oilcake and bran for when the animals come back to the *dera* before noon for milking. Milking is done by all adults. There are no taboos in milking. In the afternoon the work-force is divided. Some adult males (both old and young) may go to the bazar with the milk products and bring back provisions. At 3 — 4 p.m. the animals are again taken to the forest.

The daily routine of the buffaloes varies from locality to locality, according to the feeding time table. In the Kunao Range the lopping of trees is done in the afternoon and the buffaloes are taken to the lopping area, where leaves are fed to them along with whatever grass is available. The animals stay out in the forest during the night. One or two men also stay with them in view of possible danger from predators, specially tigers. Early in the morning lopping is again done and the animals are fed the leaves. After the feeding the animals are brought to the *dera* around 10 — 11 a.m. In the *dera* all the lactating, pregnant and ill buffaloes are given oilcake and bran, often mixed with water and the leaves of trees. Dry buffaloes are given oilcake and bran in smaller qunatities. After the feeding in the *dera* the lactating buffaloes are milched. The buffaloes are then taken to water, where they sit in the water for some time.

In the Haldugodam Range the routine is somewhat different. Here the animal do not stay out in the forest during the night. Around 5 or 6 a.m. the animals are fed with *pural* and then led to the forest for grazing, where the herdsman also lops the leaves of trees. Around 10 — 11 a.m. the animals come back to the *dera* and are fed with oilcake and bran before milking. After milking the animals are led to the water and then to the forest for grazing and feeding of leaves. The animals come back to the *dera* before nightfall.

It will thus be seen that in two different ecological situations the routine of the animals is changed by the herdsmen, who are keenly aware of the different conditions as well as of the availability of resources. In the Kunao area, although desirable flora are available in plenty, the unfavourable weather conditions and drying up of the water holes compels moving out to a locality where the weather and watering conditions are favourable but where desirable flora are scarce. Besides, there is a prohibition on lopping certain kinds of trees, which makes it necessary to change over to a different type of fodder which is available by purchase only.

In all situations the milking routine is constant. The Gujar milk their buffaloes only once in twenty-four hours, just before noon. After the milking the buffaloes are led to water holes, ponds or rivers, where they are allowed to sit and rest for about an hour every day.

Usually after milking or when they are taken out for grazing in the forest the buffaloes are given rock salt to lick. Intake of salt is helpful in the metabolic process of the animals and at the same time the feeding of salt at the *dera* is an attraction to the animals, which prompts them to come to the *dera* on their own at the appointed time.

Rock salt is purchased in the market and boiled in an empty canister. Usually the twigs of the *bhoomal* (*Grewia oppositifolia*) are first boiled in water and the fibres removed. To the extract rock salt is added and put to boil. When the solution has cooled it solidifies. The solid mass is then broken into piecess which are given to the buffaloes for licking. According to Kasam Chauhan, a Gujar herdsman, the consumption of rock salt is about 60 kg for 40 buffaloes in 5 months. That is 12 kg per month which comes down to about 300 gm per buffalo per day.

Salt is given to the animals only on two days in a week, Mondays and Thursdays. In some cases it may be given on other days of the week according to convenience, but Mondays and Thursdays are a must.

In the organisation of daily routine, apportioning of time, specially the period between dawn and dusk, is very important. The Gujar do not possess watches and clocks to guide them, but like every pastoral community they have learnt to tell time from natural indicators.

1. Early dawn is signalled by the position of *kirgiti* (a constellation of six stars) and the *loi tara* (morning star) over the *dera*. The Gujar also recognise that the shrieks of the *ghughu* (owl) indicate the dawn.
2. During the day, between sunrise (*dhyda chadna*) and sunset (*dhyda chhipha*), they divide the time according to the sun's trajectory through early morning, mid-morning, noon, afternoon, and so forth.
3. The lengthening and shortening of the shadows of trees also indicates the different quarters of the day.

EMOTIONAL ATTACHMENT

The Gujar's total dependence on their herds for life support also leads to mutual emotional attachment between man and animal. The naming of a buffalo is an important element of this process. Most of the time the name given to the buffalo (specially females) is after the physical attributes of the animal such as:

1.	Pund (poond)	Completely black
2.	Raayee	Upright horn and iron colour
3.	Arani	Spiral horn (two or three spirals)
4.	Kadani	Horns bent backwards
5.	Kanchar	One with glassy eyes
6.	Paini	One with pointed horns

7.	Seti	One horn bent and one horn straight
8.	Waali	Horns bent towards the neck and depressed
9.	Rosi	Forehead, tail and feet half white
10.	Gatera	Horns bent downwards
11.	Raj	Colour brown, mouth white and small udders
12.	Tasni	One foot white and one horn white at root
13.	Sunni	Good-looking (beautiful)
14.	Chandu	White spot on the forehead

The following song is in praise of the desirable attributes of a buffalo:

Saing sunhi de, bang-bang kundalay
Thann keley di phaliyan
Dodh Sunni da semtu mithada
Jau misri di daliyan

Horns or Sunni, the beautiful, are like spirals
and udder like the plantain,
Milk is sweet as a lump of sugar candy.

There is no naming ceremony as such, but female calves (*katdi*) are given names between the ages of 1 and 3 years. By the time a calf matures and attains reproductive age, that is 3—4 years, she already has a name and answers to that whenever called by her owner. The animal becomes familiar with its name through the feeding of oilcake, bran and fodder, as it is called by name. Here one can see the relationship of dominance and symbiosis between man and the animal. Man's dominance over the herds is to be seen in the submission of the herds to the cultural regime in a context of mutual support. The behaviour of the beast is radically changed through a process of behaviour formation that are influenced by the circumstances of imprinting and nomadization. Imprinting among pastoral animals is given the meaning of learning and socialization, which is different from the meaning originally assigned to it.

Usually the Gujar drink milk by directly suckling the udder of a buffalo. In this process there appears to be a close emotional integration between man and animal. There is a story that has general currency among the Gujar to highlight the process:

Bar baras Jumla ayee bayees jhottee leke

Jumla came home after twelve years along with twenty-two female offsprings.

Once two Gujar were travelling together. Each had a pregnant buffalo with him. On the way one Gujar fell asleep while the other was awake, and at that time the buffaloes foaled. To one was born a male calf and to the other, a female calf. The buffalo of the Gujar who was awake gave birth to a male calf but he changed it with the other's female calf. They went their separate ways with their respective buffaloes but interchanged calves.

After twelve years the Gujar whose female calf was changed visited the Gujar who had changed the calves. In the morning the guest sat under the udder of his host's buffalo to drink milk straight from the udder. The moment the *pahali dhar* was in his mouth he exclaimed, "It is my buffalo". The thought crossed his mind that his host had changed the calves at the time of birth. A dispute arose and they took it to the king. The king listened to both and decided to put them to the test. He threw a feast to which both men were invited. Secretly the king had several maunds of barley fed to buffaloes. The barley was then extracted from their excreta (buffaloes cannot digest barley). The barley thus collected was ground into flour, out of which *halwa* was cooked and served to the guests. Everyone ate the *halwa* with relish except the Gujar who was laying claim to his buffalo. The king asked him why he was not eating. The Gujar said, why should one eat something which has already been eaten? Realising the Gujar's ability to discriminate, the king ordered that his buffalo Jumla, along with her twenty-two progeny, should be returned to him. On this the Gujar was so happy that he sang the song:

Barah baras Jumla ayee bayees jhottee leke

It is, however, noticeable that such attachment is demonstrable mostly with female calves and lactating adults, evidently for economic reasons. The male calf is unwanted.

Knowledge System

The Gujar have a fairly good knowledge of the various diseases their buffaloes suffer from. These diseases are not peculiar to Gujar buffaloes as the livestock of the region as a whole suffer from them, but what is of special interest is that the Gujar over the generations have preserved the knowledge of a curative system which is traditional and indigenous. Earlier little medical assistance was available, as there were very few veterinary hospitals or dispensaries within easy reach of the Gujar. The situation is somewhat better today as, apart from veterinary hospitals in bigger towns such as Dehradun, Saharanpur, Haridwar and Rishikesh, there are dispensaries in the smaller towns where the Gujar can take their buffaloes for treatment. But this course of action is only taken recourse to when their own curative system has failed.

When the characteristics of a disease are evident, the Gujar try their indigenous curative system. Various diseases and their cures are thus described by the Gujar:

(1) *Khurpaka* (foot-and-mouth disease). It is an acute and contagious disease of hoofed animals. The characteristics are well recognised by the Gujar, who treat the diseased animal with a decoction of *kaduwi* (*Pierasma quassioides*).

(2) *Galghontu* (Haemorrhagic septicaemia). The characteristics of this disease are recognised as choking and the release of excessive saliva. The buffalo is unable to eat. Young calves are afflicted with greater frequency. The traditional cure is to singe the undersurface of the throat.

(3) *Nakada/thanela* (mastitis). Swelling of the udders and drying up of lactation. The buffalo is fed with red chilli powder mixed with oilcake and bran.

(4) *Taku* (*epifemoral fever*). Dryness in the nostrils and hardening of the udders as a result of no lactation. The buffalo may also become lame. The Gujar try to treat this fever by administering a mixture of powdered carem seeds and sal ammoniac in water.

(5) *Rinderpest*. The Gujar describe this as blood dysentery. Rinderpest is a usually fatal and the animal generally dies within one or two days of contracting the infection. It is characterised by high fever, diarrhoea and lesions of skin and mucous membrane. It is also known as cattle plague and in epidemic form causes devastating loss of livestock. The Gujar do not know of any effective indigenous treatment and cure is sought through serum injections.

(6) *Surra* (trypanosomiasis). Often fatal, infectious disease caused by a bood infecting protozoan parasite, *Trypanosoma evansi*, transmitted by the bite of horseflies. The disase is characterised by fever, anaemia and emaciation. The Gujar recognise these characteristics and also (i) watering of the eyes; (ii) neck hanging to one side; (iii) muddy urine; and (iv) bouts of unconsciousness.

According to the Gujar, who consider the disease a sure killer, there is no effective cure. Nevertheless they try a mixture of jaggery, pepper, cumin and powdered fenugreek seeds in water or milk, but ultimately fall back on modern medicine based on antibiotics.

In addition to the various diseases caused by organisms, the Gujar are aware of the afflictions caused by various weeds including lantana and poisonous grasses or creepers. They have indigenous prescriptions in which concoctions of roots and tubers as well as a mixture of ash and whey are administered to the afflicted animal.

Decrease in the milk yield of a buffalo or even stoppage is sometimes ascribed to the evil eye, which the Gujar call *tokala*. The remedy for this is to burn carem seeds, chillis and loban, etc., in a iron pan and make the affected buffaloe inhale the fumes. In addition, some incantations are uttered and a talisman is tied around the neck of the animal.

In almost all cases, be it a disease, infection, affliction by poisonous grass or weed or affection by the evil eye, the Gujar first resort to incantation *maulavi* or a knowledgeable Gujar followed by indigenous curative methods. Modern medicines such as injections and other antibiotic prescriptions come last.

The Gujar are anxious to maximise milk yield and therefore give individual attention to their buffaloes, specially lactating ones. They are also anxious to ensure optimum fertility performance of their female buffaloes through their reproductive life spans and have indigenous prescriptions to make them conceive in every event of heat. When a buffalo fails to conceive they feed the animal with oilcake of linseed with bran and tie a talisman around the neck of the animal, chanting incantations.

CARE OF BUFFALOES ON CALVING

After a calving a buffalo is given special feed, consisting of boiled *urad*, jaggery and fenugreek, for three days. The buffalo is also fed with its own fresh milk mixed with oilseed and bran. The milk yield of a buffalo on the average is 6 — 7 litres and it lactates from one-and-a-half years to two years. However, the yield descreases continuously during this period. For the first six months it may be 7 — 8 litres. On completion of one year the yield may be 4 — 5 litres,and it may come down to 1 — 2 litres at the end of two years.

Female calves are allowed full feed for the first six months while male calves are allowed only half feed. Gradually the feeding, even of female calves, is reduced and they only suckle the udder of the mother buffalo briefly before milking to make her release milk. If a calf were not to suck her teats first, the buffalo would hold up her milk. After milking, the calves are allowed to suckle for the remainder, when the teats become soft and empty. The feed of calves is supplemented by oilcake, bran and other fodder. Male calves are allowed very little milk deliberately as part of the culling process.

The Gujar's dependence on milk is so great that they want the maximum yield. Towards that end they often take recourse to cruelty. When a calf dies either naturally or through culling, the mother buffalo may withhold milk. In that event the Gujar resort to:

(1) *Fuke dum deve*, vaginal irritation in which the tail of the buffalo is inserted into

its vagina to make the animal release its milk. Sometimes a man may insert his hand to cause great irritation. This is done only by the few who know about it.

(2) Administering posterior pituitary injection to the buffalo, which makes her release milk.

Both these operations are defined as cruelty and are punishable criminal acts. In the first case there may be imprisonment up to 6 years and a fine of Rs. 10,000. In the second case a fine of Rs. 2,000 may be imposed. However, according to veterinary doctors, rarely is a case of cruelty registered against a Gujar. They live in forest areas where it is not easy to lodge a report against them even though it is well known that they indulge in such acts of cruelty. In the Chila region it was reported that a vendor visited Gujar *deras* every morning with post pituitary injections which were sold for fifty paise apiece.

Cosmology and Belief System

According to Gujar belief, God (*khuda*) created the whole universe in six days. On the first day he created the angels, on the second day the earth, on the third day the sky, on the fourth and fifth days the stars, moon and sun, and on the sixth day humans and animals.

SKY (HEAVEN)

God created seven skies (heavens) one above another. The stars occupied the first sky. In the second and third reside the angels (*farishtas*). In the fourth sky there is a house near a berry tree where spirits live and from where they go to hell or heaven, wherever assigned. In the fifth sky there is a big pond the water of which is extremely hot, and when the farishtas strike the water with sticks, lightning flashes across the sky which falls on sinful trees and plants (trees and plants that do bad deeds, that is, cause harm to humans and animals) causing them to wither away. The sixth sky has a cold-water pond from which rise three streams: first the Gangaji, second the river of Baghdad Sharif and the third theNeel (Nile) river of Misr (Egypt). As these streams rise in heaven their waters are considered sacred. In the seventh sky resides the sun, who has seven eyes. The sun is on a throne around which 600 angels keep circling, which gives the impression that the Sun circles the earth. After death every mortal has to pass through the seven layers of skies to attain *bahisht* (heaven).

EARTH

The Gujar believe that there are seven earths one beneath the another, just as there are seven skies. It takes 500 years to cover the distance between one layer and another. In the first layer are humans, demons and animals, in the second there are suffocating fumes; in the third the sloves of hell; in the fourth the sulphur of hell; in the fifth the serpents of hell; in the sixth the scorpions of hell; and in the seventh the Devil and the Angel. Our earth, that is the layer on which humans live, is held by an angel on its shoulder. The angel is on a rock of jewels (*mani*) which is balanced over the horns of a heavily built bullock. According to the Gujar our earth is like the lap (*anchal*) of a mother on which humans live and die. It is also believed that earthquakes are caused by the movements of the bullock on whose horns all else is balanced.

FIRE

It is said that God created fire by means of the friction caused by rubbing the green boughs of two trees. Fire is considered sacred, but there is no fire worship as such.

WATER

The Gujar say that according to the holy Kuran, water separates heaven (sky) and earth. God has created all living beings with water as an essential in all creatures. Six different kinds of water have been described by the holy Kuran: the waters of rain, rivers, waterfalls, wells, oceans and ice. Water has been sent by Allah from *jannat* (*heaven*) to cleanse the earth as well as for the growth of trees and plants.

ECLIPSES

Gulamuddin says that the Gujar equate the eclipse with indebtedness. It is said that once the sun and the moon incurred heavy debts which could not be redeemed in time. That indebtedness is said to be the cause of solar and lunar eclipses. At present the Gujar suffer from heavy indebtedness at the hands of the *banias* with whom they have their economic transactions. This has overshadowed their lives. Perhaps this feeling is equated with the phenomenon of eclipse and hence the myth. There are some who believe that the sun and the moon are proud of their brightness and therefore God, to break their egos, covers them for some time. It is a sort of punishment meted out to the sun (*dhyda*) and the moon (*chaan*) by God, and any child or calf born during an eclipse may become disabled. That is why expectant mothers and buffaloes are kept hidden during the eclipse.

SUN AND MOON

Haji Mir Ali (78 years) narrates a belief that a mother had two sons, Suraj (sun) and Chand (moon). Suraj was cunning, disobedient and hot-tempered, so the mother gave him a curse that he would remain thus burning hot. But Chand was sweet-natured and obedient, so the mother blessed him so that he would shine during the night and that people would feal happy and joyous seeing him. Another version of the legend is as follows:

> Moon and Sun were two sons of a mother. One day the mother asked Moon and Sun to scratch her itching body. Sun got a thorny bush to scratch the body of his mother, which left many marks. The mother cursed him that he would always be ablaze, "You will rise every day blazing and inflaming and set blazing and inflaming. No one will be able to look at you." On the other hand the Moon soothed his mother's body with a soft cotton swab. She was happy and blessed him and said, "you will always remain cool and people will feel soothed in your shade". Since then the mother has lived with the moon and is visible as the black spot on it.

STARS AND CONSTELLATIONS

About the stars the Gujar belief is that there are seven types of stars in the sky: Johra, Amreekh, Jhal, Samsukmar, Mustari, Kutub tara. However, they have little or no knowledge about the orientation of these stars except Kutub tara and Loi, which are known to be time indicators.

SOME GUJAR BELIEFS

1. On doomsday the letters of the Kuran will be reversed. The sun will face towards the earth (at present it has its back towards the earth) and this world will come to an end.
2. After a dead man is buried, angels call him out and he sits up in his grave. Then judgement is pronounced as to whether he will be sent to heaven or to hell. After he has served his term in heaven he is sent back to the earth.
3. Small children should not be left alone in the house, otherwise spirits will possess them.
4. If the shade of a tree falls on a pregnant woman it can have a bad effect on the unborn child, including still birth.
5. Ganga water is considered sacred. A buffalo may contract *khurpaka ijar* if its feet do not come in contact with Ganga water. Sprinkling of Ganga water on its

feet cures the disease.

6. It is a sin to point the feet towards a cemetery or towards Makka and Madina.
7. Before leaving the *dera* the Gujar say, "God, in your care" (*Allah tere hawale*).
8. Performing Haj cleanses one of all sins.
9. When a person is possessed by evil spirit (*jinna*) he stamps his feet and hands on the ground and starts behaving as though he is mad. A *maulavi* can cure him by exorcism. Sometimes a chicken has to be sacrificed.
10. If dogs or jackals wail it may bring illness or some ill-event.

From Nomadic Pastoralism to Sedentarisation and Rehabilitation

In 1976, when I first had the opportunity to make a quick survey of the Gujar of the central and western Himalayas, a trend of change from pastoral nomadism to sedentarisation was clearly noticed. In the Kashmir Valley the Gujar were settled during the time of Maharaja Ranbir Singh, who started settling the Gujar from Jammu in the Valley. In the Jammu region there was a noticeable difference between the Dudh Gujar, who followed pastoralism with transhumance, and the Zamidar Gujar, who were settled on land and practised agriculture. Among the Dudh Gujar also, a change towards agro-pastoralism was noticed. In Himachal Pradesh and the Uttar Pradesh hills the trend towards sedentarisation was evident from the fact that the winter encampment areas were becoming larger and larger and taking on a semi-permanent shape, as quite a number of them were not abandoned as in the past. There was clearly a preference for remaining in the Siwaliks for easy availability of grazing for their herds within the forest area and access to market centres for their produce. The desire for change was also expressed by the Gujar themselves as they wanted to have a settled life so that they could enjoy the fruits of development, their living conditions could improve and their children could get education. However, they wanted the permanent settlement within the Reserve Forest area and already had voiced their demand for land in Asarodi and Mohand Forest Ranges of the Siwalik Forest Division of Dehradun (Negi and Raha, 1982).

After about fifteen years, when the present pilot survey was undertaken among the Gujar in the Garhwal region, there was a partial change in which a sizeable number of Gujar *deras* gained permanent to semi-permanent status in the Siwaliks and the lower regions of Garhwal. For instance, 42 families have been settled in Kunao and about 25 families in Chila, remaining in the Siwaliks all the year round. They have given up the practice of seasonal migration to high altitudes. In the Siwalik forest also there are a number of families who have either given up seasonal migration or follow it partially in the sense that only a few members of a family migrate while the rest remain behind in the winter encampment area. Gradually the transhumant mode of subsistence is being abandoned due to the multifactoral changes which have already been discussed. However, the most important change has come in the relationship between man and animal on the one hand, and man, animal and nature on the other. The relationship has been rendered exploitative and parasitical due to the phenomenal growth of human and animal populations and depletion of resources due to overutilization.

The pastoral Gujar have perceived the change in this relationship and would like to readjust the adaptive strategy. As a matter of fact they have started making efforts in that direction. Reduction in the number of migrant *deras* to high altitude pastures is a step in the process of sedentarisation. Taking up horticulture and agriculture in their semi-permanent winter encampment areas is another step towards giving up nomadic life. It is true that the Gujar are yet reluctant to completely give up the pastoral mode of subsistence, but they are aware that it is no longer a successful adaptive strategy as it used to be, and in the changed situation needs either to be modified or given up altogether.

At present the Gujar are heavily dependent on nature, in other words forest and pasture, in both winter and summer encampment areas. But there are limiting factors. They are constrained both in the Rajaji National Park area in the Siwaliks and in the high-altitude areas where the entire region of Rawain, Rupin and Supin (Tons valley) has been declared a Protected Area (Govind Pashu Vihar). The Forest Department, in the interest of conservation of natural resources and environmental protection, is gradually imposing restrictions on issuing of permits to the Gujar both in the Siwaliks and in high-altitude pastures. They would rather have the Gujar move out of the forest and also give up their transhumance. The Gujar for the time being have choosen an easier option, amounting to deception with the connivance of minor forest officials. They do not disclose the actual number of livestock, always giving a lower figure. As for humans, there has not been an accurate census and only estimates of the population are available. The strategy is to keep the figures at a level which may be considered sustainable in the forest environment. But this play cannot work for long and the Gujar will have to be pursuaded to settle. However, while doing so they should be taken into confidence and their rehabilitation outside the forest area must be done in a manner that allows them to pursue their life-style and also enjoy the fruits of development. At present the Government of Uttar Pradesh has a rehabilitation scheme for the settlement of 512 Gujar families in the Pathri Reserve Forest area about 20 km south of Haridwar.

an isolated patch of 2,400 ha of planted forest immediately south of the Siwaliks. The rehabilitation scheme at Pathri envisages giving them pucca houses and space for raising six buffaloes per family, who would be stall-fed. There is to be provision of water and other amenities. The Gujar will also be alloted land for cultivation, which would initially supplement their subsistence and gradually may become their primary occupation. Houses and other amenities for 512 Gujar families have already been created at considerable cost.

Table 2.10
U.P. Government Scheme for the Rehabilitation of the Gujar of the Rajaji National Park

		Expenditure in lakhs of Rs.
1.	House construction for 512 families Rs. 40,000/unit	204.80
2.	Cattle shed and store Rs. 2,500/ family	12.80
3.	Roads 4 km	0.50
4.	Two tube wells with electric connection	4.00
5.	Drain for irrigation	0.06
6.	Demarcation and levelling of land	0.16
7.	Community hall and school	3.00
8.	Electrification	7.42
9.	Drinking water (handpump/3 families)	2.53
10.	Food subsidy at 25% Rs. 4,212 for 6 buffaloes or 3 years	64.71
	Total	300.00

The Gujar are not yet fully convinced about the rehabilitation scheme. Their scepticism is natural and they will need a lot of persuasion and a humanitarian approach to finally make them move. Their viewpoint should be accommodated wherever feasible. For instance, they would like to have a minimum herd of ten buffaloes per family as they have the apprehension in their minds that less than that may not sustain their life-style. Till such time as there is a shift in their mode of subsistence this may be true, but the change may come in when they actually take up horticulture and agriculture or streamline dairying operations on a cooperative basis. However, there are exterior forces such as NGOs, activists and agitationists who for their own ends would like the Gujar to resist change altogether. One such NGO has just submitted a document to the Government of India that in view of the fact that 1993 has been declared by the United Nations as the Year of Indigenous Peoples, the Gujar should be given the management of forests, including the Rajaji National Area, and allowed to continue to live there. For one thing, the claim that the Gujar are indigenous people in the Siwaliks is far from true. They have a history of immigration into this area for only 100 to 150 years. Second, the Gujar are an illiterate people. They cannot even manage their trading relationship with the local *bania* and get exploited in the process. How they are expected to manage the forest and its conservation is difficult to understand. The NGO has already assumed the leadership role of a faction of the Gujar *biradari*.

The Gujar may have a deep knowledge of the forest as is claimed, but at present they use this knowledge for the over-exploitation of forest resources, allowing little or no opportunity for regeneration. This is a crisis situation and against the interest of the Gujar themselves in the long run. For instance, the excessive lopping that has been indulged in by the Gujar has already damaged the trees and the forest. The accumulation of dung in natural streams has choked them and created environmental hazards. The only solution, therefore, is that the Gujar must be pursuaded to move out of the forest and settle in the periphery, where they can still have the benefit of forest resources in a controlled manner that will allow regeneration of resources.

Appendix - I

Human Diseases and Curative System

The Gujar likewise do identify some human diseases and have their own curative system. In case of human too the recourse to the modern medicine is taken as a last resort.

Human Diseases and Their Cures

Sl. No.	*Name of Disease*	*Symptoms*	*Treatment*
1.	*Kan peer* (earache)	Extreme pain in the ear and pus formation	Heat garlic in mustard oil, make thin paste and use as ear drops.
2.	*Haddi paigyan* (bone fracture)	Severe pain subsequent swelling	Thick paste made of wheat flour and bark of *maida* wood

			(*Litsaea sebifra*) boiled in linseed (*Linnum usitattisium*) oil and milk is applied on the fracture.
3.	*Sojja* (swelling) of body	—	Heat *swagan* (*Moringa oleifera*) leaves and apply on the affected part of the body.
4.	Malaria	Fever with shivering	Leaves of *ateesh* (*Aconitum heterophyllum*) taken with a small quantity of water.
5.	*Khurk* (itching)	—	Massage of deciduous oil. If the cause is excessive heat, extract of *kimala* (*Ficus glomenta*)/ orange (*Citrus aurantifolia*)/ *nimboo* (*Citrus medica*) is given to the patient.
6.	*Phingari* (boil)	Boils in the body turning sceptic after a few days	Rub on the boil a paste of ground leaves of *dhamni* (*Punica granatum*) in oil.
7.	*Dhat girana* (lucorrhoea)	Discharge of white substance	Avoid chilli and tea. Take only pulses and chapatis made of maize flour. Gum of *bajaishal* tree is soaked in water and put in a pot on the roof without a cover so that during the night dew falls into it. The patient is made to drink that water for 4 or 5 days continuously.
8.	Tuberculosis	Pain at the back of the chest; suffocating feeling during movement	Take dried intestines of hen with honey twice a day. Take root of *mindars*.
9.	*Jad peer* (toothache)	Extreme pain in tooth; swelling of jaw	Put under the tooth milky secretion of *aakh* (*Catotropis procera*) on cotton swab. Take fruit of *kantagaree* (*Caesapima dacapetta*)

10.	*Catguan* (bleeding)	—	Rub *parijja* (*Cenchurus ciliasis*) grass on the cut.
11.	*Pet peer* (stomachache)	Pain in the stomach; severe discomfort	Salt and sugar solution in hot water.
12.	*Najla* (fever)	—	Ground cumin seed and black pepper in tea.
13.	*Akha peer* (eye ache)	Eyes become reddish	Single drop of honey so that dirt comes out.
14.	*Kamalbai* (jaundice)	Eyes, nails and body become yellowish, urine yellowish	*Kaulbai* (*Clemalis connata*) leaves used as *mala*.

Appendix - II

Flora

Hindi Name	*Botanical Name*
Achmehandi	Lycium europaceum
Amaltas	Cassia fistula
Arjun	Terminalia arjuna
Aam	Magnefera indica
Amda	Spondias magnefera
Anzori	Ficus palmata
Anwala	Emblica officinalis
Asna/Sain	Terminalia alta
Aru	Ailanthus excelasa
Ayar	Lyonia ovalifolia
Akara	Alangium salvifolium
Akashneem	Millingtonia hortensis
Amli	Antidesma acidium
Imli	Tamarindus indica

Ikdarnia	Bridelia retura
Imrai	Ulmus wallichaiana
Kakronda	Blumsea cacera
Kachnar	Bachunia variegata, Bachunia purpurae
Kathal	Artocaspus heterophyllus
Katera	Solanum surattense
Kadai	Flacurtia indica
Kathsagan	Haplopnragma adenophyllum
Kaner	Nerium indicum
Karzua	Caesalpinia crista
Kaizilia	Kigilia pinnata
Keekar Bilayati	Parkinsonia aculeata
Kuchla	Strychnos nuxvomica
Kuchle Ka Malang	Viscum monicum
Kumka	Alacia senegal
Kekra	Phoeba lanceolata
Kala Sirus	Albizia leblock
Kala Tendu	Diosphyrous melabrica
Kanju	Holoptelea integrefolia
Kaphal	Myrica esculanta
Kathber	Zizphus glaberrima
Kandhara	Xylosma longifolium
Kapoor	Cinnamomum comphora
Kathmara	Listsea monopitalu
Kaula	Machilum odoratissima
Kirmaull	Aur oblongum
Kumbhi	Caruya arborea
Kusum	Schleichera oleosa

Kanak champa	Plerospermum
Khardala	Sterkulia pallens
Khabar	Ficus rumbhii
Khajeda	Prospis spicigeria
Khagra	Teema politoria
Khazoor	Phoenix sylvestris
Khair	Acacia catechu
Khadik	Celtes tetrandra
Khurpat	Garuga pinnata
Khatti	Bahunia malabarica
Khaina	Ficus semicordata
Khamri	Ficus palmata
Ganera	Themidia quadrivalis
Gadmawa	Engelhardtia colebrookiana
Gair	Olea glandulifera
Gainthi	Bochimeria rugulosa
Gundala	Sterculia villosa
Gogina	Sauruja napaulensis
Gular	Ficus racemosa
Gammar	Cimelina arborea
Gutel	Trewia mudifloria
Genjra	Cochlospermum gogsipium
Gul Khekar	Althaca officinalis
Godela	Cordia vestita
Gong	Perris scandens
Chuka	Croton rox
Chamrod	Ethritia laevis
Chandana	Distsaea glutinosa

Chilkia	Wendlandia excreta
Chilla	Caseuria elliptica

Appendix - III

Fauna

Local Name	*Zoological Name*
Asian elephant	Elphas maximus
Tiger	Panthera tigris
Leopard	Panthera pardus
Leopard cat	Felis benglensis
Sloth bear	Melursus ursinus
Sambar or swamp deer	Urvus unicolor
Cheetal	Axis axis
Kakar or barking deer	Muntijacus muntjae
Para or flogdeer	Axis procinus
Neelgai	Bosephalus tragocamelus
Goral	Nemorrhaedus goral
Wild boar	Sus-Scrofa
Himalayan yellow throated martin	Marces falvigula

Appendix - IV

Kinship Terminology of the Gujar

Sl. No.	*Relation*	*Addressing terms in Gojri*
1.	BS	Bhatija
2.	BD	Bhatiji
3.	DD	Dohti
4.	DH	Jamain
5.	DHF	Samdhi

6.	DS	Dohta
7.	F	Abba
8.	FF	Dada
9.	FM	Dadi
10.	FZ	Phuphi
11.	FZDC	Vivi
12.	FZD(Y)	By name
13.	FZH	Phupha
14.	H	Gharwala
15.	HV(e)	Jeth
16.	HB(y)	Dewar
17.	HBD	Bhatiji
18.	HBW(e)	Didi
19.	HBW(y)	By name
20.	HF	Mama/Saura
21.	HM	Mami/Sasu
22.	HZ(e)	Nanad
23.	HZ(y)	By name
24.	HZD	Bhanji
25.	HZS	Bhanja
26.	M	Amma
27.	MB	Mamu
28.	MBW(e)	Mami
29.	MBW(y)	Mami
30.	MBS(e)	Bhanja
31.	MBS(y)	Bhanja
32.	MM	Nani
33.	MZ	Khala

34.	MZD	Bhatiji or by name
35.	MZH	Mausa/Mamu
36.	MZS	By name
37.	SD	Poti
38.	SS	Pota
39.	SWF	Samdhi
40.	SZ	Beti or by name
41.	WB(e)	Sala
42.	WB(y)	Sala or by name
43.	WBS	By name
44.	WBW	Bahu
45.	WF	Saura/Mama
46.	WM	Sasu/Mami
47.	WZ	Sali
48.	WZD	By name
49.	WZH	Bhai
50.	ZH	Bahnoiya
51.	ZHF	Mama/Saura
52.	ZHZ	Sali
53.	ZHB	Sala

Key

B	—	brother	D	—	daughter
F	—	father	H	—	husband
M	—	mother	S	—	son
W	—	wife	Z	—	sister

Appendix - V

Glossary of Gujar Terminology

Hindi	*Gojri*	*English Equivalent*
Material Culture		
(i) *Dress*		
Choti bandhne ka	Paronda Pleat	
Chooridar pazama	Sootanh Trouser	
Kambal	Lui	Blanket
Kurta	Kurta	Shirt
Tahmat	Lungi	
Maflar	Malfar	Muffler
Vasket	Fatoi	Waistcoat
Topi	Topi	Cap
(2) *Ornaments*		
Chandi ki mala	Hamel	Silver necklace
Hath ka kada	Bang	Bangle
Hansali	Sire	Half-shaped silver necklace
Kan ka jhumka	Bunda	Ear-ring
Long	Tilli	Nose-pin
Moti ki mala	Tasvi/Manka	Taveej
(3) *Food*		
Dal	Dadh	Pulses
Dahi	Khattai	Curds
Hari Sabji	Sag	Green vegetable
Matha	Lassi	Curd shake
Namak	Loonh	Salt
(4) *House*		
Char diwari	Bad	Four-walled structure

Chauki	Beeda	Stool
Chaukhat	Pwado	Base of door frame
Chapper	Chhan	Hut (dwelling)
Chapper ka Thumb	Tham	Basal support
Darwaja	Pet	Door
Deewar	Bra	Wall
Khal-chokar dene ka sthan	Twala	Feeding place
Pattiyan	Pat	Wooden pieces

(5) *Live stock*

Apong	Beenga	Handicapped
Bhainsa	Jhotha	He-buffalo
Bhains ka Bachha	Katdu	Calves
Bhains panane ka sthan	Baik	Milking place
Dudharu	Laity	Milch buffalo
Dudh Na Dena	Fandar	Dry buffalo
Gai Ki Bachdi	Bachhu	She calf of cow
Than	Odha	Nipples (buffalo/cow)
Vyahta Bhains	Gabanh	Pregnant buffalo

(6) *Cosmology (five elements)*

Aag	Aag	Fire
Asman	Asman	Sky
Baad	Pani chadna	Flood
Barsat	Barsad	Rain
Chikkal	Bukkal	Bark
Chandrama nikalana	Chand chadna	Moonrise
Chandrma dubna	Chand dubna	Moonset
Garmi padna	Swa padna	Hot weather
Hawa	Vu	Wind

Jada	Syad	Winter
Koyla	Koda	Coal
Konpal	Patchh	Bud
Kohra	Kora	Fog
Khud ruka hua pani	Talai	Natural pond
Khud roka hua pani	Dabar	Self-made pond
Mol padna	Panchh Padana	Growing buds
Nark	Dozakh	Hell
Pani	Panhi	Water
Ped ka kata hissa	Mand	Part of tree
Rakh	Swa	Ash
Swarg	Jannat	Heaven
Suryodaya	Dhyada chadna	Sunrise
Suryast	Dhyada dubna	Sunset
Surya	Tulu	Sun

(7) *Miscellaneous*

Bichhona	Binna	Cloth used for sitting
Chikitsa	Ilaj	Treatment
Dost	Yar	Friend
Dulha	Lada	Bridegroom
Dulhan	Ladi	Bride
Dushman	Bari	Enemy
Gundna	Gundhna	Tattooing
Ghumavdar	Teda-meda	Curved
Kala	Mosa	Black
Khojna	Gwachna	Searching
Kona	Kahna	Corner
Lakdi	Laddad	Firewood
Mathha banane ka	Madi	Churning

Manh	Chalisa	10 kg
Massul	Panchni	Grazing fee
Parda	Pallv karna	Veil
Pardhan	Painchh	Chief
Path	Sabak	Lesson
Samooh	Tal	Group
Var-par	Tapna	Crossing a river
Vida	Ruksat	Parting
Vivah ka Nyota	Trimor	Marriage invitation

References

Atkinson, 188, Gazetteer of N.W. Province, Himalayan Districts.

Bhasin, C.L., 1979. *Gujar Samasyaon ka Adhyayan tatha Punarvas.*

Clason, A.T., 1977. 'Wild and Domesticated Animals in Prehistoric and Early Historic India'. *The Eastern Anthropologist*, 30, 3.

Crooke, W., 1896. *The Tribes and Castes of North-Western India.*

Cunningham, A., 1871. *Archaeological Reports*, Vol. II (cited in Crooke 1896).

Darlington, C.D., 1969. *The Evolution of Man and Society.*

Evans-Pritchard, E.E. 1940. *The Nuer.*

Grierson, George A., 1916. *Linguistic Survey of India*, vol. IX, pt. IV.

Gulliver, P.H., 1955. *The Family Herd.*

Manku, D.S., 1986. *The Gujja Settlement — A Study of Ethnic Geography.*

Negi, R.S., 1982. 'Population Structure of a Pastoral Nomadic Community of the Himalaya'. In P.K. Mishra and K.C. Malhotra, (eds.), *Nomads in India.*

——— and M.K. Raha, 1982. 'The Gujar of North West Himalayas: From Pastoralism to Settlement'. In K.S. Singh, (ed.), *Economics of the Tribes and Their Transformation.*

Nityanand and K. Kumar, 1989. *The Holy Himalaya.*

Puri, G.S., 1960. *Indian Forest Ecology.*

Walton, H.G., 1989. *Gazetteer of Garhwal Himalaya* (reprint).

3

Sacred Groves and Sacred Trees of Uttara Kannada

M.D. Subash Chandran
Madhav Gadgil

There has been, of late, enormous interest in the study of nature conservation by traditional societies. The protection of patches of forest as sacred groves and of several tree species as sacred trees belong to the religion-based conservation ethos of ancient people all over the world. Although such practices became extinct in most parts of the world, basically due to changes in religion, and during recent times due to changes in resource use patterns, sacred groves and sacred trees continue to be of much importance in religion, culture and resource use systems in many parts of India. Despite many references to the sacred groves and sacred trees of India in early literature, the scientific study of them was initiated by Gadgil and Vartak (1975, 1976, 1981). Gadgil (1985) pioneered the view that sacred groves and sacred trees belong to a variety of cultural practices which helped Indian society to maintain an ecologically steady state with wild living resources. This view has been fortified by many later studies (Gadgil, 1985, 1991; Gadgil and Iyer, 1989; Malhotra, 1990; Subash Chandran and Gadgil, 1993a; and Joshi and Gadgil, 1991). There is also an increasing number of studies on the subject, and references to some of them have been made in this paper.

The present study on the sacred groves and sacred trees of Uttara Kannada, carried out under the aegis of the Indira Gandhi National Centre for the Arts, was started in January 1991. The authors had been making studies on the sacred groves and sacred trees of Uttara Kannada as part of their regular ecological programmes in the district for the last many years. But here the emphasis has been more on sacred groves and sacred trees forming part of the village landscape and land use, both present and past. The work has been carried out mainly in Siddapur taluk.

Plants Related to Religion

The concept of the sacredness of plants "enters into every form of religion. . . . It rests on the earliest conceptions of the unity of life in nature, in the sense of communion and fellowship with the divine centre and source of life." The sacred tree is said to be deeply rooted in the primitive religious ideas of the human race: "In the history of religious development it lies behind the historic era" (Hastings, ed., 1934).

In the primitive totemic religion of the hunter-gatherer, as among the aboriginals of Australia, there existed within a clan's hunting territory sacred locations identified by distinct landmarks like rocks, trees, lakes, rivers and ravines where the clans kept their sacred hoards. The essential feature of totemism is belief in a supernatural connection between a group of people and a group of objects like certain animal species, sometimes plants, or more rarely other objects. Usually there is a taboo on killing or eating an animal totem (Tokarev, 1989).

In totemism we find that plant species may be totems just as animal species or rocks are. On the other hand, the protection of plant species or groves or their planting on grounds of sacredness could be considered a more advanced stage in the evolution of religion. Such groves and sacred trees are associated more with agricultural and pastoral societies.

Thus in the Caucasus mountains each community had its own sacred grove. Especially worshipped were sanctuaries built among enormous age-old trees which were never to be cut down. The ancient Slavic people worshipped the spirits of nature, especially of woodlands. The German tribes also had their own sacred forests, which were the venue of public offerings and various rituals. When tribes began uniting, these sites became centres for inter-tribal religious worship. For the Germans the sacred groves served the purpose of sanctuaries and temples (Tokarev, 1989).

Hughes (1994), in his study of the environmental problems of the ancient Greeks and Romans, gives us a rare portrait of the sacred groves of the Mediterranean region, glimpses of which are given in the following few paragraphs.

The Greek and Roman landscapes were dotted with hundreds of sacred

> places. Sacred enclosures formed one of the major categories of land use. These usually contained groves of trees and springs of water; within them the environment was preserved, as a rule, in its natural state. As Seneca (1st century AD) remarked, "If you come upon a grove of old trees that have lifted up their crowns above the common height and shut out the light of the sky by the darkness of their interlacing boughs, you feel that there is a spirit in the place, so lofty is the wood, so lone the spot, so wondrous the thick unbroken shade."

Ovid said, "Here stands a silent grove black with the shade of oaks; at the sight of it anyone could say, 'there is a spirit here!' "

In Virgil (1st century BC) is found a reference to the rural folk wondering on seeing an old tree-covered capitoline hill: "Some god has this grove for He also noted that the dwelling!" Gods favour wild trees "unsown by mortal hand".

Pliny the Elder (AD 23-79) indicated that trees were the first temples of the gods, and "even now simple country people dedicate a tree of exceptional height to a god . . . ."

Aquelus spoke of travellers praying under the trees on "a little sacred hill fenced all around". But the grove of Daphne was ten miles in circumference. A grove near Lerna stretched all the way down a mountainside to the sea. Alexander the Great found an entire island dedicated to a goddess identified as Artemis (Hughes, 1994).

The Romans often personified the spirit of plant life. The 'forest king' was the human personification of the spirit of the sacred tree, the oak, his living double (Frazer, 1935).

The ancient Greeks represented the spirit of conservation in the shape of a formidable protector of animals and plants, the goddess Artemis. She was the protector not only of wildlife but of the wilderness itself. In ancient religious thought, Artemis endowed the wilderness with sacredness (Hughes, 1990).

Frazer, in *The Golden Bough* (1935), traces the beginnings of sacred groves to the hunting and gathering people of the palaeolithic. Among the Kikuyu of Africa, he says, "Groves of this tree (the migumu) are sacred. In them no axe may be laid to any tree, no branch broken, no firewood gathered, no grass burnt; and wild animals which have taken refuge there may not be molested. In these sacred groves sheep and goats are sacrificed and prayers are offered for rain or fine weather or in behalf of sick children".

The Mbeere tribe of East Africa had many sacred groves, areas ranging from a quarter of a hectare to three hectares, where tree cutting was taboo. Some of these groves survived up to the 1970s, providing excellent sites for examining the vegetation that had existed a century earlier, as several species of trees were rare or not seen at all elsewhere (Little and Brokensha, 1987).

The abundantly productive sycamore (*Ficus sycamorus*) and the date palm (*Phoenix dactylyfera*) were represented in the temple architecture of ancient Egypt. The worship of trees and groves was prevalent in Arabia, Persia, Assyria, the British Isles, Scandinavia, China, India, Ceylon and many other parts of the world (Anonymous, 1971).

In the Cyclops Mountains, as elsewhere in New Guinea, tribal stories concerned with descent, beliefs and taboos are closely connected to the forest, its animals and land, with conservation as a value inherent in most traditional beliefs and reflected in them. The Sentani and Tabla people respect the peaks of the Cyclops Mountains as the resting places of their ancestors. Nature has such an overwhelming influence that various clans refrain from hunting birds like the cassowary, the wagtail, lorries (a species of parrot) and hornbills due to a totemic relationship with these species (Michell, De Fretes and Poffenberger, 1990).

The Indonesians have a striking cultural similarity with Indians. The banyan tree, *Ficus benghalensis,* is considered sacred. Springs are often found under mature banyan trees. Indonesians believe that holy spirits reside in the trees and ensure the availability of clean water. For the Javanese, sacred spirits dwell deep within forests. Shadow plays like *Gunungan* have a figure that illustrates the forest ecosystem in which plants, animals, human beings, holy spirits and devils live together (Sastrapradja, 1988).

There could be many reasons why the groves vanished from Europe. A kind of multiple use was allowed in groves. Although they were strictly protected in Greece and Rome, religious use of their resources was allowed. As much wood might be taken as was necessary for sacrifices. Animals in the grove, such as goats and deer, might be captured and offered to the deity. Trees in the grove could be used in building a temple inside it or even away from it. Wood from the sacred trees was believed to keep its magical powers when fashioned into other objects and was used for making a variety of objects like statues of gods, staffs, sceptres, etc. Wood was even supplied to private persons at a fixed price for sacrifices (Hughes, 1984).

It seems the groves also suffered from the pressures of urbanization, as baths, stadia, gymnasiums, schools, etc., were established in them. At times they also had to cater to the timber needs of the military. What caused the final downfall of the groves in Europe? In the words of Hughes (1984) :

> The groves lasted as places of economic and religious importance down through the Christianization of the Roman Empire. As centres of pagan worship, they became the objects of Christian zeal, again both religious and economic. The emperor Theodosius II (5th century AD) issued an edict directing that the groves be cut down unless they had already been appropriated for some purpose compatible with Christianity. A few of them became monastery gardens and churchyards, and here and there in the Mediterranean even today one will find a gigantic old tree that is supposed, however unlikely it might seem, to have sheltered Plato or Hippocrates, and has been spared for that reason.

Sacred Groves and Sacred Trees: The Indian Scenario

Due mainly to the rise of dogmatic religions like Christianity and Islam, which advocated faith in one god and were explicitly for the eradication of 'pagan' practices, the tradition of maintaining sacred groves and sacred trees vanished from most countries. Though Brahmanic Hinduism has not been opposed to several of the local cults involving the worship of sacred groves and sacred trees, there has been an almost imperceptible transformation of the grove into the temple. Hinduism itself has grown out of the amalgamation of scores of local cults which are often nature-based. Therefore the worship of plants, groves, animals and natural objects like rivers, mounts, ant-hills and rocks continues to have some place in it. Outdoor sanctuaries were the first temples of the gods. A sacred place demarcated for a deity was called *temenos* in Greek and *templum* in Latin.

Brosse (1989) observed:

> The sacred grove was at the origin of the temple, whose columns were initially trees, and later of the Christian church which still evokes it by the alignment of its pillars, the semidarkness within it, and the soft coloured light that filters through its stained glass windows.

India has rich folk traditions of the conservation of biodiversity and the sustainable use of natural resources, to which at least its 'ecosystem people' still adhere to varying degrees (Gadgil and Vartak, 1976; Gadgil, 1991). The protection of whole communities as sacred ponds and groves is a remarkable feature of the Indian subcontinent. One of the most widespread of the traditions in India is the protection given to trees of the genus *Ficus*, which dot the countryside and are often the only large trees in the midst of towns and cities. They are now recognized by biologists as keystone resources of tropical forests, 'fruiting' often at times when most other species are without fruits (Terborgh, 1986).

Says Ashton (1988), a tropical forest ecologist, on the traditional Indian perceptions of the sacred in nature:

> The Indian sub-continent is without doubt the world centre of human cultural diversity. . . . The Hindus have inherited perceptions of a people who have lived since ancient times in a humid climate particularly favourable for forest life. Settled people, they see themselves as one with the natural world, as both custodians and dependants. The people of India continue to harvest an astonishing diversity of products from the forest. Forests of the mountains and watersheds have traditionally been sacred; springs and the natural landscape in their vicinity have attracted special veneration. The Hindus learned from their predecessors millennia ago, a mythology, sociology and technology of irrigation that has enabled the most intensive yet sustainable agriculture humanity has so far devised.

It is mainly in the hilly and mountainous areas of India like the Himalayas, the Western Ghats and central India that ancient practices survive, sometimes in their pristine form. Studies on sacred groves reveal that they are priceless treasures of great ecological, biological, cultural and historical value. In the evolution of religion sacred groves once played a vital role, but perished often without leaving a trace as in Europe, Central Asia and the Middle East. The situation in India used to be quite different, at least until the early British period. This is quite evident from the observations of D. Brandis, the first Inspector General of Forests in India:

> Very little has been published regarding sacred groves in India, but they are, or rather were, very numerous. I have found them in nearly all provinces. As instances I may mention the Garo and Khasia hills which I visited in 1879, the Devara Kadus or sacred groves of Coorg . . . and the hill ranges of the Salem district in the Madras Presidency. . . .well known are the Swami Shola on the Yelagiris, the sacred grove at Pudur on the Javadis and several sacred forests on the Shevaroys. These are situated in the moister parts of the country. In the dry region sacred groves are particularly numerous in Rajputana. In Mewar they usually consist of *Anogeissus pendula*, a moderate sized tree with small leaves, which fall early in the dry season. . . . Before falling the foliage of these trees turns

> a beautiful yellowish red, and at that season these woods resemble our Beech forests in autumn. In the southernmost States of Rajputana, in Partabgarh and Banswara, in a somewhat moister climate, the sacred groves, here called Malwan, consist of a variety of trees, Teak among the number. These sacred forests, as a rule, are never touched by the axe, except when wood is wanted for the repair of religious buildings, or in special cases for other purposes (Brandis, 1897).

Brandis also referred to a "remarkable little forest of Sal (*Shorea robusta*)" near Gorakhpur being maintained by a Muslim saint, Mian Sahib. The forest was in good condition and well protected. Nothing was allowed to be cut except wood to feed the sacred fire and "this required the cutting annually of a small number of trees which were carefully selected among those that showed signs of age and decay".

In the sacred forests or *devarakadus* of Coorg also, firewood and construction materials were removed only for the temple's sake (Shri Satyan, 1971). The *Imperial Gazetteer of India*, Vol. XI (1908), noted that in Coorg *devarakadus* were set apart for Ayyappadeva. These were "untrodden by human foot and reserved for the abodes or hunting grounds of deified ancestors".

Rao (1969-70) observed that the sites of the *gramadevatas* (village goddesses) in Andhra "are almost always in the vicinity of trees".

All over Chota Nagpur, Risley (1908) remarked,

> there are many jungle-clad hills, . . . the favourite haunts of bears, which beaters of the Animistic races steadfastly refuse to approach until the mysterious power which pervades them has been conciliated by the sacrifice of a fowl. Everywhere we find sacred groves, the abode of equally indeterminate beings, who are represented by no symbols and of whose form and functions no one can give an intelligible account, which have not yet been clothed with individual attributes; they linger on as survivals of the impersonal stage of early religion.

Kavus, the sacred groves of Kerala, are "sacred places where trees and plants were allowed to grow undisturbed and where reptiles, birds and animals could have free living without fear of poaching or interference by man". These *kavus* are of two kinds. Some are in the midst of human habitation and in most cases attached to households or not far away from them. These *kavus* used to have the serpent (*sarpakavu*) or Durga (*durgakavu*) as deities; but of late these distinctions got blurred due to both being worshipped in the same *kavu*. The *ayyappankavus*, on the other hand, exist in the mountain ranges engulfed in forests (Nayar, 1987).

A serpent *kavu*, an abode of snakes, was an indispensable adjunct to well-to-do Nair and Namboodiri houses in Kerala. An early 19th century estimate states the number of *kavus* in the erstwhile province of Travancore in south Kerala as 15,000 (Pillai, 1940).

Sacred trees like *Ficus* and *Mimusops elenji*, remnants of sacred groves, or intact groves with rare plants and sacred ponds, are associated with the Bhagavati or Mother Goddess temples of Kerala. Behind the facade of *vela* and *pooram*, the colourful cultural festivals of the beautiful temple complexes of Kerala, with their caparisoned elephants, men masked as demons or deities, sword-wielding oracles dressed in red and dipping blood, the exhilarating *panchavadya* — the music from five instruments, with the drum in the lead — are the rapidly fading folklore about entangled groves and their mysterious deities.

Ramakrishnan (1992) observes that the climax vegetation at higher elevations in Meghalaya, as at Cherrapunji, is today represented only by sacred groves. According to A.S. Chauhan of the Botanical Survey of India, the sacred groves of Meghalaya, totalling about 1000 km^2 of undisturbed natural vegetation, are found scattered in small pockets all over the Khasi and Jaintia Hills. With heavy pressure of population on the land, these groves remain the last refugia for 700 rare plant species (*Down to Earth*, 1994).

Early travellers like Hunter in 1879 and Gurdon in 1914 made frequent mention of the very conspicuous groves of evergreen forests on the Khasi plateau in Meghalaya (Rodgers, unpublished). Bor (1942) stated that all evergreen forest patches on the Khasi plateau were either sacred groves or land unfit for cultivation.

In the Nepal Himalayas Murton (unpublished) observed sacred trees, small groves and larger sacred forests. Such groves and forests are often the only remains of the original vegetation, whose presence in the landscape is dramatically observable on large deforested and terraced slopes.

Not only did sacred groves exist in more favourable climatic conditions, but their presence is noticed even in the deserts of Rajasthan. For instance the Bishnois, a sect of Hindus, are known for assiduously protecting *khejadi* (*Prosopis cineraria*) trees and groves (Sankhala and Jackson, 1985).

Sacred Groves and Trees: Scriptural and Historical References

The *pipal* tree or *asvatta* (*Ficus religiosa*) has had a conspicuous position in the cultural landscape of north India and human collective memory for more than 5,000 years. It was depicted even on Mohenjo Daro seals. Buddha himself found enlightenment under a *pipal* tree (Mansberger, 1988). Buddha is reported to have been born in a sacred grove, Lumbinivana, full of *sal* trees (Gadgil, 1985).

The conservation of forest patches, groves and trees probably dates back to the pre-epic period in Indian history. Karve (1974) and Gadgil and Guha (1992) state that the introduction of iron in India about 1000 BC was instrumental in the march of agriculture and pastoralism into the forest-clad Gangetic Valley. The combined use of iron and fire made it possible to bring the middle Gangetic plains under intensive agricultural-pastoral colonization with wet paddy cultivation as a key element. The destruction of forests with their wild animals amounted to weakening the resource base of the food gatherers. The burning of the *khandavavana* on the banks of Yamuna by Krishna and Arjuna, though couched in terms of a great ritual sacrifice to please the fire god Agni, was evidently to provide land for Arjuna's agricultural-pastoral clan.

Vana, though meaning forest, could have been sacred forest. Sita was kept captive in the *ashokavana*, or forest of *Saraca indica*, by Ravana. This beautiful small tree is a sacred tree of India and grows in the shade of humid tropical evergreen forests. The authors have seen the *ashoka* tree growing in many *vanas* (*bana* in Kannada) which are sacred to the people of Uttara Kannada. Early Buddhist literature reflects the agrarian landscape of the pre-Buddhist period. Around the *gama* (village) or suburban area lay the pasture or *khetta*, its woodland where the people gathered their regular biomass requirements, and its primeval uncleared forests like *andhavana* of Kosala, *sitavana* of Magadha, etc., which were retreats haunted by wild beasts and woodland spirits (Rapson, 1935) just as most sacred groves are the abodes of spiritual deities even today.

The Hindu scriptures, though they do not have much to say about sacred forests, do highlight the importance of planting trees and groves of trees. For instance the *Vriksotsavavidhi* of the *Matsyapurana* attaches great importance to the planting of trees and even to the celebration of the tree festival. The same *purana* states: "A son is equal to ten deep reservoirs of water and a tree planted is equal to ten sons". Other *dharmsastras* also prescribe the planting of trees: "Just as a good son saves his family, so a tree laden with flowers and fruits saves its owner from falling into hell, and one who plants five mango trees does not go to hell" (Kane, ed., 1958).

For Hindus the *bel* tree, *Aegle marmelos*, is associated with Shiva, *tulasi* with Vishnu, and fig (*Ficus glomerata*) with Dattatreya, the son of Trimurty. Pillai, (1986) refers to the *sthalavrikshas* associated with temples, the mango tree of Kanchipuram, the *jambu* tree of Jambukehavaram near Srirangam, and the *tillai* forest of Chidambaram.

In the association of gods with particular plant species we have a parallelism with the ancient Greeks. Oaks were said to belong to Zeus, willows to Hera, olives to Athena, laurel to Apollo, pines to pan, poplars to Hercules, and so on. However, inside the grove the deity was not identified with any special plant species (Hughes, 1984). This is also true for India.

Nakeera, the Tamil poet of the Sangam period, states that Lord Muruka could be found in the forest, in a place surrounded by water, rivers, tanks, meeting places under trees, new-grown groves, etc. The *kadampa* tree is likened to Lord Muruka himself. Sangam tradition holds that he is the owner of all the hilly tracts with rich groves (Ramachandran, 1990). Ayyappa, Aiyanar and Sasta (all considered to be the same) of south India is essentially a deity of the woods, whose province is to guard the fields, crops and herds of the peasantry and to drive away their enemies (Alexander, 1949; Pillai, 1939).

No temples existed in India during the Vedic period. They were not to be found in the pre-Buddhist period except for wooden ones. The ancient Buddhist sacred place was the *stupa* (Hastings, ed., 1934). The various gods and goddesses whom the indigenous population of peninsular India worshipped were not accustomed to dwell in the secluded atmosphere of temples; they loved the open air. Even today, for the *gramadevata* (village goddess) of south India there are no temples in many villages. The deity may be in the shadow of a big tree. Generally they are lodged in small shrines. In a good number of villages no object is placed to represent the deity and the tree itself is regarded as the embodiment of the deity (Ramanayya, 1983).

An interesting stage in the transformation of the sacred tree into the anthropomorphic form was observed by the Italian traveller Della Valle, who visited India in 1623–25. He found in Surat the worship of Parvati in the form of a tree. Her face was painted on the tree and offerings were of vegetable origin (Wheller and Macmillan, 1956).

The History of Sacred Groves and Sacred Trees

Gadgil and Vartak (1976) identify four important regions in India for sacred groves. These are (a) Khasia and Jaintia hills of north-east India, (b) the Western Ghats of Maharashtra and Karnataka, (c) the Aravalli hills of Rajasthan, and (d) Sarguja, Chanda and Bastar areas of central India. Uttara Kannada, where the authors have been engaged in ecological studies for more than one decade, was chosen for a case study of the sacred groves and sacred trees.

THE SETTING

Uttar Kannada or North Canara is a district of Karnataka situated towards the middle of the west coast of the Indian peninsula. The hills of the Western Ghats, seldom rising beyond 600 metres but lower than 900 metres, cover the major part of the district except a narrow coastal strip, the continuity of which is broken by wide river mouths and backwaters. In common with the rest of the Western Ghats and the west coast, Uttara Kannada receives copious rainfall during the months of June–September. The mean annual precipitation is as high as 5000 mm along the crestline, with the coast, receiving 3000 mm; the drier east, which merges with the Deccan Plateau, receives only 1000 mm. The hilly landscape is full of narrow valleys, streams, gorges of rivers and breathtaking waterfalls, chief of which are the Jog falls along the river Sharavati with a sheer drop of 253 metres, the highest in India.

Bountiful rainfall and relatively low population promoted the growth of luxuriant forests which, though subjected to heavy commercial pressures during the last 150 years or so, still cover nearly 70 per cent of Uttara Kannada's 10,200 km^2 land surface. It is a meeting place of several ecosystems, namely marine, estuarine, riverine and a variety of land-based ones. The forests belong to the tropical evergreen, semi-evergreen, moist deciduous and dry deciduous types. There are also extensive savannized lands, degraded scrub jungles, remnant mangrove patches in the estuaries, barren lateritic plateaus and hills of the west coast, and sandy beaches lined with *Calophyllum inophyllum*, coconut and screw pine (*Pandanus* spp.).

The waters support rich fisheries. Though cultivation is confined to only 13 per cent of its land surface, there is a bewildering variety of cultivated crops which include rice, coconut and arecanut, spices like pepper, cardamom, ginger and nutmeg; cocoa, cashew and fruit trees like mango, jack, *Garcinia, sapota*; other fruits like banana and pineapple; and a variety of vegetables which include cucurbit, brinjal, lady's finger, onion, *Amaranthus, Basella*, radish, cauliflower, *knolkol*, and tuber crops like sweet potato, *Dioscorea* and aroids. Groundnut and other legumes are also popular. Millets, cotton, etc., are grown towards the drier eastern parts. Small patches of sugarcane are found all over the district.

THE HISTORY

It would be of some interest to speculate on the antiquity of the sacred groves of Uttara Kannada. The origin of the groves here is likely to have followed the introduction of agriculture. Palynological study in the district reveals a major vegetational change here, beginning 3500 years B.P., in the form of a decline of forests and the spread of savanna dominated by grasses. There was also a decline in the mangrove forests of esturaries. The reason is stated to be a climatic change towards drier conditions (Caratini *et al.*, 1991).

Major civilizations of the world declined during the fourth millennium B.P. During this period of aridity the prosperity of the urban Harappans seems also to have declined. It was a period of the emergence of pastoral nomadism and of the abandonment of agriculture by pastoralists (Khazanov, 1986).

Despite this climatic change, we have no compelling reason to think of the natural replacement of forests by savanna and of the decline of mangroves, at least along the west coast and the lower portions of the Western Ghats. Some sacred groves also lend support to such a view. Here rainfall is of the order of 3,000 to 6,000 mm per annum and most natural forests would be of the evergreen type. The onset of drier conditions in all probability heralded the agricultural colonization of the wetter Uttara Kannada and other portions of South-west India (Subash Chandran, 1993). Agriculture was already being practised 3500 years ago by the Neochalcothic farmers of Hallur in the Tungabhadra Valley, towards the immediate east of Uttara Kannada (Alur, 1971).

With the climatic change during the fourth millennium B.P., when Harappan centres towards the creek of Saurashtra and the marshes of Kutch became less suitable for the cultivation of crops like rice, we may expect a stream of agriculturists moving south along the more humid and rainy west coast. Thus would begin reclamation of the fertile estuarine areas of Uttara Kannada through earthen embankments as well as by filling the shallower parts with soil dug from the coastal hills. The naturally fertile estuarine fields, called *gajani*, cleared of mangroves, and flooded during the rains, would be ideal for growing salt tolerant rice varieities like *kagga*, as is being done to this day. The beginning of estuarine agriculture would have been the major cause of the decline of mangroves (Subash Chandran, 1993). Moreover, the estuarine habitat continues to be suitable for the growth of mangroves, and there exists even today a sacred mangrove grove in Kumta. Interestingly, folklore says the legendary Parashurama retrieved the west coast from the sea and made it fit for human settlement.

All the species of forest plants found in the palynological studies of Caratini *et al.*

(1993) in the untrammelled primeval forests continue to occur in Uttara Kannada. Some trees like *Dipterocarpus indicus* are found mainly confined to just a couple of sacred groves of Katlekan in Siddapur taluk and Karikan in Honavar taluk. The natural occurrence of *Vateria indica*, another Dipterocarp, is exclusive to just a single grove in Mattigar in Siddapur. Savannization and slash-and-burn cultivation would have been the main reasons for the hygrophilous Dipterocarps to vanish from most of Uttara Kannada. Since population was thin and forest patches cleared for cultivation small, the forests must have recovered in most places except in lands maintained as savannas through periodic burning. Therefore the vegetation of sacred groves, the relics of which remain to this day, dispute the theory of climatic change as the reason for forest decline and spread of savannas in Uttara Kannada (Subash Chandran, 1993).

Since the soils of the wet tropics are notoriously fragile, being prone to quick loss of fertility and massive erosion, the farmers who occupied the hilly interior of Uttara Kannada would take to permanent cultivation of rice in the narrow valleys and slash-and-burn cultivation for millets along the hill slopes and tops around their village settlements (Gadgil and Subash Chandran, 1988). Burnt ash enriches the soil with nutrients and has a neutralizing effect on soil acidity. Unlike the fire-sensitive and tall primary forest trees of evergreens, the secondary vegetation which sprouted on the cultivation fallows would provide more usable biomass like easily harvestable leaf manure and coppice shoots and hardwoods and bamboo for a variety of purposes. At the same time, the loss of evergreen forest would result in a decrease in scores of useful plant species like pepper, jackfruit, mango, cinnamon, *Garcinia*, etc., and canes for basketry. Streams and springs are adversely affected and fire-proneness increases in the ecosystem. The village communities would therefore learn to set aside substantial area of forest close to their settlements as safety forests. Before the arrival of organized religions, including Hinduism, when paganism, with deities in the groves or mountain cliffs or water sources would be more common, the safety forests would naturally turn into sacred places as well. Tree cutting here would be taboo, which is true to this day in many parts of the country.

Evaluating the small-scale refugia of peasant socieities, Joshi and Gadgil (1993) argue that such a system may permit biological resource use at near maximal sustainable level, while keeping the risk of resource extermination low. Such an interpretation is consistent with the fact that in the tribal state of Mizoram, the village woodlot subject to regulated use is termed the supply forest, while the adjacent sacred grove is called the safety forest (Malhotra, 1990).

KANS AS SACRED GROVES

We have thus noted that the *kans* forests are patches of often climax evergreen forest protected by shifting cultivators primarily on religious grounds. These *kans*, rich in biological diversity, are also places of worship for pre-Brahman peasant societies. All along the Western Ghats shifting cultivation was a very important form of land use which involved the clearing of primary forests, at least initially. However, there is growing evidence to suggest that the shifting cultivators followed certain ethics while dealing with the forest ecosystems. The most important aspect is the retention of often sizeable patches of forests from few hectares to a few hundred hectares as inviolable sacred groves. The *kans* of Uttara Kannada and neighbouring Shimoga district belong to this category of forest (Subash Chandran and Gadgil, 1993a; Subash Chandran, 1992b).

In the sacred *kans* timber felling became a taboo, insuring their preservation through the ages. But collection of various non-wood produce and sometimes of fallen leaves for manure was carried out, if the community had no other source, without endangering the ecology of the *kans*. Obviously referring to such sacred *kans*, Dr. Francis Buchanan (1870), emissary of the British East India Company who travelled through Uttara Kannada, remarked:

> The forests are the property of the gods of the villages in which they are situated, and the trees ought not to be cut without having leave from the *Gauda* or headman of the village, whose office is hereditary, and who here also is priest (pujari) to the temple of the village god. The idol receives nothing for granting this permission; but the neglect of the ceremony of asking his leave brings his vengeance on the guilty person.

The taboo on cutting trees in the sacred *kans* continues to this day among the peasantry of Uttara Kannada, in spite of difficulties in getting forest biomass. Buchanan's statement referring to village gods is relevant here:

> Each village has a different god, some male, some female, but by the Brahmins they are called *Saktis* (power), as requiring bloody sacrifices to appease their wrath.

From this we may infer that the forests were virtually under the control of village communities with well-defined territories. Thus the common property resources of a village, like forests, were used by a small number of people under a well-regulated social system without the need for policing. The sacred groves, with their deities requiring bloody sacrifices, were evidently under the control of pre-Brahman peasant societies (Subash Chandran and Gadgil, 1993).

The *kans* undoubtedly were and still continue to function as temples of worship all along the hilly tracts of Karnataka. In spite of the Brahmanization of primitive deities that has swept through the plains of India and most of the west coast, in the interior villages of Uttara Kannada *kans* continue to be the centres of primitive cults, where religion in its early form is still in vogue.

Kans as Safety Forests

In the Uttara Kannada of the pre-British period *kans* existed contiguous with ordinary supply forests called *kadu* or *adavi*, from where people gathered their regular necessities of fuel, leaf manure, minor timber, etc., and shifting cultivation fallows in different stages of vegetational succession, pastures, fields, spice gardens and ponds with corridors of streams and rivers, creating a very heterogeneous mosaic congenial for the rich presence of wildlife. Landscape ecology stresses the high positive correlation between landscape heterogeneity and biodiversity (Forman and Godron, 1986).

Many pre-British travellers referred to the richness of wildlife in Uttara Kannada, which included tiger, panther, gaur, elephant, bear, wild pig, deer, etc., and several birds and reptiles (Campbell, 1883). Daniels (1989) reported 419 species of birds occurring in Uttara Kannada. The *kans*, with a taboo on hunting within them, in addition to acting as sanctums for wildlife, would also have provided ample food especially for frugivorous animals.

The *kans* are often found to be associated with water sources like springs and ponds. The Government of Bombay (1923) highlighted the watershed value of the *kans* of Uttara Kannada:

> Throughout the area, both in Sirsi and Siddapur, there are few tanks and few deep wells and the people depend much on springs . . . . Heavy evergreen forests hold up several feet of monsoon rain . . . . If an evergreen forest is felled in the dry season the flow of water from any spring it feeds increases rapidly though no rainwater may have fallen for some months . . .

Wingate (1888), the forest settlement officer for Uttara Kannada, noted that the *kans* were of "great economic and climatic importance. They favour the existence of springs, and perennial streams, and generally indicate the proximity of valuable spice gardens, which derive from them both shade and moisture".

Tropical forest ecologist Peter Ashton (1988) characterizes the *kans* of Sorab, in the neighbourhood of Siddapur taluk of Uttara Kannada, our focal area, as the "prototypes of a technique currently being promoted as a new approach to forestry: agroforestry. In a region dominated by deciduous forests (Sorab is bordering on the drier Deccan Plateau) that were annually burned, the *kans* stood out as belts, often miles long, of evergreen forest along the moist scraps of western Ghat hills. Assiduously protected by the villagers, these once natural forests had been enriched by the inhabitants through interplanting of such useful crop species as jackfruits, sago and sugar palms, pepper vine, and even coffee, an exotic."

The *kans*, being mostly patches of climax evergreen forest, played an important role in the conservation of biodiversity and helped in the regeneration and restoration of degraded forests around (Subash Chandran and Gadgil, 1993a).

DECLINE OF THE KANS

It is probable that the practice of maintaining *kans* as inviolable reserves suffered an early setback when the spice gardens were set up, often in the vicinity of the *kans*, by the Havik Brahmanas. The gardens derived not only water and shade from the *kans* but also much-needed leaf manure. These Brahmanas pay obeisance to *kan* deities, who are often wild spirits but who come lower in hierarchy than the higher gods of Hinduism. Nevertheless the spice gardeners realized the ecological value of the *kans* and, by and large, abstained from any cutting of trees in them.

The amalgamation of the primitive deities into the Hindu pantheon, often followed by temple construction, was another early threat to sacred groves all over India, including the *kans*. We have observed several such temples along the Western Ghats tract and the west coast, which obviously replaced the sacred groves or led towards their decline. The Talacauveri temple in Coorg may be cited as a classical instance from Karnataka, and the Ayyappa temple at Sabarimala in Kerala as another where dense sacred forests which occurred once were obviously cut down to build the temple complexes. But temple construction activity at the expense of the *kans* was not so pronounced in Uttara Kannada.

The major threat to the *kans* arose from the state laying its claim over all the forests, including the *kans*, under the British regime. The state domination over the forests would have led to the villagers' losing their hold over the *kans*. Following the Indian Forest Act of 1878 people's rights in the *kans* were curtailed to certain minor concessions like the collection of dry fuelwood, as in eastern parts of Sirsi and Siddapur (Government of Bombay, 1923). As the forest resources went out of community control the common lands conceded to the people for enjoyment of their traditional privileges were subjected to unregulated exploitation. Evidently the *kans* were also subjected to heavy pressures. Thus Collins (1922) reported that in eastern Sirsi and Siddapur the *kans* were getting infested with the prolific weed *Lantana*, which gave shelter to the pig to the detriment of agriculture. The *kans* also started shrinking in area due to the heavy pressures on them.

Collins (1922) pointed out that as a variation from its policy of strict protection of *kans*, the Government allotted *kans* in many villages of the Sirsi-Siddapur area to spice-gardeners as *betta* or leaf manure forests. In eastern Sirsi 769 hectares of *kans* were added to the minor forests open for exploitation by all.

The state takeover of the *kans* was followed by the introduction of the contract system for the collection of non-wood produce. The impact may be described in the words of Wingate (1888):

> I am still of the opinion that the system of annually selling by auction the produce of the *kans* is a pernicious one. The contractor sends forth his subordinates and coolies, who hack about the *kans* just as they please, the pepper vines are cut down from the root, dragged from the trees and the fruits then gathered, while the cinnamon trees are all but destroyed . . . . I was greatly struck with the general destruction among the Kumta evergreens, they were in a far finer state of preservation 15 years ago.

As the *kans* contained mostly softwood, unmarketable at that time, no timber exploitation was carried out in them during most of the British period.

EXPLOITATION BY FOREST-BASED INDUSTRIES

During the 1940s *Dipterocarpus indicus*, found sheltered only in some of the *kans*, was supplied to the railways and a plywood company. A working plan for the forests of Sirsi and Siddapur brought under it 73 *kans*, totalling over 4000 hectares, for the felling of industrial timber (see Appendix 1). Another working plan for Sirsi included the *kans*, of 10 villages totalling over 670 hectares. A *kan* was even clear-felled and converted into a *Eucalyptus* plantation in Menasi village of Siddapur taluk. In 1976, the village *kans* of the Muroor-Kallabbe village forest *panchayat*, which were in excellent state of preservation, were leased out to a plywood company which extracted hundreds of logs, also creating enormous incidental damage.

Thus a look at the forest history of Uttara Kannada tells us that the resources of the masses have been rapidly destroyed during the last nearly two centuries of forest management by the state (Gadgil, 1989).

The British, although they realized the watershed value of the *kans* and reserved them as state forests, did not see them as a part of the people managed landscape of the villages of Uttara Kannada. The Forest Settlement Officer Wingate (1888) brought it the notice of the administration that these distinct patches of valuable evergreen forests were not even properly demarcated on the maps. We may take it for granted that many such groves, therefore, lost their identity and merged with the ordinary forests and were treated like them. Even today it may be possible for one to distinguish some such sacred groves by the artefacts present in them.

Agroforestry, according to Ashton (1988) "is a new and unfamiliar technique, still resisted by foresters of Western training, but on a deeper level it represents a very different perception of the forest and our interdependence with it".

A Case Study of Siddapur

Sacred groves and sacred trees had a prominent place in the early religion of the indigenous people of the Western Ghats. This practice suffered a setback due to several reasons, the more important of which are stated here:

1. The arrival of Christianity and Islam, which professed faith in one god and were against the paganism of the local people.

2. The acceptance of Hinduism, as we know it today, by the masses, with faith in one supreme god, mostly Shiva or Vishnu. Several other divinities like Parvati, Durga, Ganapati, Krishna, Muruka (Subramanya) and Ayyappa, related to the supreme gods in one way or another, also adorned the central places of worship. Most often the worship was that of icons prepared according to Hindu iconographic texts and frequently installed in elaborately built temples which replaced the sacred groves or trees. In spite of the fact that trees like *pipal* (*Ficus religiosa*) and *bel*(*Aegle marmelos*) or small clumps of trees are associated with the temples, Hinduism, as it is being practised today, clearly brought about an attitudinal change towards nature, the temples and the professional priesthood coming in the way of the communion of the people with nature.

3. The influx of migrant shifting cultivators like the Kunbis from Portuguese Goa and the Kumri Marathis from Maharashtra during the past few centuries evidently interfered with the landscape management practices of the southern Western Ghats, of which sacred groves formed an integral part.

4. The takeover by the state of the forests of the west coast and the Western Ghats, beginning with the British period early in the 19th century, was a major intervention in the traditional resource management systems of the region with ravaging consequences for the landscape. Timber became the major commodity for sale. Shifting cultivation was prohibited and at least in Uttara Kannada, 80 per cent of the land came under the direct control of the forest department. Even the sacred *kans*, which were places of worship for a sizeable section of society, were not spared. Elsewhere along the Western Ghats of Karnataka, Kerala and Tamil Nadu, large areas of forest, particularly evergreens, with very little timber value then, were released to Europeans and to affluent Indians for creating plantations of tea, coffee and rubber. The local peasants in most places forfeited their traditional hold over the forests, including the sacred groves.

A 25 km^2 area in Siddapur taluk of Uttara Kannada was selected for a case study by the authors. The reasons for the selection of this area for detailed study were:

1. Christianity and Islam have had practically no impact on the religion of the people.

2. Siddapur taluk as a whole is well known for the spice gardens maintained by the Havik Brahmanas, with Shiva and Ganapati as their major gods. These ubiquitous Brahmanas, who depend on priesthood and horticulture for their livelihood, have a strong influence on the religious life of the traditional non-Brahmana peasantry of Uttara Kaṇnada. Their blend of pre-Vedic paganism with faith in the supreme gods of Hinduism was often followed by the worship of anthropomorphic deities and temple construction with certain adverse consequences for the maintenance of the once luxuriant sacred groves. But the 25 km^2 sample area, with just one family of Havik Brahmanas and two of Karad Brahmanas, exhibits a certain immunity to the Brahmanic priesthood even today.

3. The sample area also remained intact during the exodus of the Kunbi shifting cultivators from Portuguese Goa and the Kumri Marathis from Maharashtra, and therefore has presumably retained until today the traits of primal faith characteristic of the region. The traditional landscape management system, with shifting cultivation as an important form of land use, also prevailed almost until the close of the 19th century.

4. In spite of the state monopoly over the forest resources of the district, Siddapur, with its evergreen forests which had very little timber value, and by reason reason of its remoteness from sea and land routes, remained free from timber exploitation until the war fellings and industrial fellings began in the 1940s.

Siddapur is located towards the south-east of Uttara Kannada, to the south of Sirsi taluk; towards the east and south it is bounded by Shimoga district of the erstwhile princely state of Mysore, and towards its west are Kumta and Honavar taluks. Densely wooded hills occur towards its west, and the plains and low hills towards the east were once well wooded. The valleys among the western hills, full of unfailing streams, have rich spice gardens growing areca, pepper, cardamom, cocoa, banana, etc. The plains towards the east have rice and sugarcane fields. The focal area of Siddapur is situated towards the south-east of the taluk with plains, low hills and gentle valleys.

POPULATION

It can be seen from Table 3.1 that only 9 per cent of the inhabitants (Sonar, Muslim and Karad Brahmana) belong to the migrants of the recent past and that their occupations do not indicate any possible intervention in the land use, religious and cultural systems of the local population. Most groups except the Brahmanas are educationally very backward and are very little exposed to the textual traditions of Hinduism in this remote forested part of the Western Ghats.

CASTE AND THE ECOLOGICALLY STEADY STATE

Of late the Indian caste system has been viewed as an ecological adaptation that has created a diversification of ecological niches with minimal overlapping, thereby promoting sustainable utilization of natural resources. Sustainable use was accomplished in two ways: by restricting access to many specialized resources in any given locality to members of one endogamous caste group, and by linking together members of different endogamous groups in a network of reciprocal exchanges and mutual obligations (Gadgil and Malhotra,

Table 3.1

Occupations of different caste and religious groups

No.	*Name of caste/ religious group*	*No. of families*	*Population*	*Traditional occupation*	*Present occupation*	*Remarks*
1.	Namadhari	135	967	Soldiers, toddy-tapping and agriculture	Toddy-tapping and agriculture	
2.	Karivokkaliga	126	939	Agriculture including shifting cultivation	Agriculture	
3.	Madival	112	727	Washermen, agriculture	Agriculture	
4.	Sonar	25	148	Goldsmith	Agriculture	Migrants from Goa
5.	Muslim	22	129	Miscellaneous labour, beedi-making	Agriculture,	Migrants
6.	Lingayat	21	123	Trade and agriculture	Agriculture	
7.	Channaya	22	107	Labour and hunting	Labour	
8.	Bovi	13	56	?	Labour	
9.	Jogi	08	48	Bangle selling	Bangle selling, agriculture	
10.	Karad Brahmana Migrants	02	26	?	Horticulture, priesthood	from Karad
11.	Havik Brahmana	01	08	Horticulture, priesthood	Horticulture, priesthood	
12.	Kelsi	06	30	Barber	Barber	
13.	Badiger	05	19	Carpentry	Carpentry	
14.	Achari	01	10	Ironsmith	Ironsmith	
	Total	499	3337			

1983). In a classic study carried out in coastal Uttara Kannada recently, the prudent resource use by caste society has been illustrated (Gadgil and Iyer, 1989).

Our study in Siddapur supports this argument. The Namadharis had toddy-tapping as their primary occupation, which is even today taboo to other castes in the region. The Karivokkaligas were shifting cultivators. The Madivals were traditionally washermen. The Lingayats were traders and agriculturists. The Channayas had a tradition of hunting and gathering. The Jogis wandered and sold bangles and trinkets. The Brahmanas specialized in priesthood and the growing of spice gardens, which requires great skill and mastery over the landscape. The Sonars were goldsmiths and the Badigers and Acharis were carpenters and ironsmiths respectively.

Game animals were abundant in the district during the pre-British and early British periods (Campbell, 1883). The Namadharis, Karivokkaligas and Channayyas hunted to a substantial extent and did some fishing. The Madivals seldom hunted, but they fished. The Brahmanas, Lingayats and Sonars never hunted or fished and depended much on milk for their protein requirements. Other castes had hardly any tradition of dependence on milk although they had begun to use some. Most of the population gathered a variety of non-wood produce from the forests for subsistence and some trade.

PREMIUM ON LANDSCAPE MANAGEMENT

The requirements of the society in the focal area during the olden days can be summarized.

Land for cultivation

Permanent agricultural fields required the addition of large quantities of leaf and cattle manure to restore fertility and maintain the soil structure, since the soils of tropical rainy regions are notoriously fragile and quickly lose fertility. To circumvent this problem, shifting cultivation was evolved in such areas (Subash Chandran, 1992b). This system, known as *hakkal* in the focal area, was widely practised once along the hill slopes and in the highlands. It involved rotation of fields, permitting the growth of wild vegetation during the fallow stages, which on being burnt after a gap of many years enriched the soil with nutrients (Subash Chandran, 1992b).

Non-wood produce for subsistence and trade

The Uttara Kannada forests are rich in biological diversity even today. The people depended on the forests for a variety of produce like edible flour from the pith of palms, bamboo grains and shoots, fruits like *Mangifera, Artocarpus, Garcinia, Phyllanthus emblica,* and *Syzygium cumini,* edible fats from the seeds of, e.g., *Garcinia* spp., spices like pepper and cinnamon, honey, and mushrooms (Subash Chandran and Gadgil, 1993b), thatching, basket- and mat-weaving materials, fibres, medicinal plants, etc.

Game

In humid and hilly Uttara Kannada, which is not favourable for sheep and where cattle are of poor breed, most of the non-Brahmanas depended on hunting and fishing for their protein needs. From the accounts of early European travellers, the Gazetteer of Kanara (Campbell, 1883) and folk history, one learns that Uttara Kannada was a haven for wildlife. The game mainly consisted of spotted deer, barking deer, mouse deer, *sambar,* hog, *gaur,* blacknaped hare, porcupine, etc., and a variety of birds like jungle fowl, peafowl, partridge, quail, plover, snipe, coot, rail and several water bird (Subash Chandran and Gadgil, 1993b). The maintenance of such animal diversity was crucial for the survival of the population. It should be noted that the lofty evergreen forests natural to the region alone would not have supported most of these game animals. Their population was promoted by a mosaic landscape consisting of elements like species-rich sacred groves, ordinary supply forests, pastures, fields and fallows in different stages of vegetational succession with several natural interlinking corridors like rivers, gorges and ridges.

Watershed conservation

The slashing and burning of forests for shifting cultivation and repeated burning for the promotion of grass growth in the *benas* (pasture) often meant tampering with the percolation of water into the soil, adversely affecting the groundwater and with consequences for stream flow. The maintenance of substantial patches of forests as *kans* played an important role in watershed protection. The role of *kans* in watershed protection was highlighted by the Government of Bombay (1923):

> Throughout the area, both in Sirsi and Siddapur, there are few tanks and few deep wells and the people depend much on springs. . . . Heavy evergreen forests hold up several feet of monsoon rain. . . . If an evergreen forest is felled in the dry season the flow of water from any spring it feeds increases rapidly though no rainwater may have fallen for some months . . . .

We are therefore to view the sacred groves of Uttara Kannada and of the Western Ghats in general not in isolation but as a vital component of the pre-British peasant-managed landscape serving a variety of purposes.

SACRED GROVES IN THE TRADITIONAL LAND USE SYSTEM

The traditional land use and resource management systems underwent radical changes in the course of the 19th century, with the state claiming common property resources like forests, pastures and shifting cultivation lands. Nevertheless the retention of essentially the same names for landscape elements by the village communities largely reflect their past uses, in addition to other ground evidence which may be present even today.

Gadgil and Subash Chandran (unpublished) made efforts to reconstruct the traditional land use system in the focal area, mainly based on landscape names and folk history as well as on other historical records like forest settlement reports. The focal area belongs fully or partially to the villages or hamlets of Kavachur, Hittalkoppa, Akkunji, Mattigar, Dugdimane, Golgudu, Harlikoppa and Kalyanpur. Table 3.2 shows the percentage of land area under different uses. Thus in the peasant-dominated landscape of eastern Siddapur, the community was once able to maintain nearly 6 per cent of land area as sacred groves. These sacred groves, along with supply forests, from where the people gathered their regular biomass requirements like leaf manure, minor timber, firewood, fibre, etc., covered about 30 per cent of the land area. The total area of wilderness could have been higher if we also take into account the *hakkal* or shifting cultivation fallows in different stages of vegetational succession.

Table 3.2

Areas under different uses under traditional management

No.	*Land use*	*Percentage of area*
1.	*Kan, bana, vatti* or *matti* (sacred groves)	5.85
2.	*Kadu* or *adavi* (supply forest)	24.14
3.	*Hakkal* (shifting cultivation area)	23.40
4.	*Bena* (grazing land)	6.46
5.	*Gadde, bailu* or *habevu* (fields)	28.19
6.	Miscellaneous uses	6.12
7.	*Kere* or *gundi* (ponds) and *hole* (streams)	2.00
8.	*Keri* (hamlets)	3.84
	Total	100.00

Under traditional management the focal area had about 146 ha of land under sacred groves alone, though there were several human settlements. There were at least twenty major groves, ranging in size from 0.5 ha (Kadkod birla bana) to 33 ha (Akkunji kanu). If this indeed was the case with the rather well populated agricultural landscape of an undulating terrain, we could hope for bigger groves all along the hilly landscape to the west. There are also a large number of smaller groves, sometimes merely clumps of trees. Our focal area had the relics of fifty-four groves.

The working plan for the forests of Sirsi and Siddapur, for instance, also includes the *kans* of seventy-three villages (Shanmukhappa, 1966; see Appendix 1 for more details). Whereas in Aigod village the *kan* was slightly over 1 ha in size, Kodkani had 735 ha and Mulkund had 1,039 ha. The firewood supply plan for Sirsi town includes for timber exploitation the *kans* of ten villages totalling 672.4 ha. The Kallabbe *kan*, about 10 km to the east of Kumta town on the Uttara Kannada coast, is about 100 ha in extent and was in magnificent form until it was subjected to logging by forest-based industry recently.

Sacred Groves of Siddapur: Their Present State

The sacred groves are on the decline due to several reasons. In the focal area, the area under sacred groves had shrunk from about 5.85 per cent to 0.31 per cent. The details of the present sacred groves in the focal area are given in Appendix - I.

It is clear that the sacred groves of the focal area have drastically declined from 146 ha under traditional management to a mere 7.5 ha. A glance through the Table shows that the deities have very little to do with the Hindu pantheon. The deities occur almost in the form they were before their acceptance and elevation by Hinduism.

Biodiversity of the Sacred Groves

FLORA

The focal area of Siddapur has an annual average rainfall of 294 cm. About 95 per cent of this is received during the south-west monsoon, that is June to October. Such bountiful though seasonal rainfall promotes the growth of evergreen forests. But human influence is very decisive in shaping the vegetation of the focal area, which, though situated at an average elevation of 600 metres, is predominantly an agricultural landscape due to the relatively flat terrain with rolling hills not exceeding 25 metres in height from ground level. Following the Indian Forest Act of 1878 the state took over control of the forests, leading to the collapse of management by the village community. As even the *hakkal* or shifting cultivation lands were taken over by the state, the community faced great difficulty in meeting its biomass requirements. The government, however, responded to the clamour for the traditional rights of the peasants in the forests, though reluctantly, and put aside portions of the forests for the biomass needs of the people. Mention may be made of the 'minor forests' and the *bettas*. The latter are forests exclusively set aside for meeting the leaf manure requirements of individual plantations of areca and spices. It should be noted that the state reserved all the good forest for its exclusive use. The minor forests were usually lands close to villages and towns which were already in savannized condition or were shifting cultivation areas (Gadgil *et al.*, 1990).

In our focal area Siddapur, greater part of the 'minor forests' were *hakkals* or shifting cultivation lands before the present century. The *kans* which were officially distinct blocks of evergreen forests (their sacredness never being acknowledged by the state) were treated as state reserved forests. In the eastern parts of Sirsi and Siddapur taluks, with larger part of the land under agriculture, the traditional rights of the villagers were reduced to certain minor concessions like the collection of dry fuelwood from the *kans* (Government of Bombay, 1923).

Tragedy of the Commons

Forest resources thus went out of community control. The 'minor forests' became common property resources open to larger numbers of people. The general scarcity of biomass for the peasantry resulted in unregulated exploitation. As a consequence the *kans* also were subjected to heavy pressures. Collins (1922) reported that in eastern Sirsi and Siddapur the *kans* were getting infested with a prolific weed, *Lantana*, which gave shelter to pigs to the ruin of agriculture. *Lantana* being a light-loving plant, obviously would have spread due to the canopy's opening and the shrinkage of the otherwise dark *kans*. In our focal area it is therefore no surprise that the *kans*, which covered nearly 6 per cent of the land area in the traditional land use system, were reduced to a mere 0.3 per cent (Gadgil and Subash Chandran, unpublished).

Even in this attenuated form the sacred groves are found to be the best centres for the conservation of plant diversity. Most of these sacred groves may be considered remnants of the climax evergreen forests natural to the region. Outside the sacred groves the vegetation consists of moist deciduous forests, thickets and savannas. Tree density is very poor in the former kind, which are of secondary nature, the climax vegetation natural to the region being tropical evergreen forests. The best patches of deciduous forest have not more than 40 trees per hectare. The species found here are

Buchanania lanzan, Careya arborea, Dillenia pentagyna, Lagerstroemia microcarpa. Lannea coromandelica, Salmalia malabarica, Syzygium cumini, Terminalia bellerica. T. paniculata, T. tomentosa, Zyzyphus jujuba, etc. The same kind of trees are present in the thickets and savannas too, but the density is poorer, the trees are more stunted, often less than 5 metres in height. The undergrowth is similar in these forests. There is plentiful growth of several shrubby species like *Allophyllus cobbe, Breynia retusa, Bridelia scandens, Carissa carandans, Ervatamia heyneana, Glycosmis pentaphylla, Helictres isora, Holarrhena antidysenterica, Ixora coccinea* and *Plectronia parviflora.* A variety of herbs, including ground orchids, grow during the favourable season. A few hardy evergreen forest trees like *Aporosa lindleyana* and *Ixora brachiata* are associated with all these forests. A prolific weed, *Chromolaena odorata*, has become a prominent undergrowth, replacing *Lantana*. There occur also a variety of herbs which grow mainly during the rainy season.

The sacred groves, in contrast, their small size notwithstanding, are richer in vegetation, with tree density exceeding 400 per hectare. The majority of tree species are evergreens, though deciduous trees are to be found towards the edges. These sacred groves act as important refugia on an otherwise impoverished landscape. Mention may be made of trees like *Artocarpus hirsuta, Calophyllum wightianum, Caryota urens, Chrysophyllum roxburghi, Cinnamomum* spp., *Dimocarpus longan, Diospyros microphylla, Diespyros oocarpa, Dysoxylum binectariferum, Ficus nervosa, Garcinia* spp., *Holigarna grahami, Hydnocarpus laurifolius, Knema attenuata, Litsea* spp., *Lophopetalum, wightianum, Mesua ferrea, Mimusops elengi, Strombosia zeylanica Syzygium canarensis, Syzygium hemispherica* and *Vateria indica*, which have their presence almost exclusively within the sacred groves. The Devaravatti *kan* at Mattigar, though only 0.85 ha in area, has, surprisingly, about 60 tree species within it. This is very good indeed for Uttara Kannada evergreen forests, where the tree species per hectare is in the range of 30 to 50. The trees of the sacred groves are large, the emergents at times over 30 metres in height.

Also exclusively to be found within the groves of the focal area are *Actinodaphne malabarica, Litsea ghatica, Schefflera venulosa, Nothopegia colebrrokeana. Celtis cinnamomea, Dracaena ternifolia, Palaquim ellipticum, Memecylon terminale, Entada pursäetha, Gnetum scandens*, etc. Vegetation so rich in structure and diversity testifies to the fact that enormous vegetational changes have taken place in the region except in the sacred groves. Even the sacred groves are undergoing rapid changes like shrinkage in area, isolation effects being disconnected islands of vegetation, windfalls and encroachment of more heliophilous drought-resistant plants.

Going by forest settlement reports, forest working plans and related documents as well as ground evidence, all over the district sacred groves were much bigger and would have supplied the community with a variety of produce for subsistence. Shifting cultivation carried out to an extreme, robbing the fertility of virgin soils, in every suitable patch of forest would mean the community losing the benefits of biodiversity to a great extent. But the conservation of the *kans* sheltered the community of early peasants from this impoverishment. The *kans* are rich in a variety of fruit trees like *Mangifera*, *Artocarpus* and *Garcinia*. The seeds of *Garcinia* also supply edible fats. The *Kandivars*, a group of Namadharis, lived often in the vicinity of *kans* in the taluks of Sirsi and Siddapur, their traditional occupation being tapping of toddy from the wild palm *Caryota urens* of the *kans*. The palm also yields edible starchy flour from its pith, and sugar could be prepared by boiling the sweet toddy. The *kans* were known for the production of wild pepper (*Piper nigrum*), which was a prime export commodity from India since the pre-Christian period. Cinnamon and wild nutmeg (*Myristica malabarica*) are also available from the *kans*. Basket- and mat-weaving materials like rattan (*Calamus* spp.), reeds (*Ochlandra* spp.) and *Pandanus canaranus* are found in the *kans*. The *kans* also have a rich variety of herbs used in native medicine.

Elsewhere in Uttara Kannada also the sacred groves have been found to be sheltering several plant species which have mostly vanished from areas in between. *Kans* ranging in size from part of a hectare to a few hundred hectares, and protected from ancient times, may be considered the best samples of the climax evergreen forests of the region. By far the finest sacred grove we have seen is the Katlekan in the south-west corner of Siddapur. A *Myristica* swamp, reported by Krishnamurthy (1960) as a rare and threatened habitat from the Western Ghats of southern Kerala, has been located in the *Katlekan*. The rare *Myristica magnifica* and *Pinanga dicksoni*, a gregarious endemic palm of the Western Ghats, are confined to this swamp. *Katlekan* is also one of the two notable refugia for *Dipterocarpus indicus* in Uttara Kannada, the other being *Karikan*, also a sacred grove, in the Honavar taluk. These two sacred groves form the northernmost habitat of this magnificent tree of the Western Ghats (Gadgil and Subash Chandran, 1989). Notable among the plants found mostly in the *kans* of the district may be mentioned *Dysoxylum binectariferum*, *Leea guinensis*, *Mesua ferrea*, *Unona pannosa* and *Vateria indica*.

Elsewhere along the Western Ghats and the west coast, sacred groves have been found to be centres of plant diversity, harbouring even rare and threatened plant species. Gadgil and Vartak (1976) reported a sacred grove in Kolaba district harbouring a solitary well-grown specimen of the liana *Entada phaseoloides*. People came from an area of at least 40 km radius to collect the medicinal bark of this plant, reputed for treating snakebite in cattle. Another grove known as Dhuprahat has preserved two magnificent specimens of the Dhup tree (*Canarium strictum*), otherwise present only in the Uttara Kannada forests about 200 km to the south of this region.

Induchoodan (1988) found five species of *Hopea* in a *kavu* of Kerala, of which four are endemic to south-west India. Mohanan and Nair (1981) discovered a leguminous climber, *Kunstleria keralensis*, in a sacred grove in Kerala, which is a new genus record for India and a new species in the genus. *Blepharistemma membranifolia*, *Buchanania lanceolata*, *Pterospermum reticulatum* and *Syzygium travancoricum* are very rare species occurring only in the sacred groves of Kerala.

FAUNA

Landscape Heterogeniety and Animal Diversity

Landscape ecology often highlights the positive correlation between landscape heterogeniety and biodiversity. The extensive amount of edge habitat with edge species, and also animals that use more that one ecosystem in close proximity, say for breeding, feeding and resting, can be found in a heterogeneous lanscape (Forman and Godron, 1986). Such a complex landscape, species-rich sacred groves of climax forests, supply forests, pastures, fields and fallows in different stages of succession, with corridors of rivers, streams, gorges and ridges, would have been responsible for the rich wildlife that existed in Uttara Kannada. The maintenance of these landscape elements was crucial for the population, which depended greatly on hunting and gathering (Subash Chandran and Gadgil, 1993b). The modern alternative agricultural systems recommended for Third World farmers, which do not need the purchase of expensive external inputs and are based on ecological principles of sustainability and stability (Altieri and Anderson, 1986) are surprisingly similar to the traditional system of Uttara Kannada.

From the accounts of early European travellers and the Gazetteer of Kanara (Campbell, 1883), as well as from folk history, one finds that Uttara Kannada was a haven for wildlife including tiger, panther, elephant, gaur, sambar, spotted deer, barking deer, mouse deer, hog, blacknaped hare and porcupine, in addition to a variety of birds, reptiles, amphibians, etc.

Wildlife in the Focal Area

The focal area in Siddapur could not have been much different from the rest of the well-wooded district in harbouring rich wildlife, especially under traditional landscape management by the village communities. This wildlife thinned away following the disappearance of forests with the forest policies pursued by the state ever since the Indian Forest Act of 1878. Even the sacred groves showed an alarming shrinkage. Nevertheless, the leading peasant communities of the area like the Namadharis and Karivokkaligas, and to a smaller extent the Madivals, continued to depend on hunting and fishing for their major supply of proteins. The former two groups even today carry out hunting, especially for barking deer, mouse deer, blacknaped hare, porcupine, pig, and several birds like peafowl, jungle fowl, patridge, quail, duck, etc. The scrub jungles of the focal area even today harbour many of these species. However, since the 1980s the Forest Department has been converting more and more areas of the wilderness around into monoculture plantations of cashew, casuarina and *Acacia auriculiformis*. These plantations are made after bulldozing the land with all its vegetation, leading to the decline of wildlife and resentment among the people.

Birds of the Focal Area

Of the 416 species of birds recorded by Daniels (1990) in Uttara Kannada, 107 have been found within the focal area. It is a rich record, taking into consideration the fact that the district is 408 times bigger than the focal area. It is likely that the bird life was even better when the ecosystems of the focal area were in a better state under community management (see Appendix 2 for a detailed list of the birds of the focal area). In the course of a fleeting survey carried out by Dr. Daniels and the authors in the focal area, 50 of these 107 birds were found to occur in the sacred groves. The 0.6 ha Jattibana at Kalyanpur, with an excellent perennial pond, harboured 20 bird species, and the 0.85 ha Devaravattikan at Mattigar had 17 bird species. Indeed, 31 of the 107 bird species recorded are typically to be found in the forests. The majority occur in the sacred groves, which are bits of evergreen forests. Of the migrant birds of the focal area we may mentioned spotted sandpiper, eastern swallow, brown shrike, Blythe's reed warbler, greenish leaf warbler and Indian grey drongo, the last one recorded in a sacred grove.

Among the typically forest species found in the focal area, mostly in the sacred groves, are the crested goshawk, lesser serpent eagle, grey jungle fowl, blossoheaded parakeet, blue-eared kingfisher, brown-headed stork-billed kingfisher, crimson-throated barbet and Nilgiri flowerpecker. The cool shade throughout the year, higher humidity, and the availability of fleshy fruits may be some of the reasons for these special birds to occur within the sacred goves.

SACRED TREES

In addition to the 54 sacred groves in the 25 km^2 area are 45 sacred trees. They belong to a variety of species, with *Ficus*, considered the keystone resources of the tropical regions (Terborgh, 1986), dominating. *Aswatha* or *pipal* (*Ficus religiosa*), widely planted in South India, is more of an introduction from the north. In our focal area of Siddapur, Sonar Shets, Brahmanized Konkani speakers, have planted two *aswatha* trees. The rest of the trees are natural to the region, notable among them being *bakul* (*Mimusops elengi*), mango (*Mangifera indica*), *Mesusa ferrea*, jackfruits (*Artocarpus heterophyllus*), *jamun* (*Sazygium cumini*), *saptaparni* (*Alstonia scholaris*), and *baini* (*Caryota urens*). The deities associated with the sacred trees are basically similar to those inside the sacred groves.

The Gods of the Groves and an Ecological Rethinking of Hindu Traditions

Almost every hamlet in the focal area has its own sacred groves and sacred trees, the latter inside private households or in public places. A revenue village might have several groves. For instance, Arendur has thirteen groves. Each sacred place has one or two deities. The deities are mostly indistinct beings represented by vacant spots, crude stones or termite mounds. Anthropomorphic forms are rare and are recent artefacts. The deities are abstracted from nature and believed to permeate entire groves. Although the Brahmanas refer to them as bloodthirsty goblins (*Bhutas*), the laity venerate them as parental figures which carry the appellation father or mother. Thus we find Bhutappa, Jatakappa and Choudamma as the most common deities. Every hamlet invariably has a male and a female deity. Birappa is sometimes regarded as a folk hero. All these deities are considered guardians of crops, cattle and humans. Two of the deities are named Mariamma: one is represented by a piece of rock; and in Hittalokoppa village, the original crude rock idol has been replaced by an anthropomorphic one and a small shrine has been built to house it recently.

The deities need to be propitiated periodically to earn their blessings and escape their wrath. Usually for the male deities, goats or fowl are sacrificed on certain occasions, but for the female deities the offerings consist mostly of fruits and milk. Many of the deities, especially Choudamma, are associated with water sources.

There is a limited degree of animal worship as well. Sacred groves and trees together, there are nine locations where the serpent (*naga*) is the deity. One of the groves in Golgudu is dedicated to the worship of *hulidevaru* or panther. Panther is a subsidiary deity in yet another grove. Panther or tiger worship is quite natural in a heavily forested district like Uttara Kannada.

In our focal area, where almost the entire population is of non-tribal Hindu peasants, interestingly, only one major deity of the Hindus is worshipped in a grove, inside a big shrine. He is Veerabhadra, considered to be an incarnation of Shiva. There are also four small shrines of Ishwara, or Shiva, of which one is in the shade of a lone sacred tree. All these five places are under the professional priesthood of Lingayats, followers of Veerashaivism, an important sect of organized Hindu religion in South India. On the other hand are the numerous deities abstracted from nature and associated with sacred groves and sacred trees. They belong to the Little Tradition, people on the periphery of organized Hinduism who make up about 94 per cent of the population of 3,300, most of them being subsistence peasants. They have no professional priesthood, nor temples of their own. The Lingayats are economically better off and specialize in growing cash crops like arecanut and pepper. The entry of Shaivism in the focal area may be regarded as the arrival of the Great Tradition into the land of the Little Tradition. Nevertheless, the laity do have some exposure to the gods of organized Hinduism. Although for the community as a whole sacred groves and sacred trees form the places, of worship, pictures or idols of Hindu deities like Shiva, Vishnu, Krishna, Ganapati, Lakshmi, Durga, etc., are popular in the households. Those who can afford it also make pilgrimages to major temples like Tirupati, Gokarna and Dharmasthala. Almost the entire population has immense faith in the Mother at Chandragutti in the neighbouring Sorab taluk, well known for the tradition of *kans*.

Of late the Karivokkaligas of Mattigar, the most tradition-bound, and backward of the peasants-cum-hunter-gatherers, who were also shifting cultivators in the past, and whose kin still live in the interior forests of the district, have started performing annual *satyanarayana pooja*, or worship of Lord Vishnu, by inviting Brahmana priests. The worship is conducted inside a *pandal* erected for the purpose in the open field just outside their major sacred grove, *Devaravattibana*, inside which the deities are Choudamma and Jatakappa, formless spirits without any icons, and believed to permeate the entire grove.

We have here two extreme phases of Hindu worship, one of primordial formless spirits abstracted from nature, permeating the grove and approachable without the medium of the priesthood. The other, considered to be supreme god, visualized in human form and with all natural forces under his control. To the lay worshipper he is inside fortified temples, guarded by a strong priesthood and with elaborate ritualism involved in his worship.

We begin our journey into Hinduism from the sacred grove at Mattigar, where the Vedic concept of *purusha* and *prakriti* or Man and Nature (the latter considered female) remains frozen through time. People here have a nearness to these 'objects' of worship. There is no professional priesthood or expenditure of money involved in the worship of these Mother and Father spirits. They are easily approachable and nearer to the hearts of the simple folk, so much so that many get possessed by these deities effortlessly. They offer only food and incense to these gods, and on days of ritual hunting the animal caught is sacrificed to win their blessings. The deities stand for the welfare in general of crops, cattle, vegetation and water.

Some of the groves have just termite mounds representing deities. About 75 per cent of the deities are represented by vacant spots or by simple natural objects like rocks or termite mounds or trees themselves. The next stage in iconic evolution to be found in the grove is anthropomorphism. Crudely carved icons represent Chowdamma under two of the sacred trees. A more perfect image of Choudamma is seen associated with one of the trees. One of the deity called Bommadevaru, all the four Gramadevaru, another named Kattedevaru, and one of the two Mariammas have anthropomorhic representations. All the four idols of Shiva and one of Veerabhadra are in accordance with iconographic prescriptions. All the nine locations where the serpent (*naga*) is worshipped have carved stones. Four of the snake images are associated with termite mounds and the others are not.

Interestingly, most of the deities (animal deities excluded) with Sanskritized names have icons. They include Gramadevaru, Ishwara and Veerabhadra. We may assume that this is due to the impact of textual tradition.

Stuck in front of several deities like Jatakappa, Bhutappa and Choudamma are iron tridents. Sticks with split ends resembling arrows are stuck in front of Choudamma and Jatakappa in the Mattigar grove. These arrows and tridents, mostly associated with the folk gods of South India, take us into the hunter-gatherer days of mankind. Devotees who go to the temple of Aiyappa in Sarbarimala traditionally carry an arrow and place it under a famous *Ficus* tree. The devotees of Murukan, a popular deity of Tamil Nadu, also might carry a *vel* or trident, his favourite weapon. These deities appear to be originally associated with sacred groves or summits or hills. Interestingly, Murukan (Sanskritized as Subramanian), as in Palni or Adichanallur, and Aiyappa of Sabarimala (Sanskritized as Sastha) are today in large temple complexes where millions of devotees throng every year.

For tribals and nomadic pastoral peoples, anthropomorphic idols of deities are rare; for them mountains, termite mounds, trees, animals of the forest, and rivers, all characteristic of untamed nature, are close to them and intrinsically divine (Eschmann, 1978).

According to Vaudeville (1989), Murukan of Tamil Nadu, Khandoba of Maharashtra, Mailara of Karnataka and the ubiquitous Bhairava and Govardhan of Braj belong to a group of ancient folk deities inhabiting forests and mountains. The predominant element in the origin of Murukan and Khandoba is the worship of the mountain in the forested tracts by hill tribes and pastoralists. Sontheimer (1989) traces the origin of Khandoba to the worship of the ant-hill, the seat of snakes. The ant-hill should not be ploughed by farmers lest they suffer great harm. For the forest tribes and pastorals the ant-hill was also the seat of wealth.

In the Sangam period of Tamil Nadu, Murukan of the Tirupparankundram hill of Madurai was referred to as a centre of nature worship. He was in the form of a spear under a *kadamba* tree. In the 8th century AD the Pandiyans established a Shiva temple there and an idol of Murukan (Sanskritized as Subramanian, the son of Shiva) was installed. He later became the son-in-law of Vishnu during the Nayaka period. This is thought to be an effort to bridge Shaivism and Vaishnavism. These scences are said to be depicted on the pillars of the temple (Nachiyappan, 1988).

In Uttara Kannada, temple construction in all probability began with the Brahmanic influence. However, temples and priesthood could not be supported to a large extent by the subsistence peasants, pastoralists and hunter-gatherers. Therefore sacred groves, sacred trees and various objects of nature continued to be places of worship. Nevertheless, with improvement in the economic conditions of the people and changes in value systems, groves and sacred trees might have given way to shrines and temples. The shrine to the *betedevaru* (hunter's god) of the Halakkivokkal peasant is evidently in the ruins of a grove. A large termite mound under a tiled roof is the original deity. A crude human image of a hunter was installed there later. In the Karikan temple devoted to Karikanamma (Mother of the Black Forest), the natural rock on a hill summit representing the deity is today covered with a metal mask depicting the Mother, considered to be Parvati. The temple, under Havik Brahmana priesthood, co-exists with a wonderful grove dominated by *Dipterocarpus indicus*, a rare tree in Uttara Kannada. This grove is today part of a reserve forest. The Shantika Parameshwari temple in Kumta, an important one for non-Brahmanas, also has a large termite mound as the deity. Here also a metal mask depicting the Mother conceals most of the mound.

Entangled inseparably in the sacred groves of Uttara Kannada are ecological and

Hindu religious history. Whereas the sacred groves of Katlekan and Karikan together shed much light on the kind of primeval endemic vegetation of the Western Ghats harbouring tall Dipterocarps or swamps of wild nutmegs (*Myristica*) and endangered mammals like the lion-tailed macaque, enshrined in the groves of Siddapur are stages in the development of the Hindu religion. It is difficult to find such a priceless heritage in most other parts of the country. Taken in totality, the groves and religion related to them widen our horizons of knowledge. They highlight the links between human groups in our country as well as champion the cause of conservation of biodiversity, the call for which will arise from the rustics or 'ecosystem people' rather than from the elite or 'biosphere people'. A lack of holistic appreciation of these traditional value systems is resulting in religion drifting from conservation and in the ecosystem and biosphere people coming together to steadily deplete biodiversity and natural resources.

There is still plasticity enough in the Hindu religion, as it does not preach any dogmatic creed. It has evolved through the ages, incorporating a megadiversity of cultures, religious cults and creeds. As Vannucci (1992) puts it: "In traditional thought in India there is no distinction between sacred and the profane: everything is sacred. Tolerance of all beliefs, and the implict recognition that everything evolves — that nothing is static and immutable except the Ultimate Reality or Brahman . . . . The essence of this tradition is to live in partnership rather than the exploitation of nature."

In the personification of Lord Shiva, for instance, we may observe the evolution of Indian traditional thought of living in partnership with nature. He is as old as Indian thought and his origin probably merges with oblivion in the Indus Valley culture. He has mountains and wild places as his abode. His entangled hair symbolizes the primeval untamed forest. The Ganga originating from his tress depicts the watershed function of sacred groves. Serpents coiled around his neck symbolize coexistence with the denizens of the ecosystem. By his trident and leopard skin attire he brings to our mind the picture of the hunter-gatherer. The sacred ash smeared on his body could be the ash of the woods, which restores fertility to depleted soils. As the fragile tropical hill soils got quickly depleted of nutrients, it was wood ash that sustained agriculture; it also neutralized soil acidity in areas of heavy rainfall. Shifting cultivation, which was widely prevalent in the hill country, involved growing and burning of wood. Shiva and his prototypes were known for their wrath. Probably this refers to their power over fire, which could reduce woods to ashes. This destruction is followed by creation; incorporating the elements (*bhutas*) from Mother Earth sprouts crops and grasses and once again forests. The sacred grove, on the other hand, was aboriginal forest which enhanced overall landscape heterogeneity and thereby greater plant and animal diversity. The necklace of *rudraksha* (*Elaeocarpus* spp.) adorning Shiva's neck also highlights his links with the forest.

The entire clan of Shiva is replete with ecological symbolism. Shiva's consort Parvati is considered the daughter of the mountain. She is the personification of Mother Earth. Apparently the female deities of the sacred groves may be identified as Parvati, her incarnations or prototypes. Thus the Mother of Karikan (Black Forest) in Honavar is addressed as Parameshwari. The termite mound in a Kumta temple is worshipped as Shantika Parameshwari. Examples abound to trace the origin of Shiva and Parvati from sacred woods.

Ganesha, the son of Shiva, is a combination of elephant and man. The elephant is worshipped in this country and even today forms an integral part of many temples and festivals. Muruka or Subramanyan, another son of Shiva, also with the trident as his favourite weapon, and the peacock as his vehicle, is a deity of woods and mountains in South India. The *bhutas*, despite their grotesque caricatures gifted from the hands of textual tradition, in all probability would be objects of worship for peasants. Scores of *bhutas* are still worshipped as the guardians of fields and cattle. *Bhutas*, unseen, simply would mean elements, of which water, the earth, fire and air, and the life-giving light coming from the sky are integral components of the ecosystem (Subhash Chandran, 1992a). No wonder Shiva is considered the supreme lord of *bhutas* and Ganesha their marshal.

The Indian tradition is strongly cosmocentric, where man lives as part of a system in which everything is related to everything else. Creation and destruction take place simultaneously. Materials and energy move from organism to organism. Matter is arranged in precise order in every organism, but in death this order is followed by disorder: cycling of materials through organisms brings order once again. But today, rapidly drifting from our traditions of sustainable use and coexistence, we seem to be entering a man-centred world that implies the decimation of nature. In religion, superstitions with wide-ranging implications for ecology are replacing superstitions of a simpler kind. Our gods, alienated from the elements of nature, are getting locked up in temple complexes which have turned out to be places of elaborate ritualism. This drift is going to revise Indians' attitudes towards nature. The view that has gained strength is of the overharvesting of natural resources, not their prudent use. As a result the sacred groves are disappearing and being replaced by housing sites, agriculture, secondary forests or even eucalyptus plantations. Temples also are replacing the groves. Thus we find that in most of Kerala, Bhagavati temples have come up in places where,

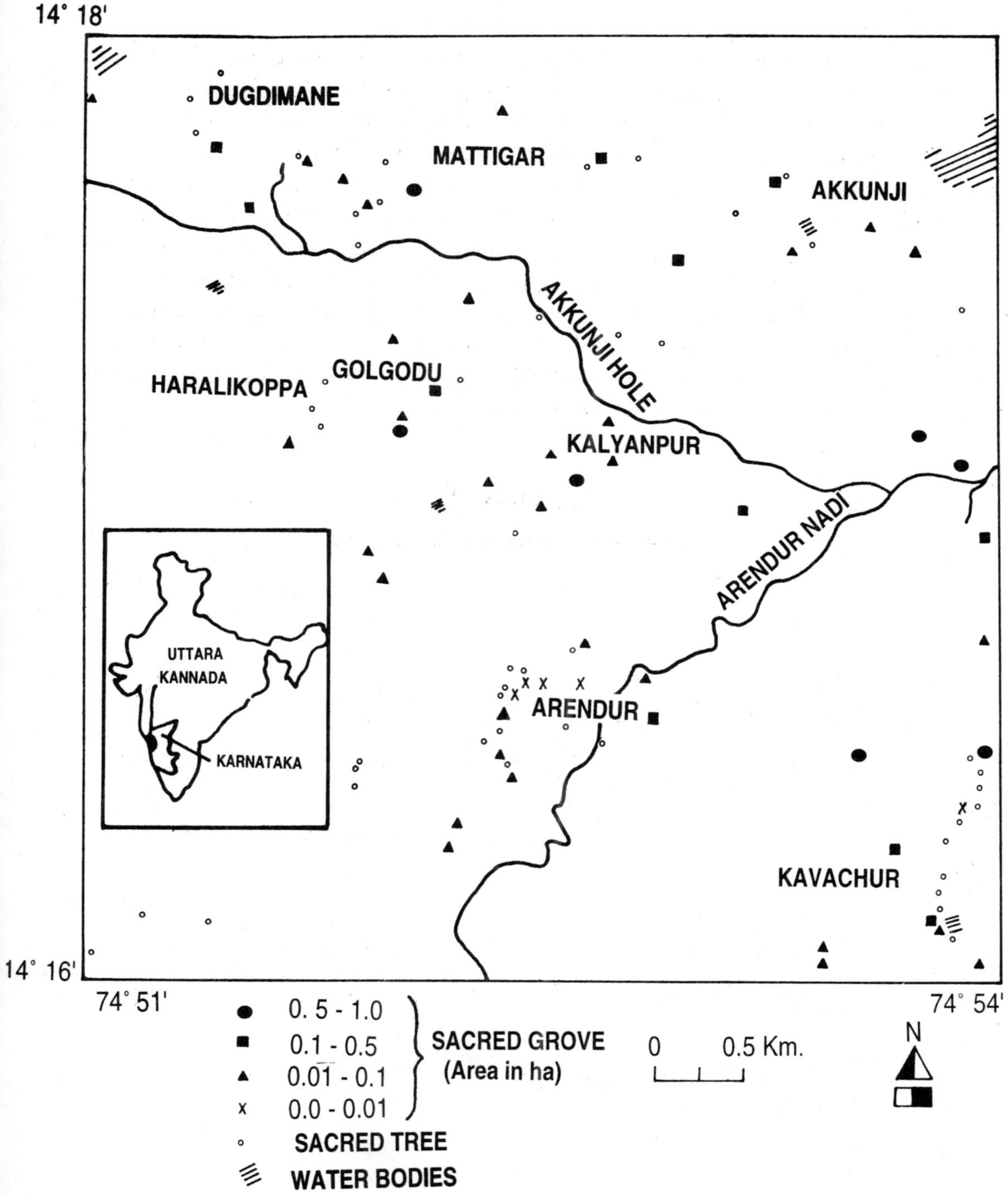

Sacred groves and sacred trees in a 25 kilometer area of Siddapur taluk (focal area).

presumably, groves existed in the past. *Bhutasthanas* or shrines for *bhutas* appear to be a major reason for the degradation of the sacred groves of Dakshina Kannada. Today at Talacauvery in Coorg, the sacred Kavery river is not gushing out from a watershed forest as it used to but from a concrete pit in the premises of a temple complex at the base of a deforested mountain! The all-powerful bureaucracy, in collusion with the industrial lobby and politicians, together forming a formidable stranglehold, too realised that the groves, once an integral part of the village landscape and ecosystem, are no more sacred. The groves became part of the reserve forests in Uttara Kannada. A number of groves were attached to arecanut gardens as leaf manure forests during the British time itself. A forest working plan of 1966 included over 4000 hectares of sacred *kans* for timber exploitation in Sirsi and Siddapur taluks of Uttara Kannada (Subash Chandran and Gadgil, 1993a; see also Appendix - II).

Appendix - I

Sacred groves in the focal area

No.	*Name of the grove*	*Village*	*Deities*	*Area in ha*
1.	Hosakatte Bhutappa bana	Kavachur	Hosakatte-Bhutappa	0.045
2.	Choudibana	-do-	Choudama	0.193
3.	Gamadevarubana	-do-	Gamadevaru, Veerakallu (hero stone)	0.375
4.	Mastikatte	-do-	Masti	0.031
5.	Kuntbhutappana kan	-do-	Kuntbhutappa	0.078
6.	Manekere Choudamma bana	-do-	Choudamma	0.040
7.	Mariamman bana	Hittalkoppa	Mariamma	0.540
8.	Jatakadevara bana	-do-	Jatakadevaru	0.144
9.	Nagarabana	-do-	Nagappa (cobra) Choudi	0.003

No.	*Name of the grove*	*Village*	*Deities*	*Area in ha*
10.	Birappa bana	-do-	Birappa	0.090
11.	Jatakadevaru	-do-	Jataka	0.525
12.	Choudibana	Arendur	Choudi	0.113
13.	Kattedevara bana	-do-	Kattedevaru Hulidevaru (leopard) Gamadevaru	0.050
14.	Gamadevaru bana	-do-	Gamadevaru	0.030
15.	Mariamman bana	-do-	Mariamma	0.012
16.	Nagarabana	-do-	Nagappa	0.010
17.	Bhutappana bana	-do-	Bhutappa	0.005
18.	Bhutappana bana	Arendur	Bhutappa	0.003
19.	Bhutappana bana	-do-	Bhutappa	0.012
20.	Devammana bana	-do-	Devamma	0.006
21.	Bhutappana bana	-do-	Bhutappa	0.046
22.	Birappana bana	-do-	Birappa	0.054
23.	Bhutappana bana	-do-	Bhutappa	0.010
24.	Holkavi Choudammana bana	-do-	Choudamma	0.041
25.	Devaravatti kanu	Mattigar	Jatakappa Chouda-mma Birappa	0.855
26.	Brahma/Nagappa bana	-do-	Brahma Nagappa	0.018
27.	Yaxi bana	-do-	Yaxi	0.075
28.	Varamakki Bhutappana bana	-do-	Varamakki-bhutappa	0.030
29.	Hulibesi Bhutappana bana	-do-	Hulibesibhutappa	0.039
30.	Kadanmattibiralu bana	-do-	Biralu	0.120
31.	Kuntbhutappana bana	Golgudu	Kuntbhutappa	0.037
32.	Hulidevarubana	-do-	Hulidevaru	0.07

No.	Name of the grove	Village	Deities	Area in ha
33.	Kappehondadabhutappana bana	-do-	Kappehondada-bhutappa	0.033
34.	Thotada Choudammana bana	-do-	Thotada Choudamma	0.048
35.	Heddarkatte Bhutappana bana	-do-	Heddarikatte Bhutappa	0.051
36.	Maddele Bhutappana bana	-do-	Maddele Bhutappa	0.050
37.	Jatakadevaru bana	Harlikoppa	Jataka Hulidevaru Nagara	0.525
38.	Choudibana	-do-	Choudi Nagappa	0.055
39.	Kadkod Choudamma bana	Aralihonda	Choudamma	0.600
40.	Kadkod Birappadevaru bana	-do-	Birappa	0.630
41.	Choudibana	-do-	Choudi	0.195
42.	Bhutappana bana	Aralihonda	Bhutappa	0.045
43.	Bommadevaru kanu	Akkunji	Bommadevaru Birappa	0.123
44.	Choudammana bana	-do-	Choudamma	0.105
45.	Kere Bhutappana bana	-do-	Kerebhutappa	0.020
46.	Akshayabhutappana bana	Kalyanpur	Akshayabhutappa	0.042
47.	Choudammanabana	-do-	Choudamma	0.021
48.	Maddelebhutappana bana	-do-	Maddelebhutappa	0.060
49.	Jattibana	-do-	Jatakappa Chou-damma (Kereyamma)	0.600
50.	Kuntbhutappana bana	-do-	Kuntbhutappa	0.029
51.	Karehondadabhutappana kanu	-do-	Karihondabhutappa	0.150

52.	Bhutappanabana	Dugdimane	Bhutappa Choudi	0.135
53.	Choudibana	-do-	Choudi	0.240
54.	Jatakadevarubana	-do-	Jataka	0.04
	Total area under groves			7.502 ha

Appendix - II

Details of the *kan* patches (safety forests-cum-sacred groves in the traditional landuse systems) of Sirsi and Siddapur taluks of Uttara Kannada which were included in the forest working plan for selection felling of industrial timbers (Shanmukhappa, 1966).

No.	*Forest village*	*Gazetted area in acres*
1.	Advalli	30-4-0
2.	Kop	23-0-0
3.	Sarda	26-0-0
4.	Kalgar	59-25-0
5.	Molinonkeri	65-39-0
6.	Herehulekal	108-33-0
7.	Heggar	6-0-0
8.	Arehalli	769-0-0
9.	Girgadde	35-33-0
10.	Aigod	61-34-0
11.	Balekop	60-36-0
12.	Ballate	130-33-0
13.	Halgaddekop	6-33-0
14.	Kangod	328-32-0
15.	Kondli	146-34-0
16.	Maddikop	11-2-0
17.	Nidgod	42-16-0
18.	Archhanhalli	87-8-0

19.	Gadihalli	121-20-0
20.	Gonur	120-28-0
21.	Margundi	38-10-0
22.	Vaddikop	45-13-0
23.	Venkatapur	39-30-0
24.	Bhasi	145-25-0
25.	Kop	214-36-0
26.	Gudnapur	273-33-0
27.	Kalli	184-33-0
28.	Doddanhalli	29-15-0
29.	Gangolli	43-38-0
30.	Kalkardi	98-4-0
31.	Kandraji	363-34-0
32.	Kuphalli	207-30-0
33.	Malalgaon	113-39-0
34.	Mavinkop	36-35-0
35.	Kodigar	49-24-0
36.	Karur	87-22-0
37.	Modur	42-35-0
38.	Gurvalli	132-25-0
39.	Kakkalli	212-0-0
40.	Kanmuski	141-21-0
41.	Menshi	48-10-0
42.	Vanhalli	410-3-0
43.	Kodgadde	44-20-0
44.	Avarguppa	228-7-0
45.	Mulgund	1039-32-0
46.	Balguli	54-35-0

47.	Tyagli	4-2-0
48.	Bidarkan	133-8-0
49.	Golikai	85-21-0
50.	Heggadmane	25-35-0
51.	Henantemane	11-14-0
52.	Kolsirsi	229-26-8.5
53.	Kunji	94-28-0
54.	Moggegar	226-7-0
55.	Muttalli	397-4-0
56.	Muttagi	198-14-0
57.	Tyarhi	32-13-0
58.	Uppadki	33-16-0
59.	Gunjgod	61-33-0
60.	Hosmanji	105-23-0
61.	Itgi	13-11-0
62.	Shigihalli	38-10-0
63.	Alwalli	26-32-0
64.	Chandraghatgi	6-12-0
65.	Hemgar	128-0-0
66.	Menshi	47-12-0
67.	Akkunji	68-38-0
68.	Arendur	33-25-0
69.	Hosur	84-3-0
70.	Muswalli	34-18-0
71.	Kodkani	735-0-0
72.	Korlkai	252-25-0
73.	Nalavjaddi	499-32-0
	Grand total of the *kan* area	10,179-11-8.5 acres or 4121 hectares

Appendix - III

List of birds observed in the 25 km^2 sample area of Siddapur taluk in Uttara Kannada. Five sacred groves were specially sampled.

Abbreviations

Mat — Mattigar grove
Ara — Aralihonda grove
Gol — Gogudu grove
village with sacred groves)
E — endemic to India

Kal — Kalyanpur grove
Kav — Kavachur grove
M — migrant;

F — typically forest species

No.	*Common name in s. groves*	*Latin name*	*Occurrence*	*Remarks*
(1)	(2)	(3)	(4)	(5)
1.	Little cormorant	Phalacrocorax niger		
2.	Little green heron	Butorides striatus		
3.	Pond heron	Ardeola grayii		
4.	Cattle egret	Bubulcus ibis		
5.	Smaller egret	Egretta intermedia		
6.	Little egret	Egretta garzetta		
7.	Openbill stork	Anastomus oscitans		
8.	Blue-winged teal	Anas querquedula		
9.	Cotton teal	Nettapus coromandelicus		
10.	Crested honey buzzard	Pernis ptilorhynchus		
11.	Crested goshawk	Accipiter trivirgatus	Kal	F
12.	Lesser serpent eagle	Spilornis cheela	Mat	F
13.	European kestrel	Falco tinnunculus		
14.	Painted partridge	Francolinus pictus		

(1)	(2)	(3)	(4)	(5)
15.	Grey jungle fowl	Gallus sonneratii	Ara	F
16.	Indian peafowl	Pavo cristatus		
17.	White-breasted waterhen	Amaurornis phoenicurus	Kal	
18.	Pheasant-tailed jacana	Hydrophasianus chirurgus		
19.	Bronze-winged jacana	Metopidious indicus		
20.	Red-wattled lapwing	Vanellus indicus		
21.	Spotted sandpiper	Tringa glariola		M
22.	Green pigeon	Treron phoenicoptera		F
23.	Indian spotted dove	Streptopelia chinensis		
24.	Rose-ringed parakeet	Psittacula crameri		
25.	Blossom-headed parakeet	Psittacula cyanocephala	Mat. Kav. Gol.	F
26.	Indian loriquet	Loriculus vernalis		F
27.	Common hawk cuckoo	Cuculus varius	Mat.	
28.	Indian baby-banded cuckoo	Cacomantis sonneratii	Kal. Ara	
29.	Indian plaintive cuckoo	Cacomantis merulinus		
30.	Indian drongo cuckoo	Surniculus lugubris		
31.	Indian koel	Eudyanamysscolopacea	Gol	
32.	Coucal/Crow pheasant	Centropus sinensis Kal		
33.	Crested tree swift	Hemiprocne longipennis		F
34.	Small blue kingfisher	Alcedo atthis		

(1)	(2)	(3)	(4)	(5)
35.	Blue-eared king-fisher	Alcedo meninting	Kal	F
36.	Brown-headed stork-billed kingfisher	Pelargopsis capensis	Kal	F
37.	Small green bee-eater	Merops orientalis		
38.	Ceylon hoopoe	Upupa epops subsp		
39.	Small green barbet	Megalaima viridis	Mat. Ara. Kav. Gol.	F
40.	Crimson-throated-barbet	Megalaima rubricapilla	Kal	F
41.	Crimson-breasted-barbet	Megalaima haemacephala		
42.	Indian small yellow-naped woodpecker	Picus chlorolophus Kav	F	
43.	Malabar golden-backed woodpecker	Dinopium benghalense		
44.	Malabar golden-backed three-toed woodpecker	Dinopium javanense	Ara	
45.	Indian pitta	Pitta brachyura		
46.	Madras bushlark	Mirafra assamica		
47.	Malabar crested lark	Galerida malabarica		
48.	Eastern swallow	Hirundo rustica		M
49.	Indian wiretailed swallow	Hirundo smithii		
50.	Indian cliff swallow	Hirundo fluvicola	Mat	
51.	Indian red-humped swallow	Hirundo daurica sub sp.	Mat	

(1)	(2)	(3)	(4)	(5)
52.	Rufous-backed shrike	Lanius schach		M
53.	Brown shrike	Lanius cristatus		M
54.	Indian golden oriole	Oriolus oriolus	Gol	M
55.	Indian grey drongo	Dicrurus leucophaeus	Mat	M
56.	Bronzed drongo	Dicrurus aeneus	Mat Kal	F
57.	Indian myna	Acridotheres tristis		
58.	Jungle myna	Acridotheres fuscus	Kav	
59.	Hill myna	Gracula religiosa	Ara	
60.	Indian jungle crow	Corvus macrohynchos	Ara Kav Gol	
61.	Blackbacked pied flycatcher shrike	Hemipus picatus	Kal	F
62.	Malabar woodshrike	Tephrodornis gularis	Kal	F
63.	Indian woodshrike	Tephrodornis pondicerianus		
64.	Orange minivet	Pericrocotus flammeus	Kal	F
65.	Malabar small minivet	Pericrocotus cinnamoneus		
66.	Peninsular Indian iroa	Aegithina tiphia	Mat	
67.	Golden-fronted chloropsis	Chloropsis aurifrons	Mat	F
68.	Jerdon's chloropsis	Chloropsis cochinchinensis	Kav	
69.	Fairy bluebird	Irena puella	Kal	F
70.	Red-whiskered bulbul	Pycnonotus jocosus	Mat. Ara Kav	
71.	Red-vented bulbul	Pycnonotus cafer	Mat Kav	
72.	White-browed bulbul	Pycnonotus luteolus		
73.	Yellow-browed bulbul	Hypsipetus indices Kal	F	

(1)	(2)	(3)	(4)	(5)
74.	Penninsular spotted babbler	Pellorneum ruficeps	Mat Kav	F
75.	Kerala scimitar babbler	Pomatorhinus schisticeps		F
76.	Black-headed babbler	Rhopocichla atriceps	Mat	F
77.	Malabar jungle babbler	Turboides striatus subsp.		
78.	Nilgiri quaker babbler	Alcippe poiocephala	Kal	F
79.	White-bellied blue flycatcher	Muscicapa pallipes Kal	EF	
80.	Tickell's blue flycatcher	Muscicapa tickelliae	Ara	F
81.	Peninsular paradise flycatcher	Terpsiphone paradisi sub sp.		Kal
82.	Indian blacknaped blue flycatcher	Monarcha azurea	Mat Kal	F
83.	Indian tailorbird	Orthotomus sutorius		
84.	Blyth's reed warbler	Acrocephalus dumetorum		M
85.	Greenish leaf warbler	Phylloscopus trochiloides	Ara	M
86.	Indian magpie robin	Copsychus saularis		
87.	Malabar shama	Copsychus malabaricus	Kal Ara	F
88.	Pied bushchat	Saxicola caprata		
89.	Malabar whistling thrush	Myiophoneus horsfieldii	Mat	F
90.	White-throated ground thrush	Zoothera citrina	Ara	F
91.	Black-capped blackbird	Turdus merula		
92.	Yellow-cheeked tit	Parus xanthogenis	Ara	F

(1)	(2)	(3)	(4)	(5)
93.	Velvet-fronted nuthatch	Sitta frontalis		
94.	Indian paddy field pipit	Anthus novaeseelandiae sub sp.		
95.	Thick-billed flower-pecker	Dicaeum erythrorhynchos	Gol	
96.	Nilgiri flowerpecker	Dicaeum concolor	Mat	F
97.	Purple-rumped sunbird	Nectarinia zeylanica		
98.	Small sunbird	Nectarinia minima	Kal Ara Gol	F
99.	Maroon-breasted sunbird	Nectarinia lotenia	Gol	
100.	Indian purple sunbird	Nectarinina asiatica		
101.	Little spiderhunter	Arachnothera longirostris	Kal	F
102.	Indian white-eye	Zosterops palpebrosa	Kal	
103.	Indian house sparrow	Passer domesticus		
104.	Indian yellow-throated sparrow	Petronea xanthocollis		
105.	Indian house crow	Crovus splendens	Ara	
106.	White-breasted king-fisher	Halcyon syrnensis		
107.	Pariah kite	Milvus migrants		

Note: This list of birds is by no means complete, as year-round observation has not been carried out. Thanks are due to Dr Ranjit Daniels for the valuable help rendered in compiling the information on birds.

References

Alexander, P.C., 1949. 'Buddhism in Kerala'. Annamalai University Historical Series, No. 8

Altieri, M.A. and K. Anderson, 1986. 'An Ecological Basis for the Development of

Alternative Agricultural Systems for Small Farmers in the Third World'. *American Journal for Alternative Agriculture*, Vol. 1, No.1, Institute for Alternative Agriculture

Alur, K.R., 1971. 'Animal remains'. in M.S. Nagaraja Rao, ed., *Protohistoric Cultures of the Tungabhadra Valley*, Dharwad, pp. 107–24.

Anonymous, 1971. *Phallic Tree Worship*, Bharat-Bharati, Varanasi

Ashton, P.S., 1988. 'A Question of Sustainable Use'. In J.S. Denslow and C. Padock, eds., *People of the Tropical Rain Forest*, University of California Press, Berkeley

Bhat, P.G., 1979. 'Pre-history of Coastal Karnataka'. *Quarterly Journal of the Mythic Society*, Vol. 70, January-June; Nos. 1–2, pp. 86–96.

Bor, N.L., 1942. Some Remarks on Geology and Flora of the Naga and Khasi Hills'. 150th Anniversary Volume of the Royal Botanical Garden, Calcutta

Brandis, D., 1897. 'Indigenous Indian forestry. Sacred groves'. *Indian Forestry-Working.*

Brosse, J., 1989. 'The Sacred Tree'. *The Courier*, January 1989, pp. 4–9.

Buchanan, F., 1870. *A Journey from Madras through the Countries of Mysore, Canara and Malabar*, Vol. 2, Higginbotham and Co., Madras

Campbell, J.M., 1883, *Gazetteer of the Bombay Presidency*, Vol. 15, (parts 1 & 2), Govt. Central Press, Bombay

Caratini, M., M. Fontugne, J.P. Pascal, C. Tissot and I. Bentaleb, 1991. 'A Major Change at *ca.* 3500 years BP in the Vegetation of the Western Ghats in North Kanara Karnataka'. *Current Science*, Vol. 61 (Nos. 9 & 10), pp. 669–72.

Collins, G.F.S., 1922. 'A Report on the General Condition of Forest Administration in Siddapur Taluka'. 15 June 1922, Forest Settlement Office, Karwar

Daniels, R.J.R., 1989. 'A Conservation Strategy for the Birds of Uttara Kannada District'. Ph. D. thesis, Centre for Ecological Sciences, Indian Institute of Science, Bangalore

Down to Earth, 1994. *The Spirit of the Sanctuary*, Vol. 2, No. 17.

Eschmann, A., 1978. 'Hinduization of Tribal Deities in Orissa'. In A. Eschmann *et al.*, eds., *The Sakta and Saiva Typology*, Tripathy Publishers.

Forman, R.T.T. and M. Godron, 1986. *Landscape Ecology*. John Wiley and Sons, New York

Frazer, J.G., 1935. *The Golden Bough: A Study in Magic and Religion*, 12 vols. Macmillan, New York

Gadgil, M., 1985. 'Social Restraints on Resource Utilization: The Indian experience'. In J.A. McNeely and D. Pitt, eds., *Culture and Conservation: The Human Dimension in Environmental Planning*, Croom Helm, Dublin

———, 1987. 'Diversity, Cultural and Biological'. *Trends in Ecology and Evolution*,Vol. 2, No. 12, pp. 369–73

———, 1989. 'Deforestation: Problems and Prospects'. *Energy Environment Monitor*, Vol. 5, No. 2, pp. 3–47

———, 1991. 'Conserving India's Biodiversity: The societal Context'. *Evolutionary Trends in Plants*, 5(1), pp.3–8

——— and K.C. Malhotra, 1983. 'Adaptive Significance of the Indian Caste System: An Ecological Perspective'. *Annals of Human Biology*, 10, pp. 465–68

——— and R. Guha, 1992. *This Fissured Land: An Ecological History of India*. Oxford University Press, Delhi

——— and P. Iyer 1989. 'On the Diversification of Common Property Resource Use by the Indian Society'. In Berkes, ed., *Common Property Resources: Ecology and Community-Based Sustainable Development*, Belhaven Press, London

——— and M.D. Subash Chandran, 1988. 'On the History of Uttara Kannada Forests'. In J. Dargavel, K. Dixon and N. Semple, eds., *Changing Tropical Forests: Historical Perspectives on Today's Challenges in Asia, Australia and Oceania*. Centre for Resources and Environmental Studies, Australian National University, Canberra

——— and M.D. Subash Chandran, 1989. 'Environmental Impact of Forest Based Industries on the Evergreen Forests of Uttara Kannada District: A Case Study. Department of Ecology and Environment, Government of Karnataka

——— and M.D. Subash Chandran, 1992. 'Sacred Groves'. In Geeti Sen, ed. *Indigenous Vision, Peoples of India Attitudes to the Environment. India International Centre Quarterly*, Spring-Summer 1992, pp. 183–87

——— and M.D. Subash Chandran, Unpublished 'Ecological Studies in Siddapur Taluk'

——— and V.D. Vartak, 1975. 'Sacred Groves of India: A Plea for Continued Conservation'. *Journal of the Bombay Natural History, Society*, 73; pp. 623–47

——— and V.D. Vartak, 1976. 'The Sacred Groves of Western Ghats in India'. *Economic Botany*, 30, pp. 152–60

——— and V.D. Vartak, 1981. 'Sacred Groves of Maharashtra: An Inventory'. In S.K. Jain, ed., *Glimpses of Ethnobotany*, Oxford University Press, Bombay.

Government of Bombay, 1923. Revenue Department Resolution No. 7211, May 1923

Hastings, J. 1934, ed. *Encyclopaedia of Religion and Ethics*, Vol. 12, pp. 448–52

Huges, J.D. 1984. 'Sacred Groves: The Gods, Forest Protection and Sustained Yield in the Ancient World'. In H.K. Steen, ed., *History of Sustained Yield Forestry*, Forest History Society, Durham

———, 1990. 'Artemis: Goddess of Conservation'. *Forest and Conservation History*, Vol. 34, No. 4, pp. 191–97

———, 1990. *Pan's Travail: Environmental Problems of the Ancient Greeks and Romans* Johns Hopkin's University Press, Baltimore

Imperial Gazetteer of India, 1908. Vol. 11. Henry Frowde, Oxford

Induchoodan, N.C., 1988. 'Ecological Studies of a Sacred Grove (Iringole, near Perumbavoor)'. M. Sc. thesis, Kerala Agricultural University, Trichur

Joshi, N.V. and M. Gadgil, 1991. 'On the Role of Refugia in Promoting Prudent Use of Biological Resources'. *Theoretical Population Biology*, Vol. 40 No. 20, pp. 211–29

Kane, P.V. 1958, ed. *History of Dharmasastra*, Vol. 5 part I: "Vratas, Utsavas and Kala etc." Govt. of Oriental Series, Class B, No. 6, Bhandarkar Oriental Research Institute, Poona

Karve, I., 1974. *Yuganta. The End of an Epoch.* Sangam Books, Poona, and Orient Longman, New Delhi

Khazanov, A.M., 1986. *Nomadism and the Outside World.* Cambridge University Press, Cambridge

Kosambi, D.D., 1970. *The Culture and Civilization of Ancient India in Historical Outline.* Vikas Publishing House, Delhi

Krishnamurthy, K., 1960. *Myristica* Swamps in the evergreen forests of Travancore. *Indian Forester*, 86(5)

Little, P.D., and D.W. Brokensha, 1987. 'Local Institutions, Tenure and Resource Management in East Africa'. In D. Anderson and R. Grove, eds., *Conservation in Africa: People, Policies and Practices*, Cambridge University Press, Cambridge

Malhotra, K.C., 1990. 'Village Supply and Safety Forest in Mizoram: A Traditional Practice of Protecting Ecosystem'. *Abstracts of V International Congress of Ecology*, p. 439

Mansberger, J.R., 1988 'In Search of the Tree Spirit: Evolution of the Sacred Tree *Ficus religiosa*'. In J. Dargavel, K. Dixon and N. Semple, eds., *Changing Tropical Forests: Historical Perspectives on Today's Challenges in Asia, Australasia and Oceania.* Centre for Resource and Environmental Studies, Australian National University, Canberra

Michell, A., Y. de Fretes and M. Poffenberger, 1990 'Community Participation for Conservation Area Management in Cyclops Mountains, Irian Jaya, Indonesia'. In M. Poffenberger, ed., *Keepers of the Forest: Land Management Alternatives in Southeast Asia*, Kumarian Press, Connecticut

Mohanan, C.N. and N.C. Nair, 1981. '*Kunstleria* Prain — A New genus Record for India and a New Species in the Genus'. *Proceedings of the Indian Academy of Sciences*, B-90, pp. 207–10.

Murton, B.J., unpublished. 'Resource Processes and Regional Integration in Western Nepal'

Nachiyappan, N., 1988. 'The Presiding Deity of Tirupparankundram'. *Journal of Tamil Studies*, 33, June 1988, pp. 11-19

Nair, N.C. and C.N. Mohanan, 1981. 'On the Rediscovery of Four Threatened Species from the Sacred Groves of Kerala'. In *Journ. Econ. Tax. Bot*, 2, pp. 233–35

Nayar, P.K.B., 1987. *Religion, Mythology and the Ecosystem.* Department of Environment and Forests, Government of India

Pillai, N.V., 1939. 'Sasta Cult in Travancore'. Is It a Relic of Buddhism?'. *Proceedings of the Indian History Congress* 3rd Session, pp. 230–49

Pillai, T.K.V., 1940. *Travancore State Manual*, Vol. I, Government of Travancore, Trivandrum

Pillai, V.R.P., 1986. *Temple Culture of South India*, Inter-India Publications, New Delhi

Radhakrishnan, S. 1949. *The Hindu View of Life.* George Allen and Unwin, London

Ramachandran, C., 1990. 'The Forest, Our Divine Source'. Seminar on Ecology and Ancient India, 28 April, Institute of Oriental Study, Thane

Ramakrishnan, P.S., 1992. *Shifting Agriculture and Sustainable Development*'. MAB Series, Vol. 10, Unesco, Paris

Ramanayya, N.V., 1983. *An Essay on the Origin of the South Indian Temple.* Ramanand Vidya Bhavan, New Delhi

Rao, B.S.L.H., 1969. 'Religion in Andhra' Ph. D. thesis, Karnatak University, Dharwad

Rapson, E.J., 1935. *The Cambridge History of India.* Vol. I *Ancient India,* Cambridge University Press, Cambridge

Risley, H., 1908. *The People of India.* Thacker Spink and Co.

Rodgers, W.A., unpublished. 'Sacred Groves: Their Evolution'

Saletore, R.N., 1973. *Early Indian Economic History.* Tripathy and Sons, Bombay

Sastrapradja, S., 1988. 'Perspective on Conservation in Indonesia'. In J.S. Denslow and C. Padock, eds., *People of the Tropical Rain Forest*, University of California Press, Berkeley

Shanmukhappa, G., 1966. *Working Plan for the Unorganised Forests of Sirsi and Siddapur.* Karnataka Forest Department, Bangalore.

Sontheimer, G.D., 1989. 'Hinduism: The Five Components and Their Interaction'. In

G.D. Sontheimer and H. Kulke, eds., *Hinduism Reconsidered*, Manohar Publishers, New Delhi

Shri Satyan, 1971, ed., *Gazetteer of Coorg District*, Government of Karnataka, Bangalore.

Subash Chandran, M.D., 1992a. 'Perceptions of *Bhutas* (Elements) in Oral Tradition of the Peasants of Uttara Kannada in South India'. Paper presented during *Seminar on Perceptions of Bhutas (Elements) in Oral Traditions*, 10–13 February 1992, Janapada Sampada, Indira Gandhi National Centre for the Arts

———, 1992b. 'Shifting Cultivation in the Western Ghats and the Conflicts in Colonial Forest Policy'. *Paper Presented in the International Conference on the Environmental History of South East Asia.*

———, 1993. 'Vegetational Changes in the Evergreen Forest Belt of Uttara Kannada District of Karnataka State'. Ph.D. thesis, Karnataka University, Dharwad

———, 1990 and M Gadgil, 1993a. Kans — Safety Forests of Uttara Kannada'. *Proceedings of the IUFRO: Forest History Group Meeting on Peasant Forestry*, 2–5 September, Freiburg, Germany, No. 40, pp. 49–57

———, 1990., and M. Gadgil, 1993b. 'State Forestry and Decline of Food Resources in the Tropical Forests of Uttara Kannada, Southern India'. In C.M. Hladik *et al* eds., *Tropical Forests, People and Food: Biocultural Interactions and Applications to Development*, Vol. 15, MAB Series, Unesco/Parthenon Publishing Group, Paris

Sankhala, K.S. and P. Jackson, 1985. 'Peoples, Trees and Antelopes in the Indian Desert'. In J.A. McNeely and D. Pitt, eds., *Culture and Conservation: The Human Dimensions in Environmenta Planning*, Croom Helm, Dublin

Terborgh, J., 1986. 'Keystone Plant Resources in the Tropical Forest'. M.E. Soule, ed., *Conservation Biology: The Science of Scarcity and Diversity*, Sinauer Associates, Sunderland

Tokarev, S., 1989. *History of Religion*, Progress Publishers, Moscow

Vannucci, M., 1992. 'Tradition and Change'. In Geeti Sen, ed., *Indigenous Vision: Peoples of India Attitudes to the Environment*, Sage Publications and Indian International Centre, New Delhi

Wheller, J.T. and M. Macmillan, 1956. *European Travellers in India*, First Series, Sushil Gupta (India) Ltd., Calcutta

Wingate, R.T., 1888. 'Settlement Proposals of 16 Villages of Kumta Taluk'. No. 210, December 1888, Forest Settlement Office, Karwar

Vaudeville, C., 1989. 'Multiple Approaches to a Living Hindu Myth: The Lord of Govardhan Hill'. In G.D. Sontheimer and H. Kulke, eds., *Hinduism Reconsidered*, Manohar Publishers, Delhi

4

Island Ecology and Cultural Perceptions

A Case Study of Lakshadweep

Makhan Jha

THE tiniest Union Territory of India, Lakshadweep, is an archipelago consisting of twelve atolls, three reefs and five submerged banks. Of its twenty-seven islands covering an area of 32 sq km, only ten are inhabited. They are Androth, Amini, Agatti, Bitra, Chetlat, Kadmat, Kalpeni, Kavarathi, Kiltan and Minicoy. Bitra is the smallest of all, with a population of only 181 in 1981, which increased to 225 in 1991. Recently a previously uninhabited island, Bangaram, has been developed by the administration for promoting tourism. As per the 1991 census there were only 61 persons on Bangaram.

Location

Although the land area is extremely small, if we consider the lagoon area of about 4,200 sq km, 20,000 sq km of territorial waters and about 400,000 sq km of economic zone, Lakshadweep is a large territory. The enchanting coral islands in the Arabian Sea were called the Laccadive, Minicoy and Amindivi islands, though they were popularly known as the Laccadives or Lakshadweep. The territory was officially named Lakshadweep on 1 November 1973. However, the Lakshadweep islands had been declared a Union Territory of India in 1956.

The earliest reference to the Laccadives is found in the records of the Dutch Company. In the 'Memorandum on the administration of the Malabar coast' by J.V.

Stein, written in 1743, these islands are referred to as 'Lekker-Diva'. Though this name was used in all subsequent Dutch records, and the British records used 'Laccadives', the local people called themselves inahbitants of the *divis* till recently. The term 'Laccadives' is derived from 'Lakshadweep', which is generally interpreted as a hundred thousand isles.

Since these islands lay directly on the trade route between India and Africa and Arabia, they are considered the landmark or the *laksh* (aim) for navigators, and hence called Lakshadweep. There are many interpretations of the origin of this term.

The islands are irregularly scattered in the Arabian Sea between 8 and 12-30°N and between 71 and 74°E. According to the Survey of India, the geographical area of Lakshadweep is 32 sq km. However, according to the revenue records it is 28.5 sq km, which represents only the land use area. The inhabited islands and the area of each are given below.

Sl. no.	*Inhabited Islands*	*Area (sq km)*
1.	Minicoy	4.4
2.	Kalpeni	2.3
3.	Androth	2.8
4.	Agatti	2.7
5.	Kavarathi	3.6
6.	Amini	2.6
7.	Kadmat	3.1
8.	Kiltan	1.6
9.	Chetlat	1.0
10.	Bitra	0.1

Present Administrative Set-Up

The history of Lakshadweep in its present form dates back to 1 November 1956, when it was made a Union Territory of India. During the medieval period the administration in the island was almost nil, as the emphasis was more on trade than on administration. Each island was almost a separate unit, though they were all under a common ruler. The islands came to be divided in 1787, when Tipu Sultan accepted the allegiance of the people of the Amindivi islands and took them over in return for a *jagir* from his territory in Chirakkal. Five islands came under Tipu Sultan's regime while the rest continued to be under Arakkal rule. This division of islands into two groups continued until 1956. However, in 1799, with the fall of Tipu Sultan in Shrirangapattana, the Amindivi islands were annexed by the British East India Company and came to form part of the South Kanara District. Meanwhile in 1791, the southern islands had passed by the conquest of Cannanore to the East India Company along with other possessions of the Beebi of Cannanore. British control was, however, nominal, and the Beebi retained the administration of Lakshadweep for an annual tribute. When the British took over the administration of the islands in 1875 for non-payment of revenue, the islands were attached to the Malabar District. This arrangement continued until 1956.

At present the adminstration of the islands is divided into four Tahsils. Each Tahsil has a Tahsildar at its head except for Minicoy, which has a Deputy Collector. The headquarters of the Tahsils and the inhabited islands under their jurisdictions are listed below.

Sl. no.	*Tahsil Headquarters*	*Island(s)*
1.	Minicoy	Minicoy
2.	Androth	Androth
3.	Kavarathi	Kavarathi Agathi Bangaram
4.	Amini	Amini Kidmat Kiltan Chetlat & Bitra

All the islands, both inhabited and uninhabited, have been kept under a single Lakshadweep District, which is headed by a District Magistrate. The District Magistrate also holds charge as the Administrator. Under the Adminstrator there is a Secretariat at Kavarathi, the headquarters of Lakshadweep, where almost all branches like census, education, fishing, agriculture, science and technology, medical, P.W.D., electricity, etc., work under a system known as "one file, one man". The Adminstrator is assisted by a

Secretary to the Adminstration at the Secretariat level. The District Magistrate also holds charge as Development Commissioner and is in overall charge of the administration. Until 1964 the headquarters of the Lakshadweep Administration were at Calicut, and there was difficulty in administering the islands from the mainland. However, when the headquarters shifted to Kavarathi, the tempo of development accelerated. Each section (or Department) is headed by a Director, who works under the overall supervision of the Administrator.

Each Tahsil is managed by a Tahsildar except for Minicoy. One Amin, usually selected from among the local *karnavars*, is appointed on each island to manage practically all matters of importance. Four C.D. Blocks started functioning, with their headquarters at Kavarathi, Androth, Amini and Minicoy, from January 1971. Amini Block was, however, bifurcated in October 1976 into Amini Block at Amini and the C.D. Block at Kiltan, which covers Kiltan, Chetlat and Bitra islands. Thus there are now five Blocks in the Union Territory. Again, to bring the administration closer to the people, all the inhabited islands along with their attached islands and islets were divided into nine Sub-Divisions in 1983, each under the charge of a Sub-Divisional Officer.

The Islands Council, under the Lakshadweep Island Council Regulations of 1988, was constituted in April 1990. This is the first democratic institution on the islands and consists of 79 members from different islands of Lakshadweep. Very recently a Pradesh Council for the U.T. as a whole has also been constituted, with elected members from each Island Council. The Pradesh Council consists of 21 members, with the Administrator as its chairman.

The Union Territory is represented in Parliament by a member elected to the Lok Sabha. The present Member of Parliament is Mr. P.M. Sayeed.

The Population

The early inhabitants of the islands are believed to have been Hindus who migrated from the Malabar coast. Later they were converted to Islam by an Arab saint and are now Muslims. They were declared a Scheduled Tribe as per the Scheduled Caste and Scheduled Tribes List (Modification) Order, 1956.

However, when we look at the social structure of the society, we find that the matrilineal kinship and a rigid caste system, characteristic of the Hindu traditions of the Kerala coast, are still retained in spite of being Muslim for several centuries. This coexistence of matriliny and Islam, which is clearly patrilineal, is most unusual.

The Koyas were the chief landowing caste. The word 'Koya' is of recent origin. Formerly they were known as *taravadis* or *karnavars*. Originally, they consisted of the principal families or *taravads* of the early migrants. The heads of these *tarwads*, known as *karnavars*, sat as jurors in the society *panchayat* and considered themselves superior to others.

The Malmis were the sailors, who were brought by the Koyas for sailing their traditional boats, known as *odam*. The word 'Malmi' is of Arab origin and means 'one who is connected with the sign of ways'. The Malmis were the tenants of the Koyas and served as sailors specially in exporting their produce from the islands to the mainland and bringing back rice and other essential goods. The piloting of boats is no longer an exclusive privilege of this class, as mechanized boats with sophisticated navigational systems have been introduced, which anybody who has acquired mastery over the nautical tables may operate.

The Melacheris, who were the original labour class, still form the major part of the population of Amini, Kadmat, Kiltan, Chetlat and Bitra islands. Their traditional occupation is climbing coconut trees to pluck the nuts and tap *neerah*, sweet toddy. The Melacheris were originally landless tree-climbers.

At Minicoy, the Manikfans are considered the highest class, at par with the Koyas of the northern islands. They alone owned private property and dictated the destiny of the other groups. While the Thakrufans were sailors, the Thakrus worked on the *odams* during voyages. The Raveries were labourers and worked as tree-climbers.

All the people, irrespective of their class distinctions, profess Islam. While there are no differences in the religious beliefs, manners and customs of these different classes, they have been compartmentalized by certain social barriers. Marriage alliances between certain groups are not allowed. A Koya boy can marry a Melacheri girl, but a Malmi or Melacheri boy will never be allowed to marry a Koya girl. On some islands, Melacheris are not allowed to perform *rathib*, a religious exercise, in certain mosques. The Melacheris also suffered some social disability in the past. For example, they were not allowed to use *chappals*, carry umbrellas or sing on occasions like marriages. But the situation has gradually changed.

The population of Lakshadweep was 51,681 in 1991. The density of population was recorded as 1,615 per sq km, while the sex ratio was 944 females per thousand males. The island-wise population as recorded in the 1991 census is given below.

Sl. no.	*Island*	*Population*	
1.	Kavarathi	8,664	
2.	Agatti	5,667	
3.	Minicoy	8,313	
4.	Androth	9,119	
5.	Kalpeni	4,079	
6.	Bangaram	61	(a newly created tourist spot)
7.	Amini	6,445	
8.	Kadmath	3,983	
9.	Kiltan	3,075	
10.	Chetlat	2,050	
11.	Bitra	225	
	Total	51,681	

When we look at earlier census records, we find that there has been a tremendous increase in the population of the islands, although migration from the mainland has been almost nil. The year-wise population figures for Lakshadweep are given below.

Sl. no.	*Census year*	*Total Population*
1.	1901	13,882
2.	1911	14,555
3.	1921	13,637
4.	1931	16,040
5.	1941	18,335
6.	1951	21,035
7.	1961	24,108
8.	1971	31,810
9.	1981	40,249
10.	1991	51,681

It has been estimated by the census department of Lakshadweep that if the population increases at the same rate, then by AD 2001 the total population of Lakshadweep will be 59,000 to 60,000.

The population of Lakshadweep lives in 6,637 household families, of which 3,013 families have been identified as below the poverty line. Of these, 2,573 had been assisted under the IRDP programme for self-occupation by the end of August 1988.

Language

Malayalam was brought in by the early settlers. In course of time it evolved into its present form, which is considerably different from what is now spoken in Kerala. The island Malayalam has many peculiarities of pronunciation, vocabulary, etc. The civil SDO of Agatti, who hails from Cochin, said that there were many words in island Malayalam which people like him failed to understand. In course of time, many Tamil and Canarese words also crept in. The old Malayalam script used to be in vogue in the islands, but *vattezhuthu* was replaced by Arabic script, which subsequently came to be known as Arabic Malayalam. This is still very popular, specially among the womenfolk. However, the present Malayalam script was introduced into the territory during the time of the British.

The inhabitants of Minicoy speak Mahl, which is related to primitive Sinhalese. It has also some similarities with the language of the Republic of Male. Mahl has a script of its own called Diwehi Thana. Besides Mahl, the inhabitants of Minicoy also speak Malayalam, which is a link language in the islands.

Education

In earlier days education in the Lakshadweep islands was confined to the teaching of the *Koran* and the elements of Islamic theology in schools attached to mosques. These schools are called *madrasas* and still function side by side with the modern schools established specially after 1956, when the islands became a Union Territory. The first government school in the islands was opened at Amini on 15 January 1904. One very old informant said that as the children had to attend the mosque schools in the mornings, the government school functioned from noon to 4 p.m. and the only subjects taught were Canarese, Malayalam and arithmetic. It was further revealed that during those days, as the Amindivi group of islands was under Karnataka, pupils came to the schools only for learning Canarese, the official language. However, in 1905, when Malayalam was declared the official language of the entire Lakshadweep islands, the teaching of Canarese was discontinued.

In 1911 an elementary school was opened in Kiltan and in 1925 a similar school was opened at Kadmat. Another temporary school was opened at Chetlat in 1927. The people of the Amini group of islands did not pay as much attention to modern education as did the people of Agatti and Kavarathi islands, which were under the management of Malabar.

Among the Malabar-controlled islands, the first schools were opened on Agatti, Kavarathi and Androth in 1875. However, on Minicoy the first school was started in 1891 with a hospital compounder acting as schoolmaster in addition to his other duties. In the 1930s measures were taken by the government to make schools more popular in the eyes of the people. Scholarships were introduced for students passing out from island schools and wishing to study further on the mainland.

From the census of 1951 we learn that literacy was only 15 per cent, which by the 1961 census had increased to 23.27 per cent. The steady progress of the territory in the field of education is reflected in broad terms in the percentage of literacy, which rose to 43.66 per cent in 1971. In the same year literacy was 60.4 per cent in Kerala and 29.5 per cent in India. The literacy rate again increased to 55 per cent for Lakshadweep by 1981, while for India the increase was up to 36.2 per cent.

Till recently there was no institution of higher education in the territory, and students had to go to the mainland. To ease this problem, the Jawaharlal Nehru College, the first of its kind in the territory, was inaugurated on 15 July 1972 at Kavarathi. It imparts teaching in mainly three groups: (1) mathematics, physics and chemistry; (ii) physics, chemistry and biology; and (iii) Indian history, world history and economics, up to the pre-degree level. The college is affiliated to Calicut University. Another similar college has been started at Androth.

Dress

The people of the Lakshadweep and Amini groups of islands dress in a very simple way, while the islanders of Minicoy wear colourful clothes. Except on Minicoy, men wear a white or coloured *lungi*, which is a rectangular piece of cloth the ends of which are stiched together. Both men and women wear a silver thread round the waist. Elderly persons draw the *lungi* through the string to hold it around the waist. Men generally do not wear anything above the waist, but on special occasions a fine piece of embroidered cotton or silk cloth is put around the shoulders. Shirts are more popular among the younger generation. The women also wear a rectangular piece of cloth, known as *kachi*, around the waist, but unlike the *lungi* its edges are not stiched. The cloth is tucked into the thread or waist belt made of gold or silver. The *kachis* are either completely black or white with black borders. Silk *kachis* are generally red with black borders. Women cover their upper bodies with a tight-fitting full-sleeved jacket. The front of the jacket has a piece of embroidered lace studded with gilt and glass pieces. The headdress of the women is known as *thattam*, which is a long scarf for covering the head and shoulders. Educated women sometime wear *saris*.

The dress of the people of Minicoy is distinct. The different classes — the Manikfans, the Thakrufans, the Thakrus and the Raveri — have their own traditional dress. While the aristocratic Manikfans wear ordinary *lungis* and the shirts, the traditional dress of men of other classes is trousers resembling jeans. They are generally of black, white, blue, bright pink or green cloth and are fastened to the waist with a cord. They have a coloured embroidered tape lining on the sides as well as around the ankles. Among the Thakrus and Thakrufans, only those who have performed a sea voyage are privileged to wear this kind of dress, whereas a Raveri can wear it on attaining adulthood. A piece of white cloth is used as a waistband over the trousers. The chest is generally bare. The headdress is confined to a red or black cloth with stripes, which is worn with two to four upward projections indicating the different classes. The younger generation, however, prefers trousers and shirts to the traditional dress.

The dress of the Minicoy woman consists of a blue or green undercloth and a long robe, known as *libus*, which goes from shoulder to ankle. Made of brick-red cloth with black stripes, it has an opening only at the neck, where there is generally embroidery. Clothing with floral designs is worn on special occasions. A piece of black cloth serves the purpose of a headdress and, of late, a white cloth is also being used by some women to cover the face down to the chin.

Ornaments

The women of the islands other than Minicoy use ornaments in profusion. An *aranchan* around the waist, *vala* or *kodam* on the wrists, *koodu* and *alikkath* on the ears and an *urukku* around the neck are the usual ornaments of a woman. The waist-belt is either of gold or of silver. It can be of two types: the *kannadi aracha*, about one inch broad with a lock; and the *adippu*, which is around chain. The *vala* is an ordinary bangle while the *kodakam* used like a bracelet. The *koodu* is an eardrop pyramidal in shape, while *alikkath* are small rings worn on the outer rim of the ear. The most popular among the necklaces is the *urukku*, a chain of black beads intertwined with gold.

Bridal ornaments, however, are more elaborate, with a variety of necklaces and other jewellery like gold or silver anklets. Minicoy women are more frugal in wearing ornaments. Certain traditional restrictions on the use of jewellery also exist. Only Manikka women (the female folk of the Manikfans) are allowed to wear gold ornaments, while women belonging to other classes wear ornaments made of silver. Earrings and a chain around the neck are their characteristic ornaments. Every woman is seen wearing a *modram*, a ring on the finger.

Settlement, Land Reforms and House Construction

There are no records of the islands showing the details of land held by individuals. In the Lakshadweep group there were *paimash*, registers showing the number of coconut trees held by an individual on *pandaram* (government land) and the amount of tree tax to be paid by him. These registers were maintained since 1892 and revised once in twelve years. In the Amini group there was a property register prepared in 1875, which was called the *Land Manual* and was corrected as late as 1935, which showed the details of coconut trees and their owners. In the past, wealth was estimated in terms of coconut trees and houses owned.

Land on the islands may be broadly classified into two groups: lands under private ownership, called *janmon* lands; and lands under Government ownership, known as *pandaram* lands. *Janmon* land may be further classified as that which is directly in the possession of the *janmi* (landlord) and that which has been transferred and is in the possession of a *kudiyan* or tenant. Government lands are also of two types: lands under the absolute control of the Government and lands which have been made over to private individuals on lease.

Three types of tenancy in private *janmon* lands existed on the islands: *nadapu* tenancy, *pattam* tenancy and house site tenancy. *Nadapu* tenancy was a peculiar system prevalent in Kavarathi, Agatti, Amini and Androth islands. Under this system tenants have to render a series of customary services to the landlord from time to time. A *nadapu* normally consisted of 30 to 40 trees granted by a landlord to his tenant.

Under *pattam* tenancy, a contract is made between the parties to render services on some occasions. For example, when the landlord goes on a voyage, he enters into an agreement with people for sailing his *odam*, for which, besides some remuneration, concessions are granted to the tenants to allow them to plant trees, etc.

Under the House site tenancy system, the house site belonged to the landlord. The tenant was permitted to build a house on the site. No rent was demanded for the site, but certain customary duties were involved, such as helping the landlord with labour on special occasions. The tenant could live in the house as long as he liked, but if the house was dismantled, the site reverted to the landlord.

These tenancy systems of the islands have undergone several changes, specially after the introduction of the Laccadive, Minicoy and Amindivi Islands Land Revenue and Tenancy Regulations of 1965, which provide, among other things, for the conferment of occupancy rights. These changes have brought a revolution in the lifestyle of the people, specially the Melacheries of the Lakshadweep and Amini groups of islands and the Raveris of Minicoy.

Land and tenancy reforms in the islands have been social and economic issues due to the peculiar system of service tenancy in vogue. Landlords depend too much on their tenants, who are obliged to serve them for favour of trees, land, boats, etc. As there were no shops on the islands where the daily necessities of life could be bought or bartered, nor was there any local market for the island produce, the only channel for procuring their needs and for selling their products was through their landlords. The ecological set-up of the island compelled landlords and tenants to depend on each other.

House Construction

Nature has provided sufficient materials to construct houses on these isolated islands. The bricks made of sand collected from the sea-shore, the jelly, which works as cement, collected from the lagoon area of the sea, the coconut leaves used for thatching roofs, these are some of the materials which have been provided by the existing ecology for constructing their houses in the Lakshadweep islands.

By a rough estimate, about 84 per cent of the houses on the islands have walls made of stone and only 16 per cent have walls made of grass, leaves and reeds. So far as thatching is concerned, the islanders use mainly coconut leaves. About 70 per cent houses have roofs made of coconut leaves while approximately 28 per cent have tiled roofs. I was told at Kavarathi that Minicoy has more tiled houses than the Amini group, nearly 60 per cent. This is due to their income from jobs such as employment in foreign shipping companies, export of fish, etc. On the economically backward islands like Agatti, Kiltan and Chetlat the standard of houses is noticeably lower than on other islands.

Communications

Communications on the islands are still in a primitive stage, although many improvements have been made after 1956. As there is no scope for road communication, there is no question of its improvement, although some pucca roads of a few kilometres have been constructed linking the circuit house or dak bungalow with the secretariat or jetty on each island.

Previously the islanders used their own country boats, known as *odams* in the Laccadive and Amini groups of islands and *odies* in Minicoy, for visiting the mainland as well as making inter-island contacts. The traditional means of transport in the territory was the country-made sailing vessel. These *odams* and *odies* are of various sizes and shapes, built to carry about 70 to 400 tons of cargo. The people of Chetlat island are expert in making these traditional vessels. On Bangaram, which is almost uninhabited, a special type of wood is found, which is used in making *odams*. Coconut wood is also used. The wood of the breadfruit tree is also used in making these country boats, which measure from 10 to 15 metres. In the past, the islanders used to build small boats without using any wood. They were made of twisted coir and fish oil was applied to make them water-tight. Not a single iron nail was used in such coir boats. However, the people of Minicoy used iron nails extensively in building their *odies*.

Sailing vessels used to operate only during the months from September to May as they were not strong enough to withstand the fury of the south-west monsoon. Their ports of call depended on seasonal winds. A traditional navigator told me that previously they did not see the people other islands for three or four months, specially during the monsoon, nor did they visit the mainland during these months.

But the situation is completely changed now, as mechanised boats have been pressed into service by the administration, specially after 1970. This has eased the problem of communication and transportation. Big ships like the *Tipu Sultan* and many other speedboats are in operation these days, and an islander can reach the mainland in 24 to 30 hours.

Other modern means of communication like telephones and fax are in operation on some of the islands, through which quick communication is possible with any part of the world. Postal facilities, bank facilities, treasury works, etc., have brought the islands close to the rest of the country and to the world. Some islands like Kavarathi and Agatti are linked with Delhi Dooradarshan through microwave.

The islanders use bicycles for moving around. A few of them have three-wheelers for carrying passengers from the jetty to their place of stay or to and from the helipad.

↑ Fig. 4.1 The grave-yard in the midst of coconut trees at Agatti island.

↓ Fig. 4.2 Fishermen of Agatti island.

↑ Fig. 4.3 The young fishermen have started dressing of Tuna fish for Mas.

↓ Fig. 4.4 Tuna fish is being smoked for Mas preparation.

↑ Fig. 4.5 Coconut tree blossomed with beautiful nuts at Kavaratti island.

↓ Fig. 4.6 The islanders carrying coconuts in their cycles at Kavaratti island.

↑ Fig. 4.7 After plucking the nuts are kept aside by the islanders for proper sun-dry.

↓ Fig. 4.8 The Odam just arrived from the mainland loaded with tiles etc.

↑ Fig. 4.9 The salt bags are being unloaded from the Odam at Agatti island.

↓ Fig. 4.10 A house, thatched with dry coconut leaf, of a Melachery (lower caste and belonging to poor economic strata) at Agatti island.

↑ Fig. 4.11 A scene of deep sea-erosion at Kavaratti island.

↓ Fig. 4.12 The *pan* (betel-leaf), imported from the mainland, for sale at Agatti island.

↑ Fig. 4.13 Two islanders are making windows of coconut trunks at Agatti island.

↓ Fig. 4.14 A group of children at Agatti.

↑ Fig. 4.15 An Ujra Mosque (with a loud-speaker) and a well at Agatti.

↓ Fig. 4.16 An *Arekkal* (a common grinding place) where many *Amnis*, *Amnis-kutti*, *Kundami*, etc. are kept for common use at Agatti.

Flora and Fauna

The surface soil of coral sand contains 95 per cent calcium, hence most of the islands are barren with little spontaneous vegetation. However, the soil and the climatic conditions are ideal for coconut cultivation, and coconut therefore forms the staple product. Coconut is the spine of the island economy, with copra and coir forming the major export items, besides fish.

Two varieties of coconut, locally called *thenga*, are cultivated here. The common tall variety does not give sufficient nuts, but the micro variety, which is about 5 or 6 ft tall, gives high yield, though the size of the nut is small. The micro variety copra has high oil content when compared with the ordinary variety. Breadfruit, papaya, drumstick, etc., are also found on all islands, though in limited quantity. The distribution of flora is more or less similar on all the islands.

There are no forests in the entire territory, although some bushes are seen. Vegetables are neither cultivated nor a part of the daily diet. However, the Agriculture Department produces some vegetables in its demonstration farms on different islands.

The fauna of any oceanic island is generally very restricted due to the difficulty of crossing an extensive barrier of sea. However, the marine life of a coral sea is very elaborate and colourful. It is almost impossible to condense the thousands of forms found in the lagoons and adjacent seas of the Lakshadweep archipelago, and therefore this description is limited to the most common fish there.

Tuna, shark, sailfish, seer, flying fish, turtles, etc., are found in the Lakshadweep sea area. Out of total fish catch, 80 per cent is of tuna. Turtles are of two types, green turtles and hawksbills. The fat of green turtles is used to make boats waterproof. Sometimes dolphins are also found in the sea but are not commonly hunted. The islanders at Agatti reported that whenever they saw whales in the sea, they avoided hunting them as their arrival was considered auspicious for the islands.

While describing the fauna of Lakshadweep, the importance of molluscan forms cannot be overlooked since they are magnificent in appearance and important from the economic point of view for the islanders. The money cowrie is abundant in the shallow waters of the lagoons and on the reefs. Cowries are picked up from the reef area at low tide, mainly by the womenfolk during their spare time, and are largely sold on the mainland.

Cattle and goats are reared on the islands in a very small way. Dearth of fodder is a major problem. As a result, the yield from these animals is very poor. Poultry also is reared. Cats are common, but dogs are almost wholly absent. There are no poisonous snakes on the islands, but they are infested with rats and mosquitoes. The rats bring about a great deal of damage to coconut trees. Different types of birds are also seen on the islands, some of which are migratory. There is a legend substantiating the total absence of the crow from Kavarathi island. A Muslim saint, Sheire Muhammad Kasim Walliwullah (17th century), once visited Kavarathi and was doing *vajju* before offering *namaj* at the Ujra Mosque when a crow defiled his dress with its droppings. The saint cursed the crow to leave the island immediately, and since then no crow has been seen on the island. However, at Pitti island, which is uninhabited and is located only 24 km from Kavarathi, crows and many other birds are found. Pitti has been declared a bird sanctuary.

ECOLOGICAL CHALLENGE TO DEVELOPMENTAL ACTIVITIES

Among the different factors responsible for shaping and influencing culture and developmental activities, the ecology of a region plays a very important role. That is why social scientists have started showing considerable interest in varying eco-structures with a view to understanding the complexities of cultural perceptions on the one hand and ecological challenges to developmental activities on the other.

Ecological Structure of the Islands

The eco-structure of the Lakshadweep islands has two broad dimensions: the natural eco-system and the man-made eco-system. This brief typology of the eco-structure of the Lakshadweep islands suggests that the natural and the man-made eco-systems are closely linked. For example, land is very limited, only 32 sq km, out of which the land use area is only 26 sq km. Thus too many developmental activities will throw off balance the natural eco-structure of the islands.

(A)

Natural Eco-Systems

Sea

Reefs Lagoons Atolls Island (on which various activities are done like coconut plantation, construction of houses, etc.)

(B)

Man-Made Eco-System

Inhabitants' houses Man's various activities

(both traditional and modern) like agro-horticulture, plantation of coconuts, animal husbandry, industries, fisheries, tourism, transportation and communication etc.)

However, the sea area is unlimited and there is enough scope for fishing and various other activities relating to the fish trade. However, the study of the island ecology shows that over-exploitation or misuse of any one system has an impact on the others.

It has been noted that the total reporting area of the land is only 2800 hectares. Out of this, 445 ha is put to non-agricultural use. There is no forest, hill or river within the islands. The Lakshadweep islands are identical in structure and formation and their tops are built up of coral reefs. The soil has been derived from coral limestone. It is essentially coral sandy soil underlined by limestone and gravel of different shapes and size. The land has 85 to 98 per cent calcium carbonate, which is totally unfavourable for any type of cultivation. Thus the natural eco-structure of these islands is not conducive to agricultural development. However, it is suited for coconut plantation, which is done here to a great extent.

Economic Peculiarities

Most developmental activities on the islands centre around fishing and coconut. Tuna is called the 'chicken of the sea'. The average annual catch of fish is 7300 tonnes in Lakshadweep. Of this, nearly 50 per cent at Agatti island, but unfortunately there is no fish processing plant there. A fish processing plant has been started at Minicoy, very far away from Agatti, and the Agatti islanders have been agitating for one. The entire tuna catch at Agatti is converted into *mas* by a traditional method of processing for long preservation. The fish is first properly dressed and then boiled with a little salt. Then, it is smoked and sun-dried. It may be kept for two years. While men prepare *mas* at Agatti, I was told women do it at Minicoy.

Mas is sold at very high prices. The islanders get the daily selling rate of fish from Cochin by telephone and then the fish-loaded boats are sent to the mainland. It is said that during the monsoon, when the islanders suspend fishing, they remain busy in disposing of their old stock. Recently a fishermen's cooperative has been established. Although it was started as early as 1962, it had not been functioning well. Only last year, with the efforts of the Administrator, did it start functioning well. At present there are 37 cooperative stores in the islands which deal in many kinds of articles.

Coir-based Industry

After the fish trade, coconuts are the largest trade of the islanders. Training is imparted in coir spinning, rope-making, mat-making, etc. There are three industrial cooperative societies and a few Mahila Udyog Samitis which were introduced in the Seventh Plan period, where knitting, handicrafts, etc., are taught to women. During the Eighth Plan period (1992-97) a sum of Rs. 13.83 lakhs has been provided for the development of coir-based industries in the islands. Emphasis has also been laid on the development of *khadi* industries, for which a sum of Rs. 22–50 lakhs has been provided in the Eighth Plan period.

In April 1988 a Vayudoot air service was introduced after commissioning the Agatti airstrip, which facilitated the transportation of men and materials. An expert committee has recommended the introduction of amphibian aircraft. If they are introduced, almost all islands of Lakshadweep can have an air service.

So far as the thrust area of economic development is concerned, 178 km of sea-shore have been identified, of which 16 km are subjected to severe sea erosion. To prevent this erosion the plantation of bushes and trees has been suggested. A scientific committee has also suggested the scientific plantation of coconut trees in the islands. About 180 to 200 coconut trees should be planted per hectare, and hybrid varieties, which may give about 200 nuts per year should be distributed. The present traditional coconut trees give only 40 to 50 nuts per year.

Out of 5,906 households, nearly 3,013 have been identified as being below the poverty line. Of these, 2,573 families had been assisted under the IRDP for self-occupation by the end of 1988. All islands have been covered by seven Primary Health Centres and two hospitals (one at Kavarathi and another at Minicoy) where the services of specialists like paediatricians, eye specialists, pathologists, surgeons, anaesthetists, gynaecologists and others are available.

Food Habits

Fish and coconut form the major part of both daily diet and ritual food. The islanders call themselves 'sons of the sea' and from childhood they learn to fish in the lagoons. Tender coconut or its water is mixed in almost all preparations. Some of the food items which I observed are described below.

Salted dishes

1.	*Kanji*	The water of boiled rice is left overnight, mixed with fish and coconut water, and is taken in the morning as breakfast. This is very popular among the aged people of the islands.
2.	*Rabe-chor*	Rice cooked in the night is taken in the morning with fish or mixed with coconut water. It forms part of the daily diet.
3.	*Tengachor*	Rice mixed with coconut cream; may also be eaten with fish curry called *miha pottichad* (Kavaratti, Agatti islands). It is also served on the occasion of marriages, etc.
4.	*Kori-chor*	Rice mixed with chicken or egg, spices, etc. It is prepared on some rare occasions.
5.	*Kalangi*	Rice, white of egg and coconut cream; popular on Androth island.
6.	*Arik-petri*	Rice chapati (bread)
7.	*Chakrachor*	Rice cooked in coconut water, with or without spices, and then wrapped in coconut cream.
8.	*Uppam*	Rice with/without egg, fried in coconut oil with onions, ginger, etc.
9.	*Kumi-uppam*	Rice and coconut cream, mixed with water of coconut and fried. Balls are made and are placed in a flat pot with sugar paste. In case *kumi-uppam* is to be made salted, meat or fish is added.
10.	*Kaivishel*	A sweet dish in which rice is cooked with egg and coconut water and mixed with sugar.
11.	*Uppam* of various types	*Bar-uppam, Manda-uppam, Matta-mala, Mattapum*

Besides these major items of food, different types of cakes are made of coconut, both sweet and salted. Names, sizes and methods of preparation vary from island to island. After food, most people chew *pan* (betel leaf), which is brought from the mainland. They may also chew tobacco and smoke cigarettes. However, they do not drink any alcohol except fermented coconut water prepared on some special occasions. Recently they have also started taking tea and coffee without milk.

Beliefs, Rituals and Festivals

The Lakshadweep islanders are all Muslims and most of them belong to the Shafi'i school of the Sunni sect. Besides the *Kuran*, they also acknowledge the authority of the *sunnet* (or customary law) as interpreted by Shafi. Other practices are the recitation of the *kalma*, an expression of faith in Allah and the Prophet Muhammad; offering of *namaz* (prayers) five times a day, *roza* (fasting) in the month of Ramzan; *Zakkat* (giving of alms), and *haj* (pilgrimage to Mecca). The islanders are orthodox and pious and they adhere strictly to their religious observances. In this connection it may be noted that the Muslims of the Lakshadweep islands are held in great esteem by the Muslims of South India, Sri Lanka, Malaysia, Singapore, Burma, etc. The high-caste Muslims, called Thangals, particularly those of Androth island, go to these countries on preaching tours locally known as *safars*. Pilgrimage to Mecca, though not compulsory, increases a persons's social status and prestige.

Besides these common features of the Muslim faith, there are some features peculiar to these islands. Special mention may be made of *ratheeb*. This is a form of religious performance conducted by the islanders to invoke the blessings of preceptors like Mohiddin Thangal and Raffai Thangal. Generally, the *ratheeb* mosques are patronised by the descendants of Sheikh Mohammad Kasim, the first Thangal. He is considered the twenty-ninth descendant of the Prophet. He migrated to the islands around 1650 and built mosques at Kavarathi, Agatti, and elsewhere which are popularly known as Ujra mosques.

The islanders believe that the celebration of *ratheeb* was started at Kavarathi under the direction of Sheikh Kasim. His grave was constructed near the Ujra mosque and became a place of pilgrimage. His cap, walking stick, flag, etc. are still kept in the Ujra mosque at Kavarathi. The grave of Sheikh Kasim is held in very high esteem by the islanders. Wherever they suffer from serious sickness, they come to his graveyard and offer petitional vows and adorations. Therefore many stories about the spiritural powers of Sheikh Kasim. Crows are not seen on Kavarathi due to a curse given by Sheikh Kasim. Only 5 to 10 per cent of women go to hospital for delivery, as a magical plate given by Sheikh Kasim is available with the people of Kavarathi for eradicating labour pains.

Another performance, very special to the islands, is *moulood*, which is celebrated to obtain divine blessings. Verses are recited in honour of the saints and food is taken together.

Apart from the majority, who belong to the Sunni sect, other sects such as Wahabis and Ahmadiyas are also found in very small numbers. Wahabis are a reformist sect in Islam who oppose all practices not sanctioned by the *Koran*. They are followers of Abdal Wahab. They are found on Agatti and Kavarathi and do not participate in *ratheeb* and *maulood*.

The islanders believe in magical rites and practices to drive away evil spirits. *Ratheeb* and *maulood* are performed before undertaking new ventures like the construction of houses, building of *odams*, etc. Magical rites are performed in the nights near the sea-shore to cure diseases, to drive away evil spirits, to bring harm to enemies, as well as for the safe return from the deep sea of fishermen.

The customs and rituals connected with marriage, birth, circumcision, ear-boring, death, etc., are more or less common to all the islands of Lakshadweep, except for some differences at Minicoy.

Brief Ritual Calendar

Although the details of the ritual calendar of the islanders have not been collected during the pilot survey work, a brief sketch of the important ritual observances is given here.

Month	*Date*	*Important rituals*
Muharram	9 & 10	The first month of the Islamic calendar. Martyrdom of Hazrat Imam Hussain. Days of fasting in Lakshdweep. No *taziya* is constructed.It has not much importance among theislanders.
Safar	11 (last Wednesday)	*Urs* of Sheikh Mohd. Kasim Wali. On this day the people of Androth island go to the sea for ritual bathing after applying specially prepared oil on their bodies. Celebrated in memory of the Prophet's recovery from illness.
Rab-Awwal	12	Milad-un-Nabi
Rab-Akhir	8	The *urs* of a saint popularly known as Kunthapurath Kazhin Jawar

Rab-Akhir	9	The *urs* of Sheikh Mudiuddin A. Geelani (there is a sight difference in the date among the islanders)
Jam-Awwal	12	*Urs* of Saint Bukhari of Padanna Puthiyapura, Androth, popularly known as Ippa Kazhinjawar
Jam-Akhar	24	*Urs* of Saint Ahmad Kabir Rifayi
Rajab	3	*Urs* of Saint Uways-i-Qurani
Rajab	27	*Miraj* (night journey of the Prophet); day of fasting for the islanders
Shahban	14, 15	*Barath* — days of fasting for the islanders; it is believed that God created everything on earth on this day.
Ramzan		The month of fasting. The fast is broken by islanders in the evening by drinking tender coconut water. They call *Ramzan Noimbu Masan.*
Ramzan	27	*Urs* of Saint Ubaidullah, who was responsible for the conversion of the islanders to Islam
Haj	9	*Arafa*
Dul	10	*Idul Azha*

Occupation

As stated earlier, the main occupations of the islanders are fishing and coconut cultivation. The islanders are busy fishing from September to May, which is believed to be the best fishing season. In the lagoon area, fishing is continued round the year, but deep-sea fishing is suspended during the monsoon. The fishing areas have been grouped oceanographically into three, the middle group of islands consisting of Kavarathi, Agatti and Amini, the north-eastern group consisting of Kiltan, Chetlat and Bitra, and the comparatively isolated islands of Minicoy, Kalpeni, Suheli and Androth. Some of the uninhabited islands like Byramgore, Perumalpar and Elikkalpeni are famous for tuna resources. Thus, sometimes the islanders go to these uninhabited islands for a week or so and camp there for tuna fishing. They carry with them the sweet water and food for and stay on the uninhabited islands in group of 10 to 15 persons. Of the numerous species of fish found in Lakshadweep islands, skipjack, tuna, different species of shark, *wahoo* (devilfish), sailfish, rays, etc., are economically important. Prawns are non-existent in the sea of the Lakshadweep Islands. Thus an important occupation is fishing, which the islanders pursue for 8 or 9 months in a year.

Next to fish, the principal articles of export and the main sources of income have always been the coconut and its products like coir, copra, jaggery, etc. A sizeable portion of the coconut production is consumed at home, and the surplus is exported. It fetches them very little income after meeting expenses on transport. Recently there has been a rise in the price of nuts and allied items as well as improvements in methods of cultivation (specially the hybrid trees). Coconuts have thus come to stay as the deciding factor in the island economy. While the menfolk are occupied with fishing, the children, women and old men remain busy in collecting coconuts, making coir ropes, mats, jaggery, etc., which fetch a good income.

However, the situation differs at Minicoy, where many able-bodied men join foreign shipping corporations as they are good sailors, those left at home going fishing. The womenfolk at Minicoy look after the *mas* processing, while it is done exclusively by the menfolk on the northern islands. Coconut, the only commercial crop in Lakshadweep, is cultivated even on uninhabited islands. At present an area of 2855 hectares is under coconut cultivation on the inhabited islands and the area on the uninhabited islands is not known.

Social Life

Under the matrilineal set-up, the social life of the islanders centres around females, and fathers have very limited rights and responsibilities over their children and in family affairs. The children are brought up in their mothers' houses and have rights of inheritance to their property. Though the father has no legal responsibility for the maintenance of his children, usually he meets part of their expenses on clothes, ornaments, education, etc. But he has an obligation to contribute towards the expenses connected with their rites of passage.

Children grow bereft of the love and care of their parents, specially the father. The matrilineal system prevailing in the territory make the situation worse as the children stay with the mother in her house. Their father visits the house only late in the night and leaves early in the morning for his house. As a result, small children seldom see or talk to their fathers.

There are two broad categories of property: Friday property, known as *velliazhcha*, and Monday property, which is called *thinkalazhcha*. While ancestral property, also known as *tarwad* property, is controlled by the eldest male member, the *karanavan*,

Monday or self-aquired property, which consists mostly of movable articles like jewellery, gold, utensils, cash, bicycles, wrist watch, radios, etc., is managed and owned by the persons concerned. *Tarwad* property cannot be sold. However, it can be mortgaged in lieu of loans. *Tarwad* property usually consists of coconut trees over a piece of land, which are not usually divided. However, the rules of partition and division state that *tarwad* property is to be divided among the members of the joint and extended family. The *tarwad*, which has been a notable feature in the islands, is now on the verge of breaking down owing to economic and social factors, specially due to the growing aspirations of modern educated youths, which are not fulfilled in it, and the impact of new ideas and the individualistic outlook of the younger generations.

Arts and Crafts

The islanders show considerable artistic skill in carpentry. Beautiful wood carvings are seen in many mosques all over the islands. The intricate carvings in wood found on the pillars and on the ceilings of the front part of the Ujra mosque at Kavarathi is the most exquisite. This is believed to be a century old. There are several legends associated with this masterly creation. According to one legend, it was done by a carver belonging to a family called Mukri Illam. He got his inspiration from the leaf of a plant in his courtyard. It is said that after completing the carving work at the mosque he thought of making the same carving at his house, but a piece of wood hit his eyes he lost his eyesight.

The construction of the floors of the mosques and the tanks adjacent to them reveal the skill of the islanders as stonemasons. Tombstones are also beautifully carved. Carvings on the tombstones, specially at Kavarathi, exhibit the islanders' delicate skill.

On all the islands there are expert craftsmen who construct the *odams*, although their number is decreasing day by day. The islanders are also good at producing a variety of handicrafts out of tortoise-shell, coconut shells, coconut fibre, corals, etc. It is said that the Chetlat islanders are expert in making hats, mats and baskets from tender coconut leaves. The Minicoy islanders decorate many of their household utensils and furniture by engraving and painting them colourfully.

In order to promote arts and crafts in the islands, several steps have been taken by the Administrator of the Union Territory, and a few small-scale factories like hosiery factory (since 1967), a decorating fibre plant (since 1968), etc., have been started. But as the islanders do not show much interest in these factories, their talents and resources have not been fully exploited.

ISLANDERS' CULTURAL PERCEPTIONS

The islanders call themselves 'children of the sea'. Their daily activities centre around the sea. From morning to night they move in and around the sea, and therefore their cultural perceptions are sea-oriented.

Knowledge of the Cosmos

At Kavarathi the Secretary of the Pradesh Council, who is believed to be the most knowledgeable person of the island, asked me to first note down how many types of Muslims there were in the islands, as their world-views differ. Of the four sects of Muslims, Sunnis are found in overwhelming numbers in all the islands except Minicoy, where 60 to 70 per cent are Wahabis. At Agatti, only 50 families are of the Wahabi sect. There is one family on Kalpeni island which belongs to the Ahmadiya sect. The Ahmadiya Muslims trace their origin to a village named Kadiani in Western Punjab. The Table Muslims keep very unusal long beards and wear *kurtas* down to their knees but are not considered true Muslims by the others. The Sunnis believe that Mohammad was the last messenger of God, but the Ahmadiyas believe that Ahmad Gulam Kadiani was the last messenger.

The islanders believe that there are seven worlds in the sky and that God lives in the seventh sky. The *Koran* was brought from the seventh sky to the Prophet Mohammad by God's angels.

The islanders believe in *panchendriyam* (five *tattva*): sky, water, wind, fire and that earth. This is an impact of the Malabar coast (indirectly Hindu impact). In Malayalam we come across the concept of *pench-bhutam*, and obviously the islanders, who migrated from the Malabar coast, brought this concept with them. The islanders maintain the sacredness of fire. They do not spit into it, nor do they throw any dirty articles in it. They consider the sea very sacred. Some of their rituals are performed on the sea-shore. Myths and legends are related to, and based on, sea voyage and various other marine matters. Many such traits of marine culture have already been lost, and those that are in vogue today will be lost soon due to the rapid changes taking place.

FISH AND COCONUTS — DUAL ENTRY POINTS

As mentioned earlier, the islanders are experts in the art of fishing, and 80 to 90 per cent of their daily catch is tuna. Fishing is carried out on a large scale in the islands. Tuna is caught not with nets but with the pole and line. A cotton line is used with a barbless fish-shaped hook attached to it.

Sea Fishing

When the boatmen sight a tuna shoal, they scatter live bait in its path. Attracted by the live bait, the tuna rush towards the boat. Then the boatmen cast the hooks. As soon as a fish bites, with a jerk of the rod it is swung into the boat. An informant at Agatti said, 'experienced fishermen can catch even three fish at a time — one in the boat, the second in the air and the third on the hook'. Five or more people can fish together in the sea depending on the size of the boat. Sometimes even a ton of tuna can be caught within half an hour. This method is very popular on Agatti and Minicoy, where nearly 70 per cent of the total catch is produced. The Lakshadweep administration is trying to popularise this traditional pole and line method of tuna fishing among other islands also.

Before the islanders leave for deep-sea fishing, they check their boats. These are now mechanised, loans being sanctioned by the administration. The present cost of a mechanised fishing boat is one lakh and fifty thousand rupees. The fishermen get up around 2 a.m. and collect the necessary materials like drinking water, food, tea, medicines and other accessories related to fishing, and then come to the sea-shore. They offer brief worship by breaking a coconut and praying to the sea-god for a good catch and safe return. Usually 5 or 6 persons go together in a boat. They return around 2 or 3 p.m. Thus they fish for 8 or 10 hours, of which 2 to 4 hours are spent in going and coming as well as in searching for a tuna shoal. After disembarking from the boat they unload the catch and start dressing the fish for *mas* preparation.

Uses of Coconuts

COCONUT AS A FOOD

Next to fish, coconut is the main food of the islanders. Even in fish curry they use coconut water. They prepare different sweet and salted dishes with coconut cream. Coconut oil is the medium of cooking and is prepared at home. However, recently palm oil, imported from Kerala, has come into limited use.

COCONUT AS FUEL

When copra is taken away from a coconut, the outer layer is dried and used as fuel. The roots, truck, etc., of the coconut are used in making windows and other parts of houses.

COCONUT AS MEDICINE

Whenever the islanders suffer from injury, headache, joint pain, etc., they apply coconut oil, fish oil, etc., as cures. Nowadays modern medicines are also available on all islands, but until some thirty years ago, the people were totally dependent upon these indigenous remedies. They still apply coconut oil mixed with camphor to their foreheads.

COCONUT LEAF AS A THATCHING MATERIAL

The long leaf of the coconut is used by most islanders for thatching their houses. Those who can afford them use red titles, imported from the mainland; but the Melacharies. Riveries, Malmis and those who are poor use the long dried leave of coconut. They also make mats of the dried leaves both for domestic use as well as for export to the mainland.

Coconut-Based Industry

Lakshadweep was once the scene of considerable *odam*-building activity, in which indigenous materials like coconut wood, coconut ropes, oil of fish and crabs, etc., were used. With the arrival of mechanised boats, *odam* building gradually declined. But other small-scale industries based on the coconut and its products came up in the islands.

Coir twisting is one of the oldest industries of Lakshadweep which has played a vital role in the history of the islanders. It is said that Arab vessels used to come to the islands to collect *cordio* (coconut rope). This continued even during British rule. But after Independence, the coir twisting industry was made a welfare scheme and many types of economic assistance have been extended to its workers. It is now a very important cottage industry in the islands. Mainly women work in this industry, which adds to their sources of livelihood.

Copra Industry

Copra is the dried kernels of coconut, used either for oil crushing or as food. Copra making is a seasonal cottage industry which starts from September and continues to May/June. The ripe nuts are first dehusked and cut into two pieces each. Then they are spread on mats of coconut leaves to dry. Once dry, they are exported to the mainland for oil crushing. Lakshadweep copra is usually exported to Calicut, Mangalore, etc. These are popularly known as *deevai copra* centres. Unfortunately no big industry has been established in the islands to extract oil from the copra.

CONCLUSION

This pilot survey of the Lakshaweep islands confirms that there is an intimate relationship between the island culture and its ecology. The islanders' cultural activities centre around fishing and coconuts, which may be called dual entry-points for studying the cultural perception of the Lakshadweep islanders. The islanders' awareness of their immediate environment, its flora and fauna, and their notion about sea, space, etc., refer to their historical background as well as to the existing ecological set-up. Some of the old traditions, folklore, folk songs, myths, magical rites, beliefs in spirits and miraculous dreams, etc., are shaped and determined by the ecological set-up. But as rapid changes are taking place in the man-made eco-structures of the islands, it is feared that old cultural values and traditions may become extinct soon. For example, the wave (tide) songs, rendered in the sea, have completely disappeared. The cyclone song has met the same fate. The *binelam*, a type of street-song, has also become extinct. It is urgently required to record such vanishing folk songs and other details of the people's cultural perceptions.

References

Administration of Lakshadweep, 1978. *Union Territory of Lakshadweep*. Lakshdweep Administration, Kavarathi

———, 1984. *The Coral Paradise*. Lakshadweep Administration, Kavarathi

Dube, Leela, 1969. *Matriliny and Islam*. National, Delhi

Ellis, R.H., 1924. *A Short Account of Laccadive Island & Minicoy*, Madras, reprinted in 1992

George, Abraham, 1985. 'Land Relations in Lakshadweep'. *State and Society*, Vol. V, No. 4

Government of Madras. Reports of various Inspecting Officers on Lakshadweep from 1886 to 1924

Gabriel, P.C. Theodore, 1989. *Lakshadweep: History, Religion and Society*. Books and Books, New Delhi

Ittaman, K.P., 1976. *Amini Islanders*, Abhinav, New Delhi

Mannadiar, N.S., ed., 1977. *Gazetteer of Indian Union Territory of Lakshadweep*. Administration of Lakshadweep, Kavarathi

Robinson, W., 1846. *Report on the Amini Islands: Report of the Inspecting Officer*. Revenue Department, Government of Madras

Robinson, W., 1848. *Report on the Laccadive Islands*. Government of Madras

5

The Mukkuvār
A Fishing Community

G. John Samuel

THIS study of the lifestyle of the Mukkuvār is an attempt to focus on the sociological and anthropological backdrops and the behavioural pattern of a fishing community in Puthur, a coastal village in Kanyakumari District of Tamil Nadu. The Mukkuvār, a fishing community believed to have emigrated from Ceylon, are today found in Kanyakumari District, coastal areas of Kerala, Lakshadweep, and in some scattered areas of Karnataka. Although they are described a homogeneous ethnic group, their present lifestyle is believed to vary according to geographical, ecological and other influences.

The fishing industry has a significant place in the Indian economy as a dollar-spinner. It is sustained largely by life-risking, hard-working and socially ill-placed fisherfolk. Their fishing techniques are not very modern and their standard of living is poor. There are few sociological and anthropological studies of Indian fishing communities. The Mukkuvārs are one among the many groups of fisherfolk in the country. Scanty ethnographic and allied information on this group is available in travelogues and in district gazetteers. Buchanan (1807), Nagam Aiya (1891, 1906), Thurston (1900, 1907), L.K. Anantha Krishna Iyer (1909), William Logan (1887), and L.A. Krishna Iyer (1937) are a few such sources. Nirmala Bai (1980) and Stephen Sam (1982, 1983-84, 1986-87) have undertaken some research on the Mukkuvār, mostly based on oral tradition and on material available on their traditional occupation. There has been no research on their lifestyle using an integrated approach. This study may perhaps serve as a pilot study on such lines.

There are more than 40 villages in Kanyakumari District engaged principally in fishing, and more than 50 per cent of their inhabitants are Mukkuvār. This study was restricted to Puthur, a small village, as a study of all 40 villages would have required much more resources and time. It was taken up as a micro-level pilot study involving 10 months of fieldwork (June 1989 to March 1990) by G. Stephen and A. George.

An effort has been made to bring out the lifestyle of the Mukkuvār, with a special emphasis on their perception of the environment; and to compare it with the life patterns, traditions and beliefs, and rituals and rites of some tribal groups and agriculturists in Puthur village.

This study is divided into sections on location, setting and ethnology; ecology and environment; fishing techniques and technology; life cycle and rituals; magic and rites; and oral traditions.

Location, Setting and Ethnology

Puthur, a fishing hamlet in Kalkulam Taluk of Kanyakumari District, Tamil Nadu, is located on the west coast above Cape Comorin. It is bounded by Maṇavāḷakuṟichi on the east, Colochel on the west, Maṇḍaikkāḍu on the north, and by the ocean on the south. The famous shrine of the Hindu goddess Maṇḍaikkāḍu Amman is just 500 meters north of Puthur.

Kaṭiapaṭṭiṇam, a village consisting mostly of fisherfolk, about 5 km east of Puthur village, and Colochel, another fishing village, are said to have been centres of maritime transportation. Within a radius of 20 km of Puthur are villages like 'Monday Market' (Thingal Sandhai), Colochel, Neyyoor, Marthandam, Thuckalay, Eraniel Rajakkamangalam, and Muṭṭam, connected among themselves and with Puthur by well-maintained roads and adequate vehicular transport. Fishermen from Puthur go to these places to sell their catch and to buy essentials and other requirements.

North of Puthur, the road from Nagercoil to Colochel runs along a lagoon. There is yet another road leading towards the north, connecting Maṇḍaikkāḍu and Monday Market. The lagoon meandering towards Trivandrum, believed to have been dug during the reign of the Travancore kings, has lost its importance as an inland waterway due to heavy silting: it is now used for bathing.

St. Lucy's church, said to have been built in 1745 and improved in 1912, is to the east of Puthur, located on the sea-shore. There is a 'kruzadi' to the west, not far from the Maṇḍaikkāḍu Amman temple, with four crosses. Other significant features are two wells, a middle school, and a training centre for cottage industries.

The land in this village has an upper layer of sand and loam, which carries the risk of erosion and denudation. Scientific investigations revealed a rich mineral content that includes silicon, monozite, garnets, silimnites, ilemnite and zircon, leading to the establishment of the Indian Rare Earth Complex near Puthur. The edaphic and climatic conditions do not permit any vegetation other than coconut. There is an appreciably rich stretch of coconut plantations embanking the lagoons. A small portion of these is owned by people of the Kuṟuppu Nāṭār, and other communities. Some of the land occupied by the dwellings of Mukkuvār families also belongs to individuals of other castes. However, the major part of the land utilised by the Mukkuvār for their housing, and pieces of land adjoining this area, called *Ūrvakai*, are treated as the common property of the village, although they are owned by ecclesiastics belonging to the Kottar diocese. The passing of such land from individual holdings to the control of the clergy seems to be shrouded in mystery. None in the Mukkuvār community owns a piece of land in that village, although recently a few Mukkuvār have purchased land elsewhere.

The Mukkuvār have turned to the ocean for their existence instead of becoming agriculturists or pastoralists on infertile land that they do not own. This lack of ownership of land has created, of late, another problem. If their seafaring and fishing expertise is to be refined further in keeping with advanced techniques, the Mukkuvār must obtain modern nets, motor-propelled boats and other equipment: but they are unable to avail themselves of bank loans as they cannot pledge any land.

The population of Puthur was recorded as 3000, females constituting 58.3 per cent. Its age-wise and sex-wise distribution is shown in *Fig.* 5. 1.

In the eligible age group, more than 70 per cent are married. The women account for a greater percentage of the unmarried, due to certain social conditions and to their contribution to family income.

Employment and educational levels among the Mukkuvār in Puthur reveal an interesting feature. Of the total population of 3000, only 26 men and 16 women have jobs, while 9 people have taken to small commercial ventures.

Education does not attract many. Only 40 (23 females and 17 males) have had a formal education, in general education or in crafts like tailoring, 10 having completed the S.S.L.C. Currently, just 139 lads and lasses attend formal school. Many children begin to drop out from the fourth standard onwards. To them, formal education perhaps has no meaning or relevance. It is the non-formal education handed down to them that has a bearing on their lives. Skill at launching boats; competence in preparing and handling the nets and other equipment; developing endurance to withstand the rough sea; learning about weather, currents, wind and stars — these constitute their real education. It is interesting to watch youngsters being ushered into the sea by their elders.

The Mukkuvār live near their constant associate, the sea. Just as they look to the sea for their livelihood, their abodes too generally face the sea. These are mostly, small huts thatched with coconut palm. Only around 10 per cent are tiled houses. Here we see a direct relationship with the environment, in that materials are chosen to suit the soil, the costal weather, and the precipitational regime. The huts are in a conglomeration, having neither a proper layout nor space of more than 3 feet between adjacent ones. Even this housing is now saturated, since there is no scope for further expansion or extension.

The huts are rectangular, with an all-purpose hall, a kitchen and a pial. The tiled houses have a kitchen, a hall and a room. Both have thatched enclosures for bathing purposes. There are no toilets, the inhabitants using open places for defecation. Schematic plans appear in *Fig.* 5.2. The Mukkuvār are spread mostly in villages on the western coast in Kanyakumari District and in a few villages on the eastern coast in that district. Other coastal villages in Tamil Nadu mostly occupied by the Parathavar, another fishing sect. Small groups of Mukkuvār are found in inland villages too, located in areas adjacent to market-places. These inland settlers do not themselves engage in fishing: they market the catch of others.

In Cochin and the coastal areas to the south, the Mukkuvār are found in smaller numbers than on the Malabar coast. Similarly, they abound in Lakshadweep, probably having migrated from the Kerala coast. It is believed that the "Mugayar" or "Mogayar", a fishing community found in South Kanara, also belong to this ethnic group. C.A. Innis states that north of Cannanore, there are some fishermen known as "Mugayar" or "Mogayar". One view is that the Mugayar are probably river fishers and the Mukkuvār sea fishers, but the distinction is not seen to hold good in fact (Innis 1951: 126). Ethnographers are of the view that Mukkuvār and Mogayar are of the same group. L.K. Anantha Krishna Iyer (1909: 266) points out that the word "Mukkuvār" is connected with the Canarese word "Moger" coming from the same root, which means 'to dive'. But J.F. Hall (1938: 64) contradicts this view, recording "Mogayars" as "Muhans". Mukkuvār are seldom seen on the Andhra coast. They are not found on the eastern coast except in parts of Kanyakumari District. The estern coast is mainly inhabited by the Parathavar group of fisherfolk.

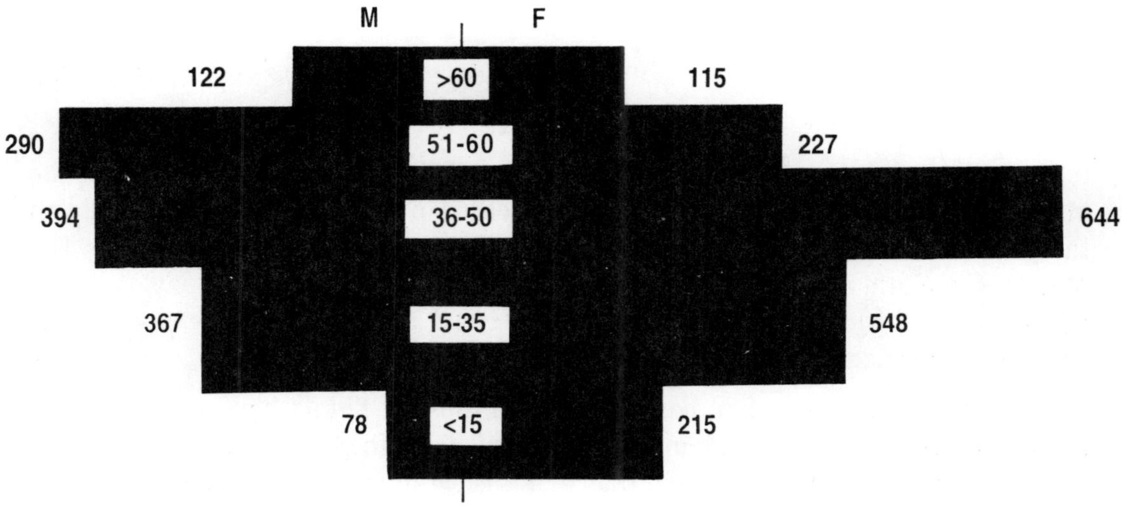

Figure 1- Puthur Population: Age and Sex

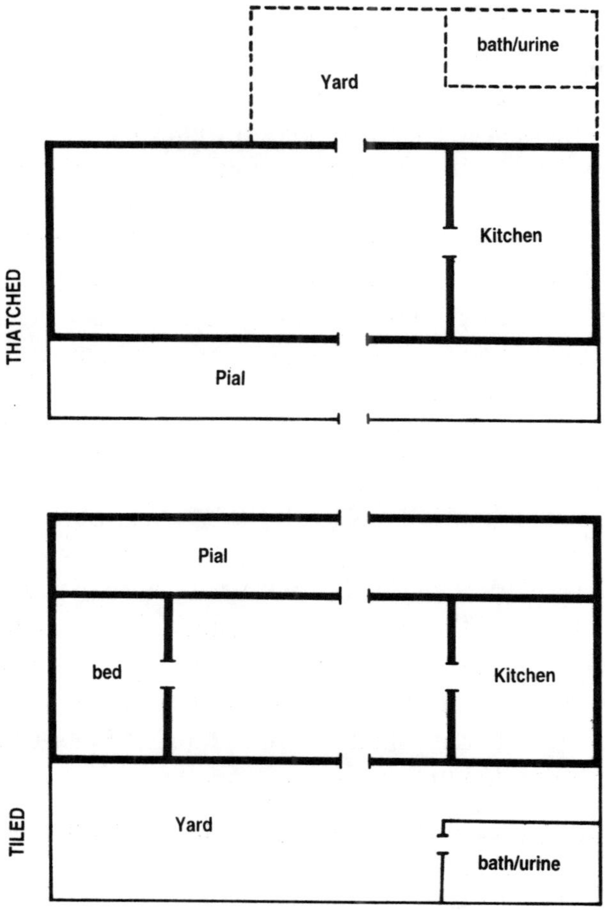

Figure 2. Puthur Houses, Schematic

According to Innis (1951: 126) and Thurston (1987: 107), it is believed that the Mukkuvār probably migrated from Ceylon and settled in Malabar. Evidence to establish this is not available. There is a reference to the Mukkuvār in Buchanan's works: "The Mucua or in plural mucuar, are a tribe who lived near the sea-coast of Malayala, to the inland parts of which they seldom go, and beyond its limits, anyway, they rarely venture" (Buchanan 1807: 527).

The Mukkuvār of Kanyakumari District and those of Kerala have a considerable affinity. Mukkuvār from Kanyakumari District sail along the Kerala coast, but they do not venture towards the east coast although it is geographically proximate. That region abounds in the Parathavar fishing community. The spoken language of the Mukkuvār shows the great influence of Malayalam. There are many Mukkuvār who are capable of conversing freely and with confidence in Malayalam. The political identity of Kanyakumari as part of the erstwhile Travancore State is also cited as one of the reasons for resemblance and ethnic connection.

Still, there are a few cultural differences between the Mukkuvār of the southern parts of the western coast and those of the northern part. An important difference is that while the northerners practise *marumakkat thayam* (matriarchal lineage), quite significant in Kerala, those of the south adopt *makkat thayam* (patriarchal system), according to C.A. Innis (1951: 126). The Mukkuvār to the north follow the 'house system' peculiar to in Kerala, as evidenced in names like 'Ponillam', 'Semmbillam', 'Karillam', 'Kachillam' (*pon*: gold, *sembu*: copper, etc.). Those of the southern areas of Kanyakumari District do not have this system. It is therefore clear that while the Mukkuvār of Kanyakumari and those of Kerala share an ethnic identity, these are also a number of cultural differences between them. There exists a good deal of professional interaction as fishermen between them; but they do not have any marital alliances.

Nagam Aiya (1906: 405) writes that a group of fishermen (Mukkuvār) was brought into certain parts of Kanyakumari District by Kesava Pillai, Dewan of Travancore during the reign of Marthanda Varman, for developing those places and improving inland communications. However, conclusive evidence is not available to establish their place of origin. It is also observed that during the regime of Marthanda Varman, special efforts were made to enable fisherfolk, workmen engaged in the dyeing industry, and other artisans, to settle in these areas: grants of land were included. Some of the ancestors of the Mukkuvār of Kanyakumari are said to have possessed land, although none can boast of land ownership nowadays.

The Mukkuvār, although fisherfolk as a group, are not without social stratification.

No 'house system' is prevalent among this community in Kanyakumari District, but there are two well-defined groups — Pulukkaiyars and Arayans. The word 'Arayan' connotes leadership. In Malabar, 'Arayan' is synonymous with 'Mukkuvār' (Innis 1951: 126; Buchanan 1807: 527; Thurston 1987: 107). Many of the Mukkuvār call themselves 'Arayans' and at the same time call their leader 'Arayan'. Arayans were the 'masters of ceremonies' in the caste, affording leadership in the religious and social matrix of life. It is interesting to note that after about 1950, the functions of the Arayan have been appropriated by the clergy. The traditional roles of Arayans during festivals and social occasions are now lost. The Mukkuvār still like to be called Arayans, as a consequence of the low status extended to them socially. According to Thurston, they were placed in the social ladder below the Thiya and artisan groups (Thurston 1987: 107). Social practice demanded that they stop 24 feet away when talking to higher-caste people (Logan 1951: 118). Because of this they resent being referred to as Mukkuvār.

Pulukkaiyars are also Mukkuvār in the real sense of the term: but there exists a deeply carved status difference between them and the Mukkuvār. Pulukkaiyars belonging as a whole to a far lower economic stratum. No marriages among the two groups are permitted. The difference is so deep-rooted that they live at appoint ends of the village. It is said that the economic differences derived from possession of fishing nets and other equipment. Until the time of the century, Pulukkaiyars did not possess any equipment for persuing their profession independently. They were treated much as 'serfs' by the Arayans, doing the work of servants.

There is an interesting anecdote about the treatment meted out to Pulukkaiyars by Arayans. It is said that when Daniel was Arayan (1950), he used to supervise work on the shore. During his visits two Pulukkaiyars held umbrellas to protect him from the sun, which one more aide carried his case containing betel leaves, nuts, etc. He would sit in a lone chair laid exclusively for him, while the Pulukkiyars stood in the hot sun and sand. During his later days there was a slow decline in his control over the Pulukkaiyars. Some Pulukkaiyars, servants of his successor Mundan, managed to obtain their own fishing net (*karamodi*). This gave them crucial self-reliance and gradually enabled them to shake off their servitude.

Pulukkaiyars are said to have been ill-treated, even to the extent of being made untouchables. It is stated that when Daniel was Arayan, some Pulukkaiyars once sat on his cot. This act so angered Daniel that he condemned all the fibre (*nār*) and fully refurbished the cot. The Pulukkaiyars had to accept whatever they were paid for their labour. They were not invited to weddings and other rituals by the Arayans.

The word 'Arayan' refers both to the leader of the Mukkuvār and to the higher group among them. The Arayan, once looked up to by all the Mukkuvār for the dispassionate dispensation of justice, slowly lost this position for the Pu̱lukkaiyars. The two groups started looking up to different people of the settling of their disputes. While the Arayans continued to resort to the Arayan, the Pu̱lukkaiyars started going to the landlord (*paṇṇaiyar*) of nearly Kūttumangalam. This landlord was from a different community — 'Kuṟuppu', colloquially called 'Krishan Vakaikkarar'. He would send for the Arayans and, after listening to both sides, would pacify them and effect an abiding reconciliation. The Arayans sometimes used to drive the Pu̱lukkaiyars away from their villages, at which they would rush to the Kūttumangalam landlord. Such clashes became more frequent and pronounced day-by-day.

During Daniel's tenure as Arayan, a group of Arayans was once learning *kaliyattam*, a kind of martial dance. Some passing Pu̱lukkaiyars seem to have jeered at them. This sparked off a riot leading to the death of 2 Pu̱lukkaiyars, serious injury to 4 more, and the expulsion of all Pu̱lukkaiyars from the village. A case was registered. Daniel appeared on behalf of the Arayans and the Kūttumangalam landlord for the Pu̱lukkaiyars.

Also disturbing to the Pu̱lukkaiyars was the discrimination they faced under the altar, where they stood as Christians. During the solemnization of weddings, bride and groom would be seated in chairs specially kept for the purpose. These chairs would be removed, however, and Pu̱lukkaiyar couples made to sit on the ground. When the Pu̱lukkaiyars attained a better economic status and started claiming equal treatment, this was denied them both by the Arayans and by the Church. Outraged by such humiliation, the Pu̱lukkaiyars decided to switch over to Hinduism and adopt Maṇḍaikkaḍu Amman as their deity. The parish priests, shocked at this, invited the Pu̱lukkaiyars to embrace Christianity again and permitted them to bring their own bridal chairs to church. Eventually the Arayans were also made to bring their own chairs, and only then did, the Pu̱lukkaiyars return to Christianity.

These contradictions have melted away of late, but not totally. Occasionally the embers of enmity may become live flames. Thre are not many differences between the social customs and life-cycle rituals of the groups.

The conflict among the Arayans and the Pu̱lukkaiyars on the ground that they belong to different castes does not hold water. The difference is not ethnic but economic. Arayans themselves accept the Pu̱lukkaiyars as Mukkuvār although they do not concede them equality. The Pu̱lukkaiyars, because they did not posses fishing equipment and were entirely dependent on the Arayans for their livelihood, were driven to such a subservient position that the Arayans felt that they stood out as a distinct class.

The fisherfolk of Puthur have generally good contacts with neighbouring fishing villages. Kaṭiapaṭṭiṇam village is mostly occupied by Puḻukkaiyars, and so is Paḷḷam. There are matrimonial alliances between the Puḻukkaiyars of Puthur and these villages. It is observed that villages west of Puthur have a preponderance of Arayans, while those to the east are mostly occupied by Puḻukkaiyars.

Mukkuvār are found in many fishing hamlets on the west coast, though Malabar to Karnataka. The fishing villages have gaps of up to 3 km between them, occupied mostly by coconut groves. Each village has an independent existence, but all maintain working relations as well as a social coherence. They exchange visits during weddings and other social occasions and rituals. Their maritime exercises too afford them opportunities to meet in mid-sea, which they are said to welcome. They speak of their career and economic difficulties, share food, discuss local occurrences and events, and help one another when situation warrant it. They stand united whenever there is a threat to any of them.

Maṇḍaikkāḍu, just to the north of Puthur, is a village where the major population is from the Nāṭār community. The temple of the goddess Maṇḍaikkāḍu Amman is quite famous in the area. People of various castes from all over Kanyakumari District visit this temple in large numbers during the annual festival in March. Puthur is also busy during this festival. Its people allow the visiting devotees to sleep in their front yards and quite often help with cooking utensils, firewood, water, etc. There is much interaction between the visitors, who come to worship a Hindu goddess, and the local people, mostly followers of Christianity. There is remarkable religious tolerance and a confluence of inland dwellers and the coastal community. A very big temporary market comes up, selling fish, condiments, sweets, fruits, etc., and a vast sea of humans competing with the sea. The fisherfolk do not mind certain inconveniences to them during this festival. There is a traditional belief that Maṇḍaikkāḍu Amman and Lucy, a Catholic saint, are sisters.

The Mukkuvār are reported to have formed a dependable corps of soldiers of Marthanda Varman, the chieftain of Travancore (Nagam Aiya, 1906: 350). It is said that women belonging to families which rebelled against Marthanda Varman were sold as slaves to the Mukkuvār (Nagam Aiya 1906: 338).

There is generally a concord and an amount of contradiction between Mukkuvār and the Nāṭār. Nāṭārs and Mukkuvār exchange their produce, like jaggery and sweet toddy from one side and fresh and dried fish from the other. The fisherfolk buy their domestic needs from shops mostly owned by Nāṭārs. Similarly, the Mukkuvār have close associations with Moplahs in Malabar, even to the extent of matrimonial relationships (Thurston 1987: 110) Such relations extend beyond these two communities. There is an eating place at the Maṇḍaikkāḍu junction, run by a Muslim. For a fisherman the day begins there, with an invigorating cup of tea or breakfast, before setting sail on the rough sea. What happens at dawn is repeated at dusk. The fishermen of Puthur take the financial support of other communities like the Nāṭārs and the Kuṛuppu. They borrow money, sometimes even without interest, and are said to be very prompt and regular in repaying it.

Though the community practises an extended family system normally, there are a few instances of nuclear familes too. The earning husband is invested with powers on larger issues like marriage, rituals and rites, and he enjoys the greatest control in the purchase of costly things. The wife, in the husband's absence — a common phenomenon — runs the family, according for daily purchases and saving a little. She has to look to her husband's decision on major items of expenditure.

The consumption of alcohol is virtually an 'occupational hazard' for the Mukkuvār fishing community. The beating of wife and children by an inebriated man is common. The women of the community are victims of sexual violence perpetrated by their strongly built husbands, roughened by their hard life, when in a state of intoxication. They are forced to satiate their men, who are indifferent to their responses, tastes and willingness.

Adequate housing facilities are not available for the growing population. The dearth of land, and economic backwardness account for this. Sons staying with parents is but a Hobson's choice, because they have neither the land for housing nor the facilities to set out to sea independently. On the demise of a man, his fishing equipment is distributed among his sons, who then run their separate families in the same precincts.

The Mukkuvār were originally Hindus. Foreign incursions into the social web influenced their religion. The Christian missionaries, with their commitment to spreading their religion, found the poverty, backwardness, social suppression and ignorance a fertile ground for their work.The higher taxes on fishing communities also added to their agony. Fr. Francis Xavier (1543) was very successful in converting many of the Mukkuvār Christianity. The missionaries tried to retrieve the Mukkuvār from their abject poverty, squalor, starvation, and lack of recognition by the higher strata of society. Christianity, known for its concern for the poor, became a ready palliative for all social and economic evils for the Mukkuvār. They were give food, clothing, relief from taxes, and many other benefits. Ill-treated by other Hindu caste people, the Mukkuvār found a totally different acceptance and equality among the Christians. Fr. Francis Xavier, with the respect that he commanded among the British officers in Tirunelveli and in stretches of erstwhile Travancore, enjoyed a good deal of public confidence.

The Christian missionaries in general had some influence with the bureaucracy, hence they could get many concessions for converts (Velu Pillai, 1940: 537–38). The Mukkuvār were permitted to wear upper garments. An inscription in St. Thomas' church at Muttam testifies to the tax relief and remissions granted to the Mukkuvār (Nagam Aiya 1906: 146). It is observed that fishermen in Travancore had to pay taxes annually and those in areas dominated by the Dutch had to give 8 pounds of fish everyday to the officers (L.K. Anantha Krishna Iyer 1909: 252). Col. Munroe (1811–15) removed the taxes levied on fishing (Nagam Aiya, 1906: 463). Due to all these factors, Christianity took firm root among the Mukkuvār.

Christianity, which offered social status to the Mukkuvār, could not in the long run afford them the relief they looked for. Deep-rooted caste differences and barriers could not be removed; the Jesuits were unable to succeed in this. This factor not only impeded the initial momentum in the spread of Christianity, is also allowed a sense of disappointment to set in among the Mukkuvār. While the foreign missionaries felt the caste system an obstruction to the speedy spread of Christianity, converts like, the Mukkuvār found that even this religion could not rise above the long-grown barriers of the caste system; ultimately both were disappointed (Forrester 1980: 42).

The Mukkuvār are addicted to alcohol, even though Christianity taboos it. Invariably, men take drinks after Holy Communion on Sundays. The Church permits them to take food only after drinking some water, and that after the lapse of an hour. The Mukkuvār take advantage of this: they overcome the taboo by taking a few drops of water before consuming alcohol.

Catholics seem to have Idianized Christianity. St. Lucy's church, in the east of Puthur, houses shrines to St. Mary and St. Lucy. As the Indian religions are Mother-oriented, so do sacred virgins occupy the prime position among the Catholics. There are many local legends prevalent, in one of which St. Lucy is called Kannamma, (meaning grandmother). According to local legend Kannamma, the religious-minded daughter of a minister, declined the marital advances of the king. Angered, the king ordered that her eyes be gouged out, but they reappeared. After her death her statue, with eyes held in a hand, was laid in a box, marked for Puthur and brought by ship to a spot near the village. Discovering it, the fishing folk of Kaṭiapaṭṭiṇam enshrined it, facing east, in their temple. To their dismay, they found the statue had moved towards Puthur, which lies in the west. Their initial reluctance to give away the statue was ended by an epidemic believed to have been caused by St. Lucy. The statue now lies consecrated in Puthur Chapel.

Although St. Mary enjoys the highest status, other saints are also worshipped by the people of Puthur. Supplications to the Lord are made through St. Mary, St. Lucy, St. Xavier, St. Thomas and St. Antony. The concept of 'family deities' also finds expression. Saints and Apostles are considered family deities and icons or pictures of them, supposed to ward off evil spirits, diseases, etc., adron houses. Angels like Gabriel and Michael are also held in reverence. Almost all are credited with various boons and functional powers related to pregnancy, disease, etc. Toeing the traditional line of the Hindus, the Catholics of Puthur too offer prayers and candles for being blessed with pregnancy.

In a similar vein, the Catholics associate St. Lucy with diseases like chicken-pox and cholera. It is believed that evil spirits, with the permission of St. Lucy, cause epidemics. An epidemic is thus viewed as a manifestation of St. Lucy's wrath: the people of Puthur then make a bee-line to her shrine, apart from seeking blessings and cures from Hindu goddesses like Maṇḍaikkāḍu Amman, who was worshipped by them before their conversion.

The parish priest, the spiritual head of the fishing folk, assumes the role of village leader too. He nominates a body which governs both the parish and the village. This body consists of educated people who abide by the rulings of the priest. Clashes and quarrels are settled, and concessions and other privileges granted, by this village committee. As the housing areas are owned by the Church, the fishing folk pay it 5 per cent of their income. This applies only to people using dragnets. Nowadays laxity has set in and the non-payment of this tax is not viewed seriously.

With the rise of the church and its power to take over land, the role of headman became insignificant. Headmanship eventually came to vest in the parish priest. The 1981 communal clashes in Maṇḍaikkāḍu can be cited as an instance. The pealing of the church bell made the people assemble. They were informed of the imminent danger and dashed to ready themselves. This practice is followed in moments of crisis, and even today government officials or police personnel meet the parish priest when an enquiry is to be initiated against anyone in the village. The granting of loans is also done through the priest.

To sum up, we may say that Christianity has had on this ethnic group an impact both positive and negative. While in the initial stages conversion afforded them succour and a social status, in the long run it failed to release them from social evils like caste. For its survival, Christianity had to absorb the traditional culture; and to consolidate its position the Church was also obliged to absorb the social structures indirectly. Gradually the land became the property of the parish and the leadership of the Arayan fell into the hands of the parish priest.

Perception of the Environment

Certain occupational groups are constantly exposed to various environmental situations and ecological conditions. This exposure inevitably leads to the acquisition of various types of knowledge, skills and talents. Different occupational groups are bound to have different kinds of experience: for example, the fund of knowledge acquired by agriculturists is quite different from that of fishermen. Each group has transmitted acquired skills and knowledge down from generation to generation. Based on changing demands, these are reworked and find their place in new settings, part of the changing total ecological setting. People also adapt to these changes and adopt new patterns of life.

That man's life is closely linked with his environment is seen clearly in Puthur. The rugged coast, the soil, the roaring sea with its tides and currents, depth unfathomed, the life within the mass of water, the wind, the sun, precipitation, all bear upon and add meaning to the Mukkuvār's life. The Mukkuvār attribute every aspect of their life to their perception of the sea. This section aims at presenting the environmental features of the village, associating them with basic primordial forces, and so interpreting various aspects of the life of the Mukkuvār.

SOIL

The interaction of water and earth has resulted in a soil condition peculiar to this area. The upper soil in the village is a mixture of sand and loam which runs just two feet deep. Below this level, down to ten feet, is black and white sand rich in minerals. Black clay is found at a still lower level.

Vettumadai, situated between Puthur and Kottilpadu, is a village projecting into the Arabian Sea. This projection of land protects Puthur from the force of the waves. Due to incessant removal of sand, however, the projection has thinned down and Puthur is now the victim of severe high tides.

Three kilometres from the shore lies a rock called Adumeichan Parai or Melakkal,

186 square metres in area and rising 2 metres above sea level. The sea is 20 metres deep in this place. Another rock, 2 km east of the above rock, is Kelakkal, about 45 square metres in area. According to local tradition, the land extended up to these two rocks in ancient times. The first mentioned rock, Adumeichan Paria, is so named because of the belief that sheep grazed there earlier.

The fisherfolk venture up to 30 km out to sea. The sea-bed gradually slopes for 4 km where the depth is only 20–25 metres. Later it becomes very deep. Sand is found up to 500 metres from the shore; up to 3 km it is pebbles, soft rocks and sand; beyond this is mud and rocks, both small and large.

There is great interaction between the life in the sea and that on the coast. Humans on the coast are very largely influenced by the sea, and Mukkuvār have a good perception of this. The vegetation of Puthur and its animal life are also interdependent with the sea's life. There is a continuous cycle of life that contributes to the richness of plankton, which in turn forms the prey of aquatic creatures big and small. These animals have a bearing on the life of the Mukkuvār, influencing their economic, social, and cultural life and being reflected in their customs, mores and cultural patterns.

FLORA AND FAUNA

The soil of Puthur is good for coconut, and in the northern part of the village it is cultivated in plenty. No more interest is shown in coconut cultivation as the land is owned by the church. Plantain is very commonly grown in houses, and trees like *Thespesia populnea*, *Hyperanthera moringa*, holly-leaved berbery, *Odina wordier*, cassia and *Jatropha curcas* are found as bathroom shelters. Papaya and guava are grown in a few homes. In the infertile, barren land Vinca Rose, *Calotropics gigantea*, the thron apple, *Sterculia foetida*, hedge-cotton, cactus, milk hedge varieties, sweet scented screw pine, *Phyilanthus niruri* and *Amranthus spinosus* are found and are used in fences. Rose, jasmine, hibiscus and table rose are a few ornamental flowers used in decorating homes.

Though numerous sea plants are found, the most commonly known are algae. Some 2 km into the sea we find *Sida hwnilis* (*kotaipaci*) floating on the water surface. Certain water plants like *satam parai* grow on rocks and are used for decorative purposes. *Vallisneria spirilas* (*patchap paci*) grows on tiny stones. Since it does not permit the fishing net to trap completely, it is called *thandapara*.

Poultry, dogs, cats, sheep and pigs are generally reared in Puthur. Sixty per cent of the houses have dogs, hens and cats; 10 per cent keep sheep; and 20 per cent rear pigs. Only one house has a cow. These apart, birds like crows, cranes, falcons, kingfishers and sparrows and animals like squirrels and chameleons are commonly seen.

A kind of sea bird resembling a duck, but small and with a long neck, locally called *karuvandu*, lives some 20 km away into the sea. The fishing folk believe that shoals of fish are more likely to be available in places where these birds live. Sea herons are found on rocks between 3 and 20 km into the sea. Also called *pullu* (which literally means 'bird'), these are seen in large numbers in the months from February to June.

Sea logs, mostly found a kilometre into the sea, are believed by the fishing folk to destroy fish on a large scale. They are considered useless and are never trapped. Sharks (*sellappillai*) are seen 20 km into the sea. Dangerous creatures, there are called 'King of the Ocean'. They are never mentioned by name by the fishing folk; and whenever sighted, they are worshipped with awe. Whales are found 3 km off to sea, like floating rocks. Catamarans are easily toppled by sharks and whales. Since modern fishing technology has not made any dent among the fishing folk of Puthur, they seldom attempt to capture sharks or whales.

Tetrodon immaculatus (*pettai*), *Diodon brachiatus* (*mullam pettai*), snakes, starfish (*katal vilakku*), *Hippocampus guttulatus* (*kudirai meen*), crabs, *murai, vanda sori, karupatti sori, alumba sori, rajatimlei* (*odukku*), *nerinji, sangu, mullan sangu, valampuri sangu, sovi sangu, kadal sippi, urula sangu, eluthani, vali sippi* and *sippukai sangu* are widely found and not edibile. *Sangu* and *sippi* varieties are used for decorative purposes. Insects found on the shore (*nariyen, odalu* and *kilavan*) are used as bait in fishing.

More than a hundred varieties of fish are found in the sea off Puthur. Table 5.3 lists them according to the nets and seasons in which they are mostly caught.

SEASONS

Human life is dependent on the changing seasons. Sunshine, rainfall, and other climatic factors contribute to the co-existence and interdependence of human beings and other living organisms. The coastal climate in the Puthur area is mainly attributable to equatorial currents, westerly winds, and the relatively large amount of sunshine. There is a considerable difference between diurnal and nocturnal temperatures. The rainfall regimen is subject to local deflections, although rain is mostly contributed by the south-west monsoon. All these have a direct bearing on the life of the Mukkuvār. Dependent on fish, the Mukkuvār classify the climatic seasons mostly with reference to the catches they get.

Kanyakumari District is marked by four seasons: dry period; summer; south-west monsoon; and post-monsoon period. December to February is a dry period. Kanyakumari District gets very little rain during the north-east monsoon. Due to low humidity, these months are generally dry. Nights are cold from November to February, but dry winds blow during the day. The temperature is unsteady, which contributes to sickness. The ratio of sea breeze to land breeze is not very constant, with dry, cold winds making the people lethargic.

From March to May is summer, when rain becomes scarce and insolation is high. There is often an epidemic of chicken pox, due to the sweltering heat, during these months. The atmosphere is generally surcharged and rarefied.

The south-west monsoon sets in June, and there is a heavy downpour until September. Sometimes this season begins at the end of May. Usually August sees the greatest rainfall, which gradually decreases in September.

The post-monsoon period commences in October, when there is no rain at all. By the end of October the north-east wind sets in, which brings some rain up to December.

The fishing folk of Puthur classify the seasons into three, according to their catches of fish: *melā mīṉ kālam*; *kīla mīṉ kālam*; and *pañca kālam*. The distinctions are based on the availability of fish and the condition of the wind. During *melā mīṉ kālam* (April to August), the wind blows from the west and there is a heavy catch of fish. In *kīla mīṉ kālam* (August to November) the wind blows from the east. High tides form in August, a furlong into the sea, reaching the shore as small waves. This is called *neṭuvāṅkal*. The fishing folk do not venture beyond this tide and the catch is therefore very small. *Neṭuvāṅkal* usually lasts for 15 days, and after it the sea becomes very calm.

Pañca kālam lasts from December to April. January to March is considered the peak of this season, when getting a catch is impossible. The people suffer a lot as they are unable to get their daily bread. The wind blows from both north and south.

OCEAN CURRENTS

Coursing through the layers of the sea are fast currents, some of them hundreds of miles long and up to a hundred miles wide. These currents are the veins and arteries of the living Earth, intriguing, unsolved mysteries. Part of the planet's system of heat exchange, they bring vast amounts of warmth from the tropics into the colder latitudes, which would be almost uninhabitable without them. Along with the winds, by which they are largely driven, the currents maintain the balanced temperatures we experience. Without them the tropics would grow gradually hotter, and the higher latitudes more and more frozen.

The movement of currents, by which the oceans 'plough' themselves, is caused by three main forces: prevailing winds, the Earth's rotation, and differences in the sea's density. Winds drive immense bodies of water before them, forming surface currents. The Earth's rotation, which deflects moving things to the right in the northern hemisphere and to the left in the southern hemisphere, causes these surface currents to move clockwise or anticlockwise.

Where currents meet or diverge, where cold or salty water sinks beneath water that is less dense, or where coastal winds blow the surface water seawards, a circulation is set up which may reach to the ocean's bottom. Surface water is then replaced by upwelling water rich in nutrient salts which stimulates new growths of marine plants. The herbivorous plankton thrive and the sea becomes fertile for fish. It is understandable that many of the world's great fisheries are found along the paths of ocean currents. The Mukkuvār are by no means students of oceanography or marine biology in the formal sense, but their profound understanding of these physical phenomena and their sensitivity to them has made them what they are. They describe and divide the currents in their own way, which is not far from the scientific approach. The currents of the ocean are determined by the seasons. The fishing folk of Puthur refer to eight types of current:

1. *Cōṇu vāṭṭu* is when the water flows from west to east and plenty of fish is available.
2. In *Cōṇu vāṭṭukkaravalu* the water flows from south-west to north-east and availability of fish is very low.
3. In *Cōṇu vāṭṭu ummaṟincavalu* the flow is from north-west to south-east. It is also called "unna etuttavalu". The availability of fish is average. *Kōḻiyā meral vaḷai, vaḷi vaḷai* and *gangoos vaḷai* are the nets used.
4. *Vāṇu vāṭṭu* is when the flow is from east to west. Nets like *vaḷi vaḷai, kaccā vaḷai, tāttuvaḷai* and *cāḷa vaḷai* are used for an average catch.
5. In *Vāṇu vāṭṭukkaravalu* the flow is from south-east to north-west and the nets used in *vāṇu vāṭu* are employed. The catch is very little.
6. *Vāṇuvāṭṭu ummaṟincavalu.* The flow here is from north-east to south-west and the same nets are used as in *vāṇu vāṭu.* The catch is average.
7. In *Nerekariyaṭṭivalu* the flow is from south to north. Almost all kinds of nets

are used without any restriction, but the catch is very little.

8. In *Nērē ummarincavalu* the flow is from north to south. All kinds of nets are used, again for a very small catch.

The use of certain nets is not determined by the current alone. The availability of different kinds of fish plays a major role in the chain of nets. When there is a criss-cross current fishing becomes impossible, and the fishing folk must return home empty-handed. Such a current is called *valu takarāru.*

WINDS

Eight types of winds exist, according to the fishing folk of Puthur. These are different from purely geographical divisions. The trade winds and westerly winds are the two major types. The usual coastal pattern of sea breeze and land breeze is also present. Winds are also associated with the deflection of surface currents.

1. *Cōlavakkāṟṟu* blows from west to east during April, May and June, when the current is *cōṇu vāṭu.* At times, specially in the mornings, the current can be *vāṇu vāṭu.*
2. *Cōlavakkarakkāṟṟu* blows from the south-west during June to September. *Cōṇu vāṭu* and *cōṇuvāṭṭukkaravalu* are the two currents during this period.
3. *Cōlavakkōṭaikkāṟṟu* blows from the north-west in the months September to November, when the currents are *vāṇu vāṭu* and *vāṇu vāṭṭukkaravalu.*
4. *Vāṭakkāṟṟu* blows from east to west during November to February, *Cōṇuvāṭu* and *vāṇu vāṭu* are the currents during this period.
5. *Vāṭakkoṉṭal* blows from the south-east during November to March. *Vāṇu vāṭu* and *vāṇuvāṭṭukaravalu* are the currents.
6. In *vāṭakkōṭai* the wind blows from the north-east during November to January. *Vāṇuvāṭṭu ummarincavalu* is the current.
7. *Kurincikkāṟṟu* blows from south to north. It is also called *adaiyakaccāṉ* and *karai kurinji* and blows during September to November. *Coṇu vāṭu* is the current.
8. *Nēru kōṭai* blows from north to south during March–April. The sea is calm and the currents *cōṇu vāṭu* and *vāṇu vāṭu* are weak.

These winds and currents do not always strictly correspond to the months mentioned.

Winds from two different directions may come into collision, which is called *kāṟṟu takarāṟu*. When caught in this situation, fishermen usually bring down their sails and just go with the wind. The link between wind and current is illustrated in Table 5.1.

Table 5.1

Winds and currents

Direction	*Wind*	*Current*	*Months*
W to E	*Cōḷavakkāṟṟu*	*Cōṇuvāṭṭu*	Apr–Jun
NW to SE	*Cōḷavakkoṭaikkāṟṟu*	*Cōṇuvaṭṭu ummaṛincavalu*	Sep–Nov
N to S	*Nērukōṭai*	*Nērē ummaṛincavalu*	Mar–Apr
NE to SW	*Vāṭakkōṭai*	*Vāṇuvāṭṭu ummaṛincavalu*	Nov–Jan
E to W	*Vāṭakkāṟṟu*	*Vāṇuvāṭu*	Nov–Feb
SE to NW	*Vāṭakkonṭal*	*Vāṇuvāṭṭukkaravalu*	Nov–Mar
S to N	*Kurincikkāṟṟu*	*Nerekariyaṭṭivalu*	Sep–Nov
SW to NE	*Cōḷavakkarakkāṟṟu*	*Cōṇuvaṭṭukkaravalu*	Jun–Sep

Generally in the months May to August, storms hit the coast at Puthur. At this time Puthur receives *Cōḻavakkāṟṟu*. If the lightning reaches the earth from the zenith (vertically), it foretells a storm. When the lightning appears the wind stops, the sky wears a pale look, and a dark arrow-like could appears on the horizon. It is believed that the storm will come from the direction of this cloud. On seeing these signs the fisherfolk on the sea return to the shore immediately. Those on the shore light a fire and wave it towards the sea to indicate the danger as well as to showing the way.

Cycles of the Sea

The speed of the waves, the currents, the wind, the rising and ebbing of the water, all vary from time to time. The fisherfolk of Puthur classify three seasons of sea cycles.

1. *Melākkaṭaḷ* denotes the months April to July. The waves direct their course from the south-west to the north-east. Cōḻavakkāṟṟu and Cōḻavakkāraṟṟu blow in this period. By neither rising nor falling fully, the water level maintains its balance. The current Cōṉuvāṭṭu is powerful and drives fish towards the shore.

This season is considered good for fishing.

2. *Kīḻakkaṭal.* In the months July to September, the water level rises and the tide leaves only a bit of land as shore. This is called *karaiyai kuṟukki aṭittal.* The season gets the *kurincikkāṟṟu* wind and the powerful current *vāṉuvāṭṭu.* Owing to the unrest of the sea, the village is severely affected as the fisherfolk do not go fishing.
3. *Cāyal* includes the months from September to April. In this season the sea is calm. The wind *vāṭakkāṟṟu* blows and the currents *coṉuvāṭṭu* and *vāṉuvāṭṭu* keep a normal course. The water level recedes and the catch of fish is small. This season is, however, good for the training of youngsters in the skills of fishing.

PERCEPTION OF THE ENVIRONMENT

The Mukkuvār of Puthur, when they are unable to control natural phenomena, even now resort to 'magical' rituals. Being Roman Catholics, they believe in the biblical allusion to the creation of the universe. They have myths about sea, wind, sky, fire and sun. Yet they maintain certain perceptions and beliefs about natural features and forces: these are manifest in many of their rituals, being related to their occupation.

The Mukkuvār personify all forms of Nature with which they are in contact, and like primitive ethnic groups, ascribe life to them. They do not venture to slight Nature in any of its forms as they cannot afford to risk its displeasure and bring upon themselves its malefic backlash and baleful influences.

THE SEA

The Mukkuvār treat the sea as sacred and attribute motherhood to it. There is a striking similarity to land, which is also treated as a woman by likening its fertility to that women (A. Siva Subramaniam, 1988: 47). This notion is clearly based on the association of land and sea with fertilization, sprouting, florescence and growth of life.

The other universal is the sanctity attached to water from the earliest days of human life. In the Indian tradition, from the Vedic period water has been regarded as a cleanser and purifier. All rituals and oblations performed by the Vedic people have been done on the banks of rivers, and water is used profusely in rituals and rites. River water, perhaps because of its finiteness and sweetness, is given this status. The same custom is seen among the Mukkuvār, although they have embraced Christianity, in respect of the sea.

To the Mukkuvār, the endless sea may once have inspired awe and fear. Gradually they turned to it as their succour and saviour. As is common among primitives, they do not till or tend: they are only gatherers. No wonder they continue to hold many primitive beliefs about the sea. They regard deaths in the sea as an infliction of the wrath of the mother. They feel that any violation of traditions or of the abstentions prescribed by lore may invite her wrath, which will lead to the annihilation of life. They believe that whenever there is a death natural of otherwise, in the sea, the sea is in fury. They ascribe the occasional high tides to the anger of the sea due to death, and believe that until the corpse is thrown ashore the sea will remain very rough. They believe that while the sea sustains them, it can also harm them when it is offended. Therefore the Mukkuvār are very careful in their life at sea and also in their references to any form of nature associated with the sea.

Another significant factor that strikes one is the traditional belief of the Hindu community in Maṇḍaikkāḍu about the sea. They too attribute sanctity to it. They treat the saline sea water as holy and sacred. The thousands of devotees who throng the temple carry away sea water as holy water.

The Mukkuvār use sea water as a purifier, as is observed in many of their rituals. They use it to ward off "shadow evil". They consider that the owls are purified after their dip in the sea and that their shadows will no longer harm children. On the twelfth day after confinement, mothers are taken to sea for a purifying bath.

The Mukkuvār believe that all water is holy and attribute fertility to it. During the lean seasons, when catches are scanty, they invite the parish priest to sprinkle water on the sea, believing that this will increase the quantity of fish. They believe in the sacredness of water, its palliative effects on the sick and the decrepit, and its role as a communion of divine grace to devotees in the temples. During phases of the life-cycle such as puberty and death, water is held to be a great purifier, capable of the removal of evils.

The Mukkuvār, have a belief that the richness and strength of the sea dwindles along with human generations. They believe that the longevity, physical prowess and talent of one generation are less than those of the previous one, and that the strength and richness of the sea is in proportion. The agriculturists of Kanyakumari District too entertain the belief that the fertility of the soil is being reduced and that the seasons are also changing. The fishermen say that the present catches are only three-fourths of what they had been in earlier generations, and believe that the currents and winds have become weaker.

WIND

Wind plays a very important role in the lives of fishermen. The direction of the wind, its velocity and force, all have a great bearing on their vocation. Wind can deflect the course of currents and can alter the stretch of fishing ground. To fishermen who are not used to modern techniques and rely on country boats and sails, the wind is an important factor. There is a folk usage; "Can any one go on the sea without taking account of the wind". Wind is perceive as the equivalent of breathing for a living human. Mores and folkways confirm this: the Mukkuvār, wind is an allotropic form of God. When the sea is rough, they say that God is awake; and when it is calm, they say that God sleeps. Gales and storms are the fierce deep breath of God. The fishermen therefore never slight the wind. They refer to death as an "extinction of breath". The occupation of fishing demands the holding of breath for long periods. To hold a breath for a while is equated with a temporary death.

THE ATMOSPHERE (SKY)

The fishermen in Puthur refer to the atmosphere as sky, or firmament. They believe that God lives there. According to them God lives in the form of clouds in the shape of humans and other living things, mountains, rivers, etc. They hold that the sky consists of Heaven and Purgatory. They believe that the souls of the dead first reach Purgatory.

There is a very popular and interesting story about this among the Mukkuvār. There lived one Uyirthan in an earlier generation. He passed away after ailing for some time. After bathing the body, his relations were about to put it in the coffin. To the surprise and awe of everyone gathered there he came to life, stood up and narrated what had happened to him. He is believed to have said that he was transported to Purgatory, where God sat in judgement. He was returned to this world again since his account was not yet complete. Incidentally, 'uyirthan' literally means 'came back to life', in other words, resurrection.

The Mukkuvār have a few taboos with regard to the sky. They do not expose the fallen milk-teeth of children to the sky, as that may hamper the further growth of teeth. Similarly, they do not expose eggs to the sky, fearing that they will not hatch. These taboos are based on fertility and also prevail among other communities of Kanyakumari District.

The atmosphere and the sky are very important for fishing. The fisherfolk of Puthur assess favourable situations for fishing, wind direction and movement of currents by cloud formations and by the positions of various stars. The converging of clouds and star at a particular place, indicates a particular weather condition. The agriculturists of Kanyakumari District hold the same belief. The Mukkuvār judge the formation of various currents from the position of such *neetāram*. If it is found in the south-east, *cōṇuvāṭṭu* current is indicated, if located in the east, the current would be *vāṇu vāṭṭu*; and so on. If the *neetāram* is straight overhead, absolute calm in the sea is predicted.

There are many perceptions of the sky among the Mukkuvār related to their occupation. The stars in the sky are believed to help them in judging direction, time, richness of catch, etc. They depend on nine such stars: *Katal velli, Aṟa mīn, Kūtta velli, Yeranhān velli, Chinna katal velli, Cothu velli, Kurusu velli, Malaimīn*, and *Kappal velli*. Based on their distance, from the sun/moon, periods of appearance, and location in the sky, these stars help in calculating time and direction of sailing as well as the seasonal availability of fish.

FIRE

Fire, another primordial element, is held very important by the fishermen of Puthur. Fire is the source of heat, and they believe that life becomes extinct when there is no heat. They equate light to divinity as well. They believe that God exists in the form of light, and they light candles in church and at shrines (*kruzadi*) as propitiation or in fulfilment of their vows. Candles are symbols of light and also a relic of primitive beliefs. Many rituals among the Mukkuvār are found to corroborate this.

Candles are kept burning around a dead body until it is removed from the home. A candle or lamp is kept burning for a further seven days or more, as darkness would invite evil spirits. Even in the graveyard a candle is kept alight for some days. This is attributed to their belief that God beckons to a soul only when there is light. The Mukkuvār have a ritual based on the belief that light will ward off evil spirit or, for that matter, natural calamities. Cholera and small-pox are supposed to be spread by evil spirits, ghosts and demons. Therefore whenever there is an epidemic, they light a camp-fire on the outskirts of the village at night, flood the village with lights, and keep awake, resorting to rituals and group singing, trusting that evil cannot enter where light prevails. To the Mukkuvār light and God are synonymous.

Fire is at times described by the Mukkuvār as an expression of the anger of God. There are occasional fires in the sea caused by climatic conditions in the oceans. The Mukkuvār dread such fires and refrain from sailing for three or four days whenever they sight a fire in the sea.

THE SUN

The fishermen of Puthur regard the sun as a ball of fire. The sun has a forceful impact on their life-cycle. They believe that if a pregnant women observes a solar eclipse, she will have a deformed child. They believe in performing certain magical rites before sunrise or after sunset, to ward off the effects of "shadow evils", on the commissioning of new nets, etc. They strongly believe that the transgression of such abstentions will affect them adversely or the desired effects will not be achieved.

THE MOON

The Mukkuvār hold the primitive belief that there are many mountainous rivers in the moon that accounts for its cool condition. Lunar ecclipses are also considered a taboo for women. There is a close association between the moon and the ocean currents, according to them. The radiant halo around the moon indicates the nature of the ocean currents. The angle of insolation of the moon is also said to have an effect on the currents.

FISH

Apart from the five natural forces, the fish that they catch have a significance for the Mukkuvār, other than their economic value and as an inexhaustible source of food. The species *Trichirus nalataricus*, popularly called *cavālai*, is believed to have been condemned by God. They believe the white gelatinous mould in the head of this species to be a stone, decreed by God as the species did not obey Him.

There is another folk belief to explain the cross-like figure on the dorsal surface of crabs. It seems St. Xavier, while walking on the shore, found a crab saluting him. As a gesture of his blessings St. Xavier made a cross on its back with his fingers. This story is analogous to that prevalent among Hindus, that Sri Rama, on seeing a squirrel trying to help his army build a bridge across the sea, affectionately ran his fingers over its back; and that the squirrel thus obtained the three stripes on its back.

Some varieties of fish seem to possess magical potency. The tail of the *Tvygon varnak* is smoked and shown to those who are believed to have been be possessed by evil spirits. Divergent views exist regarding the pollution caused by fish. On certain occasions fish may be considered holy too (Enthoven 1924: 217).

There is a stray reference to the migration of fish. Normally the migration of fish is due to currents: but the Mukkuvār attribute the migration of fish from Quilon to Puthur to the blessings of St. Lucy. They believe that St. Lucy brings all the catch from Quilon and does not allow it to go to the next village, Pallam, before the Mukkuvār have taken what they need. They never attempt to catch whales since that is beyond their capacity. They fear them too, and whenever they confront them closely they draw a cross on their backs and trust they would leave them unhurt.

Fishing: Tools and Techniques

Very early in his existence, man was induced to venture afloat in search of food in the form of fish, an inexhaustible resource. Among the earliest traces of human existence in India are implements made of coral, which is an indication that he ventured at least as far as the low waterline. Against the backdrop that fish has formed part man's food from the early days, and that he has caught it in the sea and in rivers, using tools and implements to suit his skills and competencies, this section analyses the fishing tools and techniques adopted by the Mukkuvār.

Though handicapped by a dearth of modern fishing technology, the fisherfolk of Puthur exhibit thorough knowledge and expertise in traditional skills and techniques. They sail either in groups or individuality, in catamarans and boats, within a radius of 30–50 km. Various fishing nets are used.

Catamarans and boats are the craft commonly used. Catamarans are built of four pieces, each 10–20 ft long, using wood like *Alpecea*, *Enythrina indica*, *Eniodindron* and *Anfractousum*, which easily floats. While two pieces form the base, the other two form the arched front and rear portions, called *aniyam* and *kaṭamaram*. These are narrow, while the *naṭumaram*, the middle part of the catamaran, is wide. The cross-wise wooden pieces fixed to the *aniyam* and the *kaṭamaram* are called *katiyal*. Before being shaped, the wood is cured in water for 10–15 days. After drying, the minute holes or pores are filled. The pieces are tied together with rope or nylon to make a catamaran. This earliest mode of transport is now common in the coastal areas of Tamil Nadu. J. Hornel (1921: 144–8) observed that the catamaran is widely found, from the Mediterranean to South American shores.

The boat may be viewed as the next stage of development. Though similar to the catamaran structurally the boat, made mostly from the mango tree, is taller and wider. The planks are fixed together with nylon. Boats are propelled by oars, sail and motors. Colochel, a neighbouring village, enjoys the possession of a good number of motor boats, there are only three in Puthur at present.

The mechanized boats of Colochel are used for fishing and also transport goods between ships and the shore. Boats are comparatively less dangerous and less accident-prone than catamarans, reason enough to refrain from transporting valuables in a catamaran.

Ōṭāvi and Vaḷḷaṅkeṭṭu are the two artisan groups among the Mukkuvār who build catamarans and boats respectively. Making use of simple tools like axe and chisel, a catamaran is easily made; while a boat is the product of hard labour and strenuous hours. The whole range of carprenter's tools is used, the planks are very closely fitted, and small holes are waxed to prevent the entry of water. The cost of labour amounts to 10 per cent of the price of the wood used in a boat. While catamarans number in the hundreds, there are only six boats in Puthur. After the day's labour or when not in use, they are dragged ashore and kept under a thatched roof called *Panna* to prevent damage by sun and rain.

Tribals and peasants use various methods and equipment other than nets. They drive the fish to shallow water or beyond a weir, where they are easily caught. These techniques date to pre-historical times (Kosambi 1989: 81). This ancient method is prevalent in Kanyakumari District.

Ropes are used in Puthur during the months of January, February and March, the lean season. In the single hook rope (*oruthanā kayiṛu*) a stone is tied to one end of a 60 ft rope and a rod is fixed some 3–4 ft above the stone. The other end of the rope is fixed to a float. The stone end of the rope is thrown into the sea, using fish or crabs as bait, while the other end is held in the hands. Small jerks or movements of the rope indicate a catch. Large fish like *cūrai, cemmīn* and *vowmīn* can be caught single-handed. This tedious method is not much liked.

The multi-hook rope (*kochu mattu*) runs to 500 ft and is made of cotton. The cotton cord is made thick and strong and is soaked in water boiled with the outer skin of tamarind seeds. In this process the cord turns crimson, which does not scare away the fish. The fishing line is made of 5 ft of gangoose rope, and more than 1000 lines are attached to the rope at intervals of 1 ft. Stones and floats are attached to the rope at intervals of 50 ft and 100 ft respectively. In mid-sea, while one person sows the catamaran slowly, another drops the bait dexterously. After a patient wait of two or more hours, the line is drawn up and the fish caught are stored in a conical basket made of palm-leaf and called *omal*.

This fishing tackle can be used only once in a day, as it involves a tedious and cumbersome process. The fixing of bait in the many hooks consumes 3–5 hours, and one can spend around 2 hours in the disentangling of the enlaced cotton and gangoose strings.

The angling hook rope (*oithu mattu*) is smaller but structurally resembles the multi-hook rope, and 50 to 60 lines attached. Apart from the baits, silk pieces of various hues — crimson, yellow, white, green — are also attached to the line. These attract fish who mistake them for moss and sea vegetation. Single-handed, this is used to catch large fishes.

Kūdu, a Tamil word, finds its equivalents in 'cage', 'nest', 'hive' or 'assemble'. This is a sort of trap made of palm-fibre or coir and is very rarely used in Puthur. The fibre is woven into box-like rectangles. This V-shaped trap has a hole of 3 cm diameter and a tiny door-like structure to trap fish. The trap is laid in stretches of sea full of rocks. Small varieties of fish are drawn inside the trap to lure prawns, which are the main catch. Although the trap is painted green to attract fish, the method is not particularly successful.

People in Kanyakumari District use a similar contrivance to fish in rivers and streams, but that is made of the ribs of palm leaves. One end of the conical trap is pointed, while the broad end is concave and nas a hole. When water flows through this, little fish enter the hole and are trapped. Highly suitable in rivulets and small streams, this is still in vogue among tribals inhabiting the hills of Kanyakumari and Chidambaranar Districts.

Nets came into use because of their greater efficiency, and modern technology has greatly influenced their quality, structure and operating techniques. Cotton was replaced by stronger, more durable nylon, which also resulted in the net's becoming a factory product. Considering the various disadvantages of cotton nets — the long hours needed to make them, their low durability and not-so-easy maintenance — the fishermen opted for nylon nets. A factory established in Maṇavāḷakuṛichi produces nylon fishing nets for the fisherfolk of Kanyakumari. Midalam, a fishing village situated in the west, 10 km from Puthur, houses a cottage industry which produces nets under the auspices of the Catholic Church.

These two units do not produce complete nets. They manufacture the smaller sections called *māl*. A *māl* has usually 100 holes but depends on the type of net for which it is meant. As the size of net varies according to an individual's economic status, efficiency, and skill, people purchase *māls* and assemble them to make their own nets. The coming of these units has robbed the womenfolk of their livelihood. Earlier the women would produce *māls* while the men were out. This labour fetched them between Rs. 5 and Rs. 10 for a *māl*.

The nets used by the fisherfolk of Puthur can be classified under two heads, circular nets and flat nets and their use depends on the seasons. Structurally, circular nets resemble *kūdu*. *Karamati*, also called *karavalai*, is one of the largest nets used.

Shaped like an hour-glass, it derives this name because it is dragged ashore after a large haul. The holes in the net are half a centimetre square. When pulled, the middle part of the net contracts. Both ends of the net are attached to floats; and to enable the net to settle on sea bed, stones are fastened. Usually 50 ft long and 20 ft broad, this net is used in lean months, i.e., January and February. As dawn breaks, a group sets sail in a boat along with the net. While two row, the rest drop the 500-ft rope attached to the floats. After the rope is laid the boat turns towards the shore, when the net is cast. While returning the rope attached to the other end of the net is slowly dropped. The net is then dragged ashore by 20 to 40 people holding both the ends of the rope.

The Katalanayan, a fishing community of coastal Cochin, possess nets which are similar to this. At present Puthur has seven such nets. The income on catches is shared among many. The following is the break-up of the profit made on the catch:

(a) 5 per cent as tax to the Church

(b) 4 per cent of *penduva* fish for the owner of the net, women, and cooking assistants

(c) 5 per cent of *kuthu* fish for labourers who put in hard work

(d) 2 per cent for the barber

(e) 5 per cent for the one who takes care of the net after the catch and who carries out minor repairs

(f) 4 per cent for the helpers who push and pull the catamaran or boat into and from the sea

(g) The rest is divided into three portions and taken equally by the owner of the net, the people who ventured into the sea with the net and those who dragged it ashore.

On the whole, a quarter of the profit is enjoyed by the owner of the net, another quarter is ued for miscellaneous expenses, and one half is equally divided among persons involved in the catch. This usually leaves them with Rs. 10 or Rs. 15 each. As the Arayans own the nets, Pulukkaiyars have always been subordinated to them.

As the land on which houses stand belongs to the Church, the fisherfolk pay 5 per cent of the profit to it as tax. A decade ago the bursar of the church used to visit households which use *karamati* with a money-box to collect this tax. This system has been abolished now, but we can see how a clan, after the introduction of tools which require collective labour, has gained from anomalous production; and how a group in possession of tools can easily enslave the have-nots. Social and economic status are determined only by the possession of large nets, as is also seen among the Jalari, a fishing community of Andhra Pradesh (Kodanda Rao 1990: 26-30).

The *taṭṭumaṭi* similar in structure to the *karavalai*, is 15 ft long and 8 ft broad. Two catamarans, with three persons in each, are employed with this net while one transports the net to the sea, the another closely follows. The net, to which are fastened stones, is dropped in fish-rich waters and the end of the rope attached to the mouth of the net is passed to the people in the second catamaran. When both ends of the rope are pulled, the net contracts and surfaces. The Katalarayan of Cochin use their circular net in the smae manner (L.K. Anantha Krishna Iyer 1909: 214).

Flat nets mark a further development in fishing technology. Six kinds are used in Puthur: *valuvalai*, *cālavalai*, *kaccavalai*, *kankūsvalai*, *tattuvalai* and *koliyameraluvalai*. Floats are fastened to the upper portion of the net while stones are hooked to the bottom. Gravitational pull makes the lower part rest on the sea bed and the floats keep the upper part near the surface. The net remains wide open and the fish swim into it and get their find entangled. The process involves two persons and takes about two hours. so that many catches are possible in a day. While one steadily rows, the other drops the line, and finally both haul in the catch. The size of the net and of the holes in it depends on the variety of fish to be caught. The flat nets need in Puthur are:

(a) *Valuvalai*: Around 13 m wide, with square holes of about 11 cm, this costs about Rs. 50,000. The largest among the flat nets, it is used mostly in shallow waters.

(b) *Cālavalai*: Used to catch the smaller varieties of fish, this is 10 m wide, with square holes of 3 cm.

(c) *Kaccavalai*: Although this too has a breadth of 10 m, its holes measure only 5 mm. It is used to catch tiny varieties of fish like *nettili*.

(d) *Kankūsvalai*: Also called '*disco*' *valai*, *parivalappu valai* and *nelattu valai*, this is chiefly used to net prawns, which dwell close to the sea bed. It is about 3 m in breadth and has holes of 1 cm. This net is made of strengthened cotton thread, which the fisherfolk twist on their own with spindles.

(e) *Tattuvalai*: Used to net sharks and other large fish, this is also 3 cm wide and has holes of 5 cm. Used in mid-sea, this net is cast among rocks and the place is marked with signs of mountains, temples, etc. The catch is taken up only after a day or two.

(f) *Koliyameralu valai*: This is an assembly of worn-out, used nets, with no specific size. The net derives its name from the *koliyameralu*, a fish usually caught with it.

An analysis of the distribution of the various types of net shows that about 20 per cent of the households of fishermen in Puthur possess one of the above types. About 10 per cent own two nets each, and around 2 per cent own even more than two nets. The possession of nets is considered a pointer to economic status. Another feature is the joint ownership of nets by two or three families so as to share the high cost. The income through such nets is shared in proportion to the monetary investment in them. All the male members in a family have a right in the use of all fishing tools, including nets. When the head of a family continues to work with the nets in his possession, married sons are given a share in the icome. However, when any lone member of the family is using a net, he is expected to give a share of the income to other male members of the family.

Kaccavalai and *cālavalai* are supposed to have followed the *karavalai*, which is considered to be the oldest type to have been used by fishermen in Puthur. The other types are of very recent origin. Twenty years ago, nets like *kaccāvalai*, *cālavalai*, *karavalai* and *tattuvalai* were made of cotton thread. The advent of nylons was exploited rightly by the Mukkuvār. The use of nylon threads helped overcome the difficulties of drying the nets during winter and the frequent decay of cotton threads. The *tattuvalai* slowly edged out the *karavalai* because of its compactness and light weight. Even youngsters can use this net.

Apart from the various types of boats and nets, there are a few other indigenous implements used by the Mukkuvār. The *ōmal* is a cylindrical basket, made of palm-leaf, used to store the catch. It is tied with a rope at the apex to facilitate opening and closing. Of late, it is also being made of nylon. The *korukacca* is a seive, with a wooden handle, made of fragments of broken nets. The implement is mostly used with the *kaṇava* type of fish, which is found near the upper surface of the sea. The gadget is also helpful in collecting the small prey caught with the fishing ropes. The *kōttumāl* is a small square container made of nylon rope, used to carry the nylon nets. The *koḻuttaṭṭi* is a piece of wood, normally a metre long, to the end of which is fixed an iron hook. This is useful in hooking out the bigger fish from *koccumattu* nets while transferring them to boats or containers.

Floats, called *pāttai* or *kāvi*, play a very important role in fishing. Until recently the Mukkuvār used floats made of *Alpecea* or *Erythrina indica*. When they found it uneconomical to change these floats frequently, and after taking to nylon nets, they began to use plastic floats. Nowadays the Mukkuvār use big plastic cans or thermocole sheets for floats.

The Mukkuvār classify four major fishing times:

Kālai maṭi (Morning catch)	:	Set out at 4 a.m. and return by 10 a.m.
Ucha maṭi (Noon catch)	:	Set out around 8 a.m. and return by 2 p.m.
Aṅtimaṭi (Evening catch)	:	Leave at 2 p.m. and return by 6 p.m.
Irā maṭi (Night catch)	:	Sail before midnight and return by 8 a.m.

The Mukkuvār carefully plan their fishing depending on the availability of catches. For example, the variety *ayila* is mostly available during nights in January and February. They will normally choose *irāmaṭi* for this catch, being fully aware that this species will swim ashore generally during the nights. There are some varieties which are lured by the stars and by moonlight. The time of making a catch is sometimes influenced by the mode and time of marketing. Catches are mostly consumed in Puthur village. Some valuable varieties like prawns are usually sent to Kerala for drying and curing. The trade is organized by big companies and the fishermen are mostly at their mercy.

Auctioning seems to be the most common method of marketing the catch in Puthur village. Immediately on returning to the shore, the Mukkuvār generally auction their catches to the crowd waiting for them. There is a group or professional auctioneers, commisssion agents, and small merchants. The professional auctioneers are usually paid 2 per cent of the sale proceeds. Occasionally the Mukkuvār carry their catches home, clean them and sell them by weight instead of by lot. The large-scale dealers from Kerala pay the commission agents in advance. In turn, the Puthur fishermen are paid in advance as part of a contract of supply valid for each season. This practice is generally disadvantageous to the fishermen because the merchants always try to pay low rate. At times such dealings lead to quarrels.

When the catch of certain types like *cālai* and *nettili* is abundant, it is cured, stored and sold for higher prices later on. Months like July, August, September and October are normally marked by abundant catches, and the Mukkuvār's purchasing power is correspondingly high. These are usually their happy months, when marriges and festivities take place in their families.

The Life Cycle

Every human has to pass through the stages of childhood, adolescence, adulthood and old age. Along with these comes a succession of roles. Apart from the economic role of bread-winner, man has to play the roles of son, brother, husband, father, etc.; which woman, the custodian of the home, has to play the roles of daughter, sister, wife, mother, daughter-in-law, etc. These roles among the Mukkuvār are discussed in this section, along with many associated rituals, folkways, modes and customs. The passage from one to another of these stages is marked by rituals that are indicative of social acceptance and are termed life-cycle rituls.

Arnold Van Gennep, in his *The Rites of Passage*, establishes three stages in every ritual connected with birth, marriage, death, etc. Although the complete scheme of rites of passage theroretically includes preliminal rites (rites of separation), liminal rites (rites of transition), and postliminal rites (rites of incorporation), in specific instances these three types are not always equally important or equally eleborated (Van Gennep 1977: 11).

BIRTH

The Mukkuvār perform many rituals before and after childbirth. The first prenatal ritual is usually performed during the seventh month of pregnancy, when the woman is taken to her mother's place. (Usually the first two deliveries are attended to by the mother's family and in her house). This ritual in the seventh month of pregnancy is a very common one among many ethnic groups. This is usually done on an auspicious day in the man's house, relatives being invited. The woman's parents and their close relatives bring sweets and other eatables. Her mother hands the sweets to the man's mother. The womenfolk, specially the husband's sisters, put new bangles on the pregnant woman and give her sweets. All the relatives are then entertained to a feast. Finally the pregnant woman is taken to her mother's place at an auspicious time, being blessed by all the relatives present. Neither her husband nor any other relatives from his side accompany her. The Mukkuvār observe a good many taboos and restrictions during pregnancy. Pregnant women are not allowed to eat horse gram, eggs, palmyra fruit or root, pumpkin, papaya, peas, and other things whose consumption is thought to harm the child in the womb. They are not allowed outdoors after dusk or during eclipses. They are prevented from seeing lightning. Such taboos and restrictions are found among many communities in Tamil Nadu. The Mukkuvār give adequate care to expectant mothers. The taboos prescribed do not suggest a total separation from the rest of the family.

The Mukkuvār have begun to take pregnant women to hospitals for delivery, though the conventional practice is to have births at home. There are midwives in whom the Mukkuvār have confidence. Natal or infant mortality are rarely reported.

The new-born is welcomed with some rituals. All women who attended the mother have oil baths. The new-born is bathed and its maternal grandmother hands it to its paternal grandmother or aunt. The lady performs the ceremony of the 'first feed' (*senai ūttal*) by touching the tip of the baby's tongue with a solution of jaggery and onion. The umbilical cord is usually buried very carefully to ensure that it is not eaten by dogs. which is considered a bad omen. The soiled clothes and bedding are given to the washerman of the village, who claims this as a traditional right.

The mother of the new-born is also given a bath and, immediately after the bath, hot food with arrack, fish curry, etc. She is also given, every morning, for about ten days, a preparation of pepper, dried ginger, garlic and a few spices, with jaggery, as a post-delivery prophylactic.

The normal period of childbed pollution extends from 12 to 41 days. After her delivery a woman is not allowed to mix freely or to move all about the home. On the twelfth day her mother brings a pot of water from the sea and bathes her. This is considered to purify her, and after it she is permitted to move about in her home. However, she is not allowed into the kitchen. On the fifteenth day her mother takes her, early in the morning, to bathe in a pond. After this bath, she is presented with a new saree by her mother. The wearing of this new saree is indicative of the ringing in of a new life, of motherhood. She is permitted to resume her normal household chores only after the lapse of forty-one days.

The new-born too is the subject of rituals. On the fourth or fifth day after its arrival, the baby is put in a decorated cradle by its maternal uncle. On the twenty-eighth day a thread is tied around the waist of the baby. This is of gold or silver, when people can afford it, or else of cotton.

Usually after 41 days the mother and the baby are taken back to her husband's place. This again involves a ritual, when the husband's family formally come to invite them with articles like rice. The mother and the baby are received at their place with all gaiety and joy. There is usually a return feast to the girl's parents and the small group of relatives who accompany them.

A woman thus passes through separation, transition and incorporation, as described by Van Gennep. Baptism is the ceremony which terminates the process of absorption. This is a happy occasion among the Mukkuvār. The new-born is given presents and gifts. These rituals signify the acceptance of the child into society. Kodanda Rao alludes to a similar practice among the Jalari, a fishing community in Andhra Pradesh.

The transition of the new-born from a state of pollution to incorporation into the social environment does not confer on it membership of the family into which it is born. The social and spiritual significance of the new-born child is recognized when it is ritually given a name and formally incorporated into the family. This formal incorporation signifies the social acceptance of its father, mother and other kin, as the kinship bonds between the child and others are ceremoniously established (Kodanda Rao 1990: 40-41).

PUBERTY RITE

Puberty, the onset of the menstrual cycle among girls, is associated with many rituals, taboos and restrictions. While this phenomenon indicates a transition from childhood to adolescence, socially it suggests the girl's responsibilities as a marriageable damsel. The Mukkuvār generally marry off their daughters soon after puberty. Age at marriage varies from 12 to 18 years.

Puberty is normally associated with joy and happiness. The rituals are held on the 3rd, 5th, 7th, 9th or 16th day of the girl's attaining puberty. Her paternal aunts and maternal uncle's wives have an important role in such rituals. They are the ones who are first informed by the girl's mother. The aunts visit the house immediately with some sweets. Normally on the third day the girl is removed from the house and taken by the aunts to a separate hut made for the purpose after an oil bath. The aunts as well as the girl are given sweets. The oil bath and the distribution of sweets are repeated on the 5th and 7th days. On the seventh day, her paternal aunt (father's sister) gives the girl a half saree, which indicates to others the attainment of puberty. The rituals may have a scientific basis. This period of a week or so is one of stress, fear, fatigue, tension and physical debility. By making it a ritual, the parents and relatives give the girl a diet rich in protein, like eggs, gingelly oil, sweets made of black gram, dhall, etc. Coconut and its milk form an inevitable part of the girl's diet.

Isolation in a separate hut formed out of green coconut leaves suggests a primitive practice, when the Mother Goddess, a symbol of energy and power, was associated with red and was feared so much that a special abode was created for her. The menarche may be considered an indication of the Mother goddess, so that the girl is accorded the same fear and respect.

But there is also another version. The girl is isolated. There are many taboos on her. She is not permitted to mix with the rest of the family. Her movement is highly restricted. She is not permitted to leave the hut into which she is ritualistically ushered, except for calls of nature. When she has to go out in the evenings she is excepted to carry an iron rod to dispel any evil spirits. Then again there are taboos on her food. She is not given green plantain, pumpkin, excessive water, jaggery, etc. Frazer gives a detailed account of these taboos and establishes that these rituals are observed on the principle of "imitative magic". The fluid out of pumpkin, raw plantain, jaggery, etc., resembles menstrual fluid in colour.

On the 16th day, all relatives and friends are informed about the onset of puberty and the isolation and are invited for a feast. On completion of ritualistic formalities the girl is given presents and the guests are feasted.

The same rituals are repeated during later manstrual periods. Separation, transition and incorporation are seen in these rituals. The girl passes through the stage of separation during the first seven days. Transition occurs through the ritual on the seventh day; and incorporation is through the ceremony on the eighth sixteenth day. The rituals have a social bearing in giving importance to aunts as a girl among the Mukkuvār is normally married to an uncle's or aunt's son. These cousins have a right to marry them. When girls are married to 'outrsiders', the cousins are compensated with a gold ring. Only then may the couple enter their new household. The ritual is called "prevention of entry" (*vācal mariyal*) (Shiva Subramaniam 1969: 291–7).

During menstruation "monthly sickness" Mukkuvār women observe many taboos. They are not permitted to enter the kitchen. The Mukkuvār are very firm about preventing women from going to the sea during menstruation. They fear that the sea might be polluted and the catch become scanty. They do not even allow menstruating women to touch fishing implements. An identical belief is held among other communities in Kanyakumari District. Women considered to be polluting are not allowed to touch seed or go near a seed bed, not permitted in a kitchen, and not allowed to coagulate milk to form curd. Such taboos are not imposed upon married women in certain communities in these tracts. On the other hand, in some parts of Tamil Nadu there are beliefs that are quite contrary to these. In the Annamalais region, Pollachi Taluk, unmarried girls are made to run around agricultural land during their menstrual periods in the belief that this will enhance the yield. Menstruation is associated with fertility (Selvaracu 1983: 119–20). In Kiḻappavūr village in Tirunelveli District, the people believe that if menstruating girls plant trees or give seeds for sowing, the yield will perceptibly increase (Josephine Violet Rani 1985:55).

In Kerala, the Bagavathiamman temple at Chenganur conducts a purification ceremony almost every month, in the belief that the goddess is also subjected to this cycle. The fourth day is supposed to be a day of purification, called *tirupūrattu*. The idol is taken back into the *sanctum sanctorum* only after this ceremony every month (Nagam Aiya 1906: 89–90). The practice has been observed in Assam as well. In the temple of the goddess Kamarupa, no idol is found except a stone with a symbolic vaginal form. It is believed that the goddess' cycle coincides with the full moon, and the *sanctum sanctorum* is closed for three days at that time. (Bhattacharya 1977: 30).

MARRIAGE

Marriages among the Mukkuvār are arranged among the parents of the boys and girls or through their relatives. No marriage brokers are encouraged to arrange marriages. Social events like marriages, temple festivals and other functions enable parents to see potential matches. The Mukkuvār believe in arranging all aspects of marriages through discussion. Demands for jewels, cash, etc., settled beforehand by both sets of parents in the presence of a few relatives.

The engagement usually takes place on a mutually agreed auspicious day. This gains social acceptance for the marriage, or recognition by the laity. It is followed by religious recognition by the parish priest in the form of *vārtha pāṭu*.

The engagement ceremony is usually held in the boy's house. The girl's party, consisting of her father, grandfather, father's brothers and uncles, visits the boy's house on a pre-arranged auspicious day. Women generally do not accompany them. It is the privilege of the boy's father to ask the girl's father the purpose of their visit and thus set the ball rolling. The girl's father then reveals their purpose formally. After the settlement of terms, the eldest among the girl's party hands over the amount to the eldest among the boy's party.

The conversation among the groups is at times in a symbolic language. The bride may be spoken of in terms of land or a plantain tree, suggesting the notion of fertility. This habit is pronounced among tribals. The Irulapallar of Coimbatore District adopt this way of asking for a girl in marriage and put it in the form of a song (Periāḷwar n.d., Vol. 19: 209).

The priests announce the purposed marriage in their parish, according to Christian tradition and the Bible. The two families are expected to remit a specific amount to the church, which is shared among the priest, the accountant, the church choir and others. The priest then conducts the ritual called *vārtha pāṭu* to assess the bride's and the groom's knowledge of the Commandments, of Holy Communion, of prayer routine, etc., and the supplement their evangelical knowledge. He educates the prospective couple on their roles and prepares them for a wedded life and to accept the responsibilities. This is normally done thrice, but there are exceptions due to exigencies. On the day of the first announcement in church, the bride and the groom wear new clothes and attend mass. The wedding invitations are usually extended after the first announcement.

GIFT

The gift to souls is a very important ritual among the Mukkuvār. It is performed in the boy's house on the day prior to the wedding ceremony. It is an invitation and invocation to the ancestors, seeking their blessings. It consists of a prayer and of the giving of a feast to some poor people who are assumed to be the ancestors. A fest for relatives is included. This ritual is performned in the bride's house also. It is a common ritual among many communities, including Brahmins, who call it *nāndhi*.

The shaving ritual, a formal one, is performed by the local barber on the bridegroom in the presence of relatives. The barber is presented with now clothes and is given Rs. 25 by the groom. Visitors also place token gifts of money in the ceremonial cup kept for the purpose. In addition, the barber is given a packet of food and groceries.

The day of the wedding begins with the groom presenting his uncles, aunts, brothers, sisters and others with new clothes. All of them then go to the bride's place. The bridegroom's party is received with honour and courtesy. The bride's uncle, brothers and other relatives welcome them with sandalwood paste, rose-water and garlands. The girl's brother presents gold chain to the bridegroom, who reciprocates by gifting a gold ring. The bridegroom is taken in a procession to the bride's place to await the emergence of the bride. All then go to the church.

The couple are seated in the special chairs brought from the bride's place (see chapter 1) and placed in front of the altar. The solemnization and mass are then conducted by the priest. The conventional *tāli*, the 'sacred tie', is blessed by the priest and handed to the groom, who ties it around the neck of the bride at the appointed auspicious time. This is followed by the traditional prayer and mass of Christians, at the end of which the newly-weds are taken to the bride's place and seated on a decorated pedestal.

The bride's mother gives the couple a preparation called *pāchōṟu*, made of boiled rice, coconut, jaggery, etc. The groom is expected to present his mother-in-law with money for this. *Pāchōṟu*, for the Mukkuvār, is associated with new life: it is cooked also whenever a new net or a new boat is commissioned. (It is similar to what is offered to deities in Tamil Nadu in the form of *ponkal*). The *pāchōṟu* is not consumed by the couple, not even tasted.

Closely following this, the priest offers prayers and blesses the couple, after which come blessings from relatives and friends. Children shower flowers and greet the couple, singing chorals. The wedding cake is cut by the couple. The couple are then taken into the house and all the guests are given the wedding feast. The guests slowly withdraw and return to their homes. The bride's brothers and the groom's sisters apply oil to the foreheads of the groom and the bride respectively, forming part of another ritual. The groom's parents and relatives then adjourn to their homes, leaving the groom in the bride's residence, where he is expected to stay for 3 to 7 days.

The groom's sisters return to the bride's place on the fourth day after the wedding for the ritual called *nālu kaḻittal* after the day on which it is done. Of late this ritual is being done on the very next day after the wedding. This ritual consists of an oil bath, being given to the couple, in the same day as on the wedding day, and the presentation of new clothes. The groom's sisters are treated to a feast, after which they return to their home.

The final phase of the rituals associated with the wedding comes generally on the fifth or the seventh day after the wedding. This is a ritual connected with the taking of the bride to the husband's house. The relatives of the boy come to the bride's house with auspicious things like plantain bunches. The newly-weds are sent to the husband's house at an auspicious time along with new vessels, groceries, fruits, sweets, etc. The next visit of the bride to her natal home is at the first Christmas after the wedding.

Separation, transition and incorporation — the 'rites of passages' — occur in the rituals of Mukkuvār weddings. The engagement ritual prepares the bride and the groom to be accepted in the new setting, separating them from their own settings. The lag between the engagement and the wedding in the church is interpreted as a transition period. Finally, incorporation is confirmed by the *vārtha pāṭu* by the parish priest. Society then accepts them as a couple, husband and wife.

DEATH AND FUNERAL RITES

Death, the leveller, to whom sceptre and crown must bow down, is also observed with a few rites and rituals by the Mukkuvār. Death is bemoaned, the funeral is attended with the same serenity as among this sect of Christians, with due Catholicity, observing traditional rites, a few of them suggesting relics of tribals. The Mukkuvār, professedly Catholics, retain some of the Hindu rites and rituals prevailing elsewhere in Tamil Nadu.

It is the duty of the barber in the village to convey the news of the death to the relatives. This is called *marāyam* among Hindu communities, although other means of quick communication have virtually taken over this role. The parish priest is also informed and the church going tolls. On hearing the news, relatives assemble in the house of the deceased. While the males condole the death, the womenfolk lament loudly.

The body of the deceased is prepared for the funeral, the rituals beginning with a sacred bath signifying purifications and absolution from sins. The parish priest sprinkles holy water on the body. The widow of the deceased is brought near him and to wear a balck scarf by the deceased's sister, after the *tāli* has been removed. The widow is taken to a corner of the house and is isolated totally for eight days. The cortege moves to the cemetery after a short mass in the church. This mass is conducted with the aim of enabling the soul of the deceased to reach God. Similar rituals are done when a wife dies. At this time new clothes are also given to the in-laws. It is to be noted that a man is not subjected to isolation when his wife dies.

The funeral is attended by all relatives. After the coffin is buried in the cemetery they return to the house of the deceased. Where there is a ritual called *mu̱rai kaḷittal*. This is mainly the smearing of oil among the in-laws of the deceased, man or woman. After this the menfolk go to the river for bathing. They return and put on the new clothes already presented to them. After a formal drink called *ilavu kanchi*, they leave. The barber takes away all the things used by the deceased and throws them in the sea. He is paid Rs. 40 by convention.

The obsequies and associated rituals are performed on the third, eighth and sixteenth days. On the third day after the bereavement, the widow's brothers come to her house with 21 balls of estables and rice gruel. The lady is given an oil bath and the rice gruel, etc. She is also given a new saree. On the eighth day a memorial service is held. On the sixteenth — or sometimes the thirtieth — day, a tomb with a cross is built. On this day all relatives are invited for a feast. The feast consists mainly of dishes which the deceased liked. Usually one person is taken to be the 'soul' of the dead person and is entertained first; only then are the others fed. Before eating they pray for the soul of the dead, this ritual being called "gift to soul".

The Mukkuvār do not bury children who die before baptism in the cemetery. They are interred in their house yards. The eldest child of a family, even when baptized, is not taken to the cemetery but is burried in the back yard of the house.

The stage of separation is marked by death and by burial at the physical level. The Puthur Christians believe that the dead person's soul travels to Purgatory first and later to Heaven or Hell. To enable the soul to reach Heaven, a copy of the Bible is placed between the dead person's hands. Personal articles are also placed in the coffin. Van Gennep makes the following observation regarding this custom:

> What is important to us in this case is that since the deceased must make a voyage, his survivors are careful to equip him with all the necessary material objects — such as clothing, food, arms and tools as well as those of a magico-religious nature — amulets, passwords, songs etc. — which will assure him of a safe journey or crossing and a favourable reception as they would a living traveller (Gannep, 1977: 153–54).

This 'transition' journey ends in the incorporation of the soul among its ancestors. The rituals of the eighth and sixteenth days after death are intended to facilitate this incorporation.

Certain practices clearly denote the status of the widow. The Mukkuvār remove the *tāli* (nuptial knot); the Jalari fisherfolk of Andhra Pradesh denude the widow of her bangles and *tāli* on the seashore (Kodanda Rao 1990: 55); the Kanikkarar community make the bereaved wife sit beside the corpse while an aged woman snaps the *tāli* and throws it before the dead husband. This custom serves the personal relationship of husband and wife and confers widowhood. In Puthur widows are considered polluted for the first eight days after the husband's death. This is the period of transition. After ceremonies she is again incorporated in the society.

Loss of life is compensated by material benefits. When a man dies, his brothers are provided with new clothes by his widow's siblings. Likewise, clothes are given to a dead woman's brothers. Compensation also takes the form of a common feast, clothes, ornaments, etc.

Rituals

Magic engaged the serious attention of primitive man for quite some time, until ideas of religion and God came to him (Chattopadhyaya 1964: 37) Magic survived and made incursions into religion also, constituting its magic-religious part. This came to be called ritual. A definition of what is magic and what is not, is difficult. The relationship of magic to religion and to science has been the subject of much debate among students of anthropology, sociology and magic itself. Sit J.G. Frazer, whose influence is widespread, believed magic to be a preliminary stage in the development of religion. To Frazer, magic is compulsion and religion is propitiation: the two exist side by side.

If we analyse the principles of thought on which magic is based, they will probably be found to resolve themselves into two: first, that like produces like, that an effect resembles its cause, and second, that things which have once been in contact continue to act on each other at a distance after physical contact has been severed. Frazer calls these the "law of similarity" and the "law of contact or contagion" (Frazer 1976: 52–53). From the first of these the magician infers that he can produce any effect he desires merely by imitating it; from the second he infers that whatever he does to a material object will affect equally the person with whom the object was once in contact, whether or not it formed part of his body. Frazer termed these "Homoeopathic Magic" and "contagious magic". The same principles are implicitly believed by the magician to regulate the operations of inanimate nature.

The Mukkuvār retain some of these old beliefs. Magic has an important place in their life. It is considered to be either positive or negative. Positive magic is intended to achieve something, while negative magic is meant to prevent something. A taboo that prevents some action by a person is positive rather than negative magic, for the breaker of the taboo is punished by having something done to him. Magic is also either black or white. Black magic is evil, for it calls into play unsanctioned forces and beings or aims at illness, injury, maiming death, dissolution of property and so on. White magic performs wonders or cures without the invocation of dark powers.

Among the Puthur Mukkuvār one can observe these four types of magic applied to various aspects of their life, avocation, marriage, ailment and general prosperity. Rituals and magical words for the general good of an individual or a group — that is, white magic — are often seen in the fields of agriculture, hunting, fishing, medicine and warface (Johnson 1980: 413).

Family feuds, ferquent ailment to children in a family, untimely death of herds and milch animals, failure or loss of careers, delay in auspicious things like weddings in a family, etc., are attributed to spirits and ghosts. This is common belief among Hindus, Christians and Muslims in Tamil Nadu and varies only in degree. The Mukkuvār performs some magical rites to be free from spirits. They take people believed to be possessed by spirits to a magician in Kaṭiapaṭṭiṇam, who prays to St. Anthony and prepares a talisman to be worn by the individual. Chantings carved in copper plate rolled in the talisman are believed to dispel evil aimed at the individual. The person who takes the talisman is expected to pray to St. Anthony for thriteen days. The magician has to observe an absolutely celibate life, and has to chant prayers 1008 times daily, in order to gain adequate strength and potency for his magic.

Magicians try to nullify the evil effects of black magic. Talismsans are used to protect people from these as well as to help them in their normal lives. These talismans are usually tied with black thread. The Mukkuvār and the magicians believe in the efficacy of the colour black in removing their difficulties. The Christians also believe that spirits cannot come near the Holy Cross, so most of them wear a crucifix. The cross is respected and feared as well. People professing other religions exploit this belief of the Christians. Stretches of land with coconut plantations along the coast and adjoining the lagoons are mostly owned by Nāṭārs. The Mukkuvār used to steal coconuts from these plantations. The Nāṭārs hit upon the idea of carving the cross on all the coconut trees. Those who respect the cross dare not put their feet on it by climbing a tree.

The Mukkuvār also resort to magic for creativity, fertility, productivity and prosperity. They adopt homoeopathic magic to ensure rains, crops, fishing and progeny. If imitative magic, working by means of images, has been commonly practised for spiteful purposes, it has also been employed with benevolent intentions. The Mukkuvār apply the principle of imitative magic, like produces like, to procure offspring. Barren women offer toy cradles, baby dolls, etc. in church, seeking offspring. This is common among many peoples in Kanyakumari.

Magical rites are performed on the same mimetic lines in fishing too. On the completion of a new net, the Mukkuvār perform magical rites to ensure a good catch as well as to ward off the evil eye. The artisan (*maṭikketti*) takes the newly made fishing net to the shore, spreads it out, and scatters bits of jaggery and pieces of coconut kernel. Later he rolls the net, takes it home and places a hatchet on it. The throwing of jaggery and coconut on the shore causes a huge crowd of children to collect. The belief is that this imitative magic will make fish flock to the net. The placing of a hatchet on the new net is to mitigate the effect of the evil eye.

The artisan and the owner leave early the next morning, carrying in six small containers the special offering made of boiled rice, jaggery and coconut. On the shore, the net is again spread and half of the offering is throw over it. Children again collect as on the previous day. The net is then rolled up and they set sail for fishing. The food remaining is thrown into the sea as an offering. After the day's fishing, a portion of the maiden catch of the new net is thrown in the air in all directions, to be taken by birds. The artisan is given a quantity of fish and the traditional wage. New nets are generally put to use in the months when catches are large.

The Puthur fishermen perform similar imitative rites when they commission a new fishing boat. On the maiden launch of the new boat, plantains and sugar are distributed to all. The fishermen believe that just as all feel happy on that occasion, they will also be happy with the new boat in the days to come. The bunch of bananas is carried in the new boat and thrown into the sea. Shark oil is applied all over the outride of the boat in the belief that its smell will charm the fish. Certain rites commonly performed by other communities in Tamil Nadu can also be seen among the Mukkuvār. For example, the parish priest is invited to sprinkle holy water into the sea when fish become very scarce.

Protective magic is meant to guard against the evil eye and 'shadow evil'. Adults, children, and also inanimate objects like fishing nets and boats are believed to need such protection. The Mukkuvār observe the principle of 'contagion'. They tie a piece of alum, chillies and limes with a black cord and hang it in the house. The evil spell on the children is believed to be transferred to these objects. It is plain that superstition rests on the 'law of contact'. In this process of transference of evil, animals, birds and some other articles are used by the Mukkuvār. For instance, a coin is fastened to a child's hand for three days. The child is then seated in front of a palm-leaf that has tasty food spread on it. This leaf, with the food in it, is rolled and waved around the head of the child by the magician. The coin fastened for the previous three days is removed and put in it. Finally the magician throws the leaf, with all the food and the coin, in a burial ground without being seen by anyone. Evil is believed to be mitigated by taking away the coin which was in contact with the child, as well as the food, which the child is believed to have consumed by a kind of optical illusion.

A few other rites are employed to cure children believed to be ailing due to the evil eye. An areca-nut slicer is soaked in water for a long time and then the ailing child is bathed in that water. There is another unique rite to cure children supposed to be suffering from the evil eye. Two of the child's uncles stand on opposite sides of the door of the house, holding a *dhotī* like a cradle. The child is placed in the *dhotī*. The uncles gently toss and roll the improvised cradle such that the child is swung across the threshold.

Another belief is that the shadows of polluted women, will cause ill health in children, calling this "shadow evil". This evil is removed by a rite involving holy water, which to them can be nothing but sea water. The maternal uncle of the child goes early in the morning to the sea, unseen by anyone. He stands on the shore holding a small vessel and counting the number of times the waves touch his feet. On the count of seven he fetches water from the sea in the vessel. The child is then bathed in that water. The shadow of a couple in coitus is believed to cause ill health to children, which must be countered similar magical rites. These practices are found among agriculturists as well as Muslims in southern Tamil Nadu, according to T. Gnanasekaran (1987: 28–29).

Some taboos among the Mukkuvār have the significance of magical rites. They have a belief that certain birds can cause harm to unborn children. If a pregnant woman is seen by an owl returning from the sea, it causes 'bird evil', which can affect the larynx and vocal chords of the child. This is why preganat women are prevented from going outdoors after dusk. They adopt a rite to cure a child who has come under 'bird evil'. Castor oil is applied to the body of the child, which is made to lie on a mat. Then a toad is buried alive in the backyard. After some time the child is bathed at that spot.

The Puthur fishermen believe that their catches dwindle whereever the evil eye is cast on their nets. Sometimes they make fish curry from the catch in that net, and give it along with rice to a dog. Only if the dog eats it do they think there is no evil eye on the net. There is a magical rite to protect a net. A virgin is asked to grind *Acorus calamous* and coconut and mix them in water. This solution is sprinkled on the net on the shore, early in the morning. The Mukkuvār believe that the virgin's grinding does all the magic: she does not have to utter a word.

The Mukkuvār believe that if a woman accosts a fisherman going towards the shore with his net or if she says anything before he leaves for fishing, the evil eye is invoked. To avert this, fishermen leave quite early in the morning with their nets and other implements. Leaving them on the shore, they return home for the morning meal. The women normally stay in the rear portion of the house and do not go to see the menfolk off to their fishing.

In northern Kerala, a barren jack tree is made to yield fruit by having a naked boy hit at its trunk with a pestle during a solar eclipse (Nambiar 1986: 66). Parallel to this is a practice among farmers in Kanyakumari District. A peasant reaches for a hatchet and raises it to strike at an unyielding jack tree. The other pleads, "Don't chop! dont't chop! The tree will yield next year." This play-acting is repeated three times in the hope of a good yield the following year.

The evil eye affects not only nets and implements but also humans. A gluttonous child experiences the bad effects produced by the hungry eyes of others. To remove this, cooked rice and fish are smeared on the belly of the child. After reciting a hymn to the Holy Mother seven times, the food is given to a dog. This is believed to reduce the ill effects. When an adult is affected, some pepper and salt are waved around the patient's head, smeared on the belly and later put in the fire after making the patient spit in it. During this, the hymn to the Holy Mother is chanted in the reverse order.

In the above practices there is evident an attempt to transfer evil effects to inanimate or non-human things. 'Shadow evil' is transferred to sea water, 'bird evil' to the toad buried in the sand, the evil eye on fishing nets to holy water or to the leaves of *erukku*, a milky shrub, that on humans to pepper, salt, etc., Children's ailments are transferred to the silver coin tied on the wrist, and the evil eye to the water used to soak, an areaca-nut slicer or to the *dhotī* of the maternal uncle. Primitive man also believed that his burdens and problems could be easily transferred to other living creatures like animals and plants.

Magical rituals aimed at the transfer of evil are also prevalent among the farmers of Tamil Nadu. Coconut, egg, lemon, salt and pepper are largely used in these rites. Coconut and egg are made to touch the affected person's body or are waved around the head so that the evil effects are transferred to them. When they are later broken, the bad effects are also destroyed (A. Sivasubramanian 1988: 34–35).

The Mukkuvār attempt to harm, injure or destroy their enemies through the application of the principle of imitative magic and also on the principle of contagious magic. They sometimes employ sorcerers, who make images of the enemies in wax, clay, flour, etc. A needle is run into the head, heart, or stomach of the image, believing that the victim will at the same moment be seized with excruciating pain in the corresponding part of his body. Another familiar example of contagious magic is the sympathy which is supposed to exist between a man and any severed portion of his person, such as hair or nails. Whoever gets possession of the severed parts may work his will, at any distance, upon the person from whom they were taken. A piece of clothing of the person who is to be enchanted or something that stands in relation to him, such as his excrement, the refuse of his food, his spittle, his footprints, etc., can be employed as the medium for a charm, combined with an incantation or the murmuring of a certain formula. This is said to have been known in India to sorcerers for thousands of years, and the practice is widely prevalent in Tamil Nadu. This charm combines homoeopathic and contagious magic, since the image which is made in the likeness of the enemy contains things which were once in contact with him (Siva Subramanian 1988: 28).

The Mukkuār do not bury the eldest child in the cemetery because they fear that the liver, spleen, skull, etc., may be stolen and used for black magic. Though the people of Puthur have faith in black magic, they have not developed it as an art or science among themselves. They hire people from outside the villages to achieve their ends.

To the Mukkuvār, life centres around fish and nets. The first thing they attempt against their foes is to jeopardise their fish catch. With the intent of impeding an enemy's catch of fish, they will stealthily take two or three fish from his net, scorch them in fire, and throw them into the sea, muttering thrice that there should be no catch on that day. It is believe that the sacred sea does not tolerate an evil like the killing of a few fish, and that all the fish in it will die. This magic is based on the principle 'like produces like'. That imagination can control ground reality is the prime principle of magic (Thompson 1980: 11).

Farmers in Kanyakumari District also believe in black magic and in taboos based on the homoeopathic influence of people on vegetation. For example, while eating jackfruit or mango one is not supposed to spit pips at the trees. If one does this, the tree may grow but will yield no fruit. Similarly, coconut trees may wither when the shells of coconuts are beaten against them or when two broken pieces of coconut are joined.

Certain rites are based on the principle that articles used by men or women can be used to make potent charms. In the Puthur fishing community there exist practices bordering on black magic. In order to bewitch or entice a man or to prolong an extra-marital relationship, a woman may prepare a *kaivalayam* or love potion. She goes this by grinding a piece of her fingernail, a piece of used tampon, mustard unbroken or unfried while seasoning, and rice found in salt. The paste is mixed with the food of the paramour, and it is believed that after taking it he can never desert the woman. There are methods to detect whether one has fallen prey to such a love potion. A paste of coriander and water is smeared on the chest of the person. If it dries up, he is unaffected; but if it remains moist, the reverse is true.

The person is made to bite and chew herbal root. If it tastes sweet to him, he is believed to be under the influence of a love potion. A person so affected is taken to a doctor belonging to a different community. The doctor induces vomiting or diarrhoea to ward off the effect.

A love potion to entice women is commonly prepared in Tamil Nadu with donkey's semen. It is to be applied to the woman's forehead. Another variety is made by drying and powdering a chameleon's head. The powder is mixed with semen and applied to the woman forehead Siva Subramanian (1988: 29). According to Gnanasekaran (1987: 91–101) many such potions are used in Vadanapatty, a village in Tamil Nadu.

Oral Tradition

Oral tradition has come to mean myths, legends, folktales, proverbs, riddles, verses and a variety of other forms whose medium is the spoken word. The folk element prevalent among the Mukkuvār can be observed in their prose narratives, lament songs, labour songs, dredge songs, etc. Their oral tradition is worthy of extensive and deep research. An attempt is made in the following paragraphs to look at it against an environmental and sociological background.

Many prose narratives found among the Mukkuvār are symbolic of their ethnic unity with other groups as well as of their clashes with them, of their migration and of religious coexistence. It was observed earlier that the Mukkuvār have an amiable relationship with the other major community of the area, the Nāṭār although there are discord and differences at times. Many stories are narrated in Mukkuvār families whose symbolic messages are not always understood.

A story often heard is about a crow, a deer and a fox. The crow and the deer lived happily in a forest. There was a famine in the forest. The crow went in search of a new fertile area. It then took its friend there and they continued to live happily. One day a fox tried to befriend the deer, aiming to take it as a prize catch to a hunter. The crow scented the evil designs of the fox and advised the deer not to be carried away by a shallow and cunning 'friend'. At last the worst happened: the fox lured the deer into the hunter's net. The crow managed to find the deer and get it out of the net. On finding the deer escaping, the hunter killed the fox.

The characters in this story represent different communities. The shift from the forest to another area represents the Mukkuvār's migration from Ceylon to Malabar and then to Kanyakumari. This story has a clear socio-historical background.

A folk saying of the Mukkuvār has some sociological bearing. "*Puraiyiṭam vāṅkiyatu Mukkuvār, anupavam eduttatu cāṇān*", means that while the Mukkuvār bought the land, the Nāṭār enjoy its produce. It was mentioned earlier that the Mukkuvār once owned land in Puthur village. While the Mukkuvār depend on fishing for their livelihood, the Nāṭār depend on toddy-tapping. The fisherfolk of Puthur bought land and handed it over to the Nāṭār to till, since they themselves did not possess adequate knowledge and experience in agricultural operations. The Nāṭār took advantage of the Mukkuvār's ignorance and exploited them.

Another hilarious anecdote on the lack of agricultural experience among the Mukkuvār is heard among the fisherfolk in Puthur and the Nāṭār in the Viḷavancode and

Kalkuḷam areas. Once a Nāṭār borrowed a sum of Rs. 500 from a Mukkuvār man at Puthur, promising to return it on a specific day. He did not keep his word. After several days the Mukkuvār went to his house, and demanded that he repay the loan immediately. He took the Nāṭār's *kalakkumattai* (a tool used to stir the toddy and mix calcium hydroxide during fermentation), shouting that he would return the implement only when the money had been repaid. The Mukkuvār then buried the implement, which is nothing but a palmyra stick. After a few months the Nāṭār brought two hundred rupees to the Mukkuvār. He pleaded for the return of his implement, promising complete repayment soon. The Mukkuvār, taking pity on the Nāṭār went to dig it out. When he found it decayed he was nonplussed. He at once promised the Nāṭār that he would make good the loss. The Nāṭār immediately exploited the situation, demanding Rs. 1, 000 to buy a new *kalakkumattai*. The gullible Mukkuvār, comparing the Nāṭār's tool with his own fishing net, shelled out the money demanded by the Nāṭār. This story points not only to the Mukkuvār's ignorance but also to his absolute lack of common sense.

There is another story reflecting the gullibility of the Mukkuvār. A Nāṭār and a Mukkuvār set out one evening for a booze. On the way they saw an iron safe. The Nāṭār told the Mukkuvār that it was not discreet to open the box when people were around. He took him away to the pub after burying the box. After drinking a good deal, both of them returned home. At midnight the Nāṭār returned to the safe, opened it, and carried away all that was inside. In the morning, pretending that nothing had happened, he took his friend to the spot, only to find an empty box after tiresome digging. Finally he told the Mukkuvār to keep the box. There are four versions of this story, but all of them concur on the gullibility of the Mukkuvār and their exploitation by the Nāṭār.

At the beginning of the nineteenth century, communal oppression and a rigid caste system were prevalent in Kanyakumari. Depressed classes as the Mukkuvār were, they were not allowed the use of umbrellas or footwear. There was a rigid taboo on wearing gold jewellery and on carrying water pots on the hip. They were not permitted to own terraced houses or to speak the language that others spoke (T.H. George 1982: 11). There were a good many restrictions on coming near or talking to higher caste people. They were subjected to severe taxation. All these oppressions perhaps led them to change their faith to Christianity. A story is in vogue among the Mukkuvār as a satire on such oppression.

A *sudra* community woman had illicit relations with a Mukkuvār. On an occasion when they were making love, the woman's husband returned home unexpectedly

Thinking quickly, the *sudra* woman took her lover out of the house. She made him pretend that he was drinking water which she poured, asking him not to touch the vessel. The Mukkuvār came out on the street loudly crying, "The *sudra* woman will give the cunt but not the kettle!" The *sudra* community, of course, is considered socially higher than the Mukkuvār.

The Mukkuvār believe that Maṇḍaikkāḍu Amman, the famous female deity of the area, and St. Lucy (Pirakasi Amman) are sisters. They believe that while Maṇḍaikkāḍu Amman came there through the mountains, St. Lucy came by sea. Quite a few stories abound on these two, particularly on the origin of the Amman's temple at Maṇḍaikkāḍu and about the origin of the goddess hereself.

Maṇḍaikkāḍu Amman is believed to be one of seven sisters in a Nāṭār family who died a young virgin. She is believed to have so died by divine grace. Her spirit is believed to still hover in Maṇḍaikkāḍu. Once a group of seven persons driving seven bullock carts reached the village late at night. They were very hungry and went in search of a place where they could get food. A maiden standing before a hut warmly asked what they wanted. They replied that they wanted food. She promised that food would soon be ready and told them to go for their bath. When they returned they found a broad spread of tasty food, of which they made a sumptuous meal. When they sought to pay for the food they could not see the maiden; their search all around was futile. They were wonderstruck and they narrated this episode to all their people. In due course the people around built a temple there and made it the abode of Maṇḍaikkāḍu Amman.

It is also widely believed that Maṇḍaikkāḍu Amman is the daughter of a Nampūtari Brahmin, who immolated herself along with her three children when she realised that she had been married for years to a low-caste (Paraiyan) man in the guise of a Brahmin scholar. This is a relic of the strong distinctions of the caste system. When the Brahmin lady found her children eating fish, she realised that her father has mistaken a Harijan for a Brahmin because of his erudition.

The fisherfolk of Puthur, hold Maṇḍaikkāḍu Amman in great esteem. They believe that the deity bathes in the sea, beautifully bedecked with jewels. During her festival the Puthur fishermen put up their fish stalls in the proximity of her temple. Expectant mothers from among the fisherfolk offer prayers to her, and it is no wonder that they address this deity as the sister of St. Lucy.

It is common for highly-placed men in any society to become the targets of public attention: apart from their failures, their personal lives are also discussed, sometimes to the point of obscenity. This feature is found in Mukkuvār folk tradition. There are a number of such obscene stories, jests, jokes, and anecdotes among the Mukkuvār.

When scientific advancements percolate through the lives of the common people, they evoke expectations, anticipations, disappointments, etc. These elements are given oral expression and form the nucleus for many forms of folklore. The common man would normally except a train to move faster than a bus. But in Tirunelveli District there is a story about a train that makes fun of its snail-like speed. The story goes that the train from Titunelveli to Tiruchendur steamed out at the scheduled hour. After some time its driver noticed a herd of buffaloes lying across the track. He stopped the train, got down, drove the animals off and restarted the train. After some time and distance he again noticed buffaloes on the track. Thinking to repeat the earlier performance, he got down: but to his surprise he found it was the same herd. Similarly, stories are heard about the social, cultural and scientific gap between urban and rural areas. In many rural areas in Tamil Nadu we may hear stories on the toilets now used in towns as well as trains. Such stories are only to compensate for inadequacies.

During the Republic Day celebration at Colochel, a cultural programme was arranged. To depict the 'konweldge gap' of a rural woman, a skit was enacted. An old mother from a village visits her daughter in city. When all retire for the might, the old lady from the village is the last to go to bed as she does not know how to switch off the tube-light. Frightened, she thinks it is a fire and shouts aloud.

The Puthur fishermen have a funny story on the origin of cinema. It seems a husband wanted to prove the infidelity of his wife in a court of law. Once when she was making love with her paramour while, as she thought, her husband was away, the husband made a hole in the wall, and by passing the sun's rays through, got their shadows on a glass to be produced in court.

New scientific ideas and developments take very long to percolate to rural folk. This has given rise to many attempts to bridge the gap and to compensate for them through imaginative compromises. The Mukkuvār have their own view of aeroplanes. Two Mukkuvār, seeing an aircraft up in the air glittering in bright sunshine, wonder how it is polished. When one raises this very genuine doubt, the other promptly replies that when the plane goes high it becomes small, so that paint can be poured on it from a tin.

Knowledge has been transmitted down the generations of human history. Experiences, trials and tribulations, failures and achivements have become the knowledge base for humanity. To what is handed down, each generation adds its own fund of experience

Life and work of the fisher folk

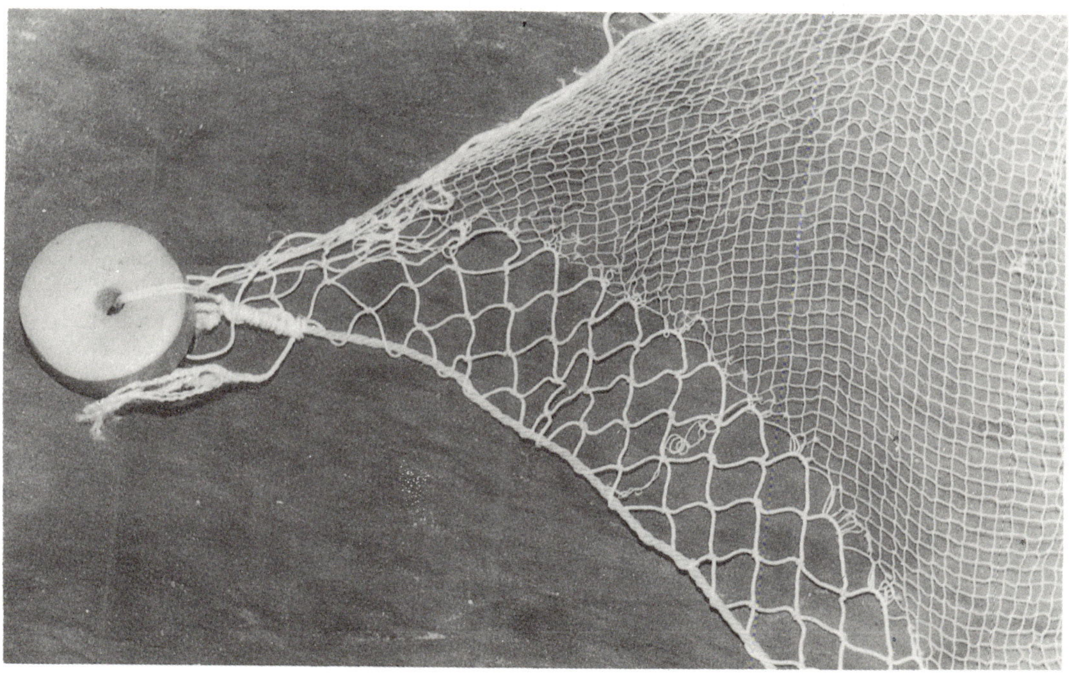

and wisdom. The Puthur fisherfolk's knowledge of water currents, wind, climatic changes, all of which contributes to their occupation and to fishing techniques, is a good example of such acquisitions and modifications.

While using the *karavalai*, the fishermen express themselves in a labour song that is called *ampa* in other coastal areas of Tamil Nadu and Sri Lanka. This song is rendered by a group of 20 to 40. While the elders provide the lead, the youngsters follow in a mostly monosyllabic chorus. The rendering of the song follows the force of the waves. When large waves push the net ashore, making the drawing process easier, the voices are low-pitched; and when the tide is weak, the pitch becomes high. This song affords perfect co-ordination in pulling the net ashore and makes the job easier (Kesavan, 1985: 30).

Karavalai songs are marked by discontinuity a characteristic of labour songs. There is no cogency or consistency in them. Love seems to be the dominant theme of the *ampa* songs of Sri Lanka (Pushpa Rajan 1976: 5–12), and it is also found in songs sung in the fishing areas of Kanyakumari District (J. Nirmala Bai, 1980: 44–55). In the songs of Ciluvai Curicil, a troupe, the names of fish figure. They also propose to consummate a marriage for the king of the ocean, the whale. This poetic imagination may be ascribed to man's meek submissiveness towards the forces of Nature.

Appendix

Zoological Names of Sea Animals

1. Holocentrus calcanifer
2. Epinephelus flavo cacrules
3. Epinephelus hexagonatus
4. Serranus sonnerati
5. Serranus bocnack
6. Meroprion Malabaricus
7. Lutianus sebae
8. Chaetodon pictus
9. Heniochus macrolepidotus
10. Mullus vittatus
11. Crenidens indicus
12. Teuthis striolata
13. Perca rubra
14. Corvina dorsalis
15. Umbrina amblyeephalus
16. Corvina aneus
17. Corvina maculata
18. Sciaena dwssumieri
19. Xiphias velifer
20. Tetrapturus indicus
21. Trichiurus armatus
22. Trichiurus malabanicus
23. Caranx mate
24. Carangoides oblongus

25. Scomber toloo parah
26. Chorinemus lyran
27. Zeus bindoo-karah
28. Zeus insidiator
29. Equula ruconius
30. Equula dussumieri
31. Scomber minutes
32. Lactarius Lactarius
33. Stromateus abbus
34. Stromateus griseus
35. Stromateus paru
36. Zeus maculatus
37. Scomber kanagurta
38. Thynnus affinis
39. Thyannus albacora
40. Scomber pelamys
41. Scomber guttatus
42. Scomber commersonii
43. Echineis albicauda
44. Sillago malabarica
45. Antennarius hispidus
46. Platycephalus vitatus
47. Gobius kora
48. Salarias unicolor
49. Mastacembeleus armatus
50. Sphyraena jello
51. Sphyraena dwssumieri
52. Fistularia Commersonii
53. Ophiocephalus gachua
54. Labrus hortulanus
55. Chaetodon maculatus
56. Chaetodon suratensis
57. Pleuronectus triocellatus
58. Pleuronectus erumei
59. Solea fumilis
60. Anius dwssumieri
61. Clanias melanoderma
62. Sanus indicus
63. Belone gracilis
64. Nemacheilus pulchellus
65. Sardinella longiceps
66. Kowala lauta
67. Hilsa ilisha
68. Clupea articauda
69. Platygaster indicus
70. Raconda russelliana
71. Dussumieria acuta
72. Stolephorus indicus
73. Stolephorous commersonianus
74. Stolephorus mystax
75. Clupea malabarica
76. Esox chirocentrus
77. Anguila marmorata
78. Muraena tessellata
79. Triacantus russelli
80. Balistes occulatus
81. Ostracion cubicus
82. Diodon brachiatus
83. Scoliodon laticaudus
84. Scotiodon acutus
85. Raja timlei
86. Trygon sephen
87. Tetrodon immaculatus
88. Trygon uarnak
89. Engraulis indicus
90. Equula ruconius

91. Caranx sausun
92. Trichiurus savala
93. Percis maculata
94. Rajafasciata shaw
95. Actobates indica
96. Triacanthus brevirostris
97. Balistes erythrodon
98. Gobius striatus
99. Gobius malabanicus
100. Percis punctata

References

Bhattacharyya, Narendra Nath, 1977. *The Indian Mother Goddess*, Delhi: Manohar Book Service.

Blackburn, Stuart, H., 1986. "Performance Markers in an Indian stroy-type", In Stuart H. Blackburn and A.K. Ramanujan (eds.), *Another Harmony: New essays on the Folklore of India*, Delhi: Oxford University Press.

Buchanan, Francis, 1807. *Journey from Madras through the Countries of Mysore, Canara and Malabar, Vol. III*. London: The Directors of the East India Company.

Chattopadhaya, Debiprasad, 1959, *Lokayata*, New Delhi: People's Publishing House.

Chattopadhaya, Debiprasad, 1964, *Indian Philosophy*. New Delhi: People's Publishing House.

Dundis, Alan, 1975, *Analytic Essays in Folklore*. The Hague and Paris: Mouton.

Dundis, Alan, 1980, *Interpreting Folklore*, Bloomington: Indiana University Press.

Enthoven, R.E., 1924. *The Folklore of Bombay*. London: Oxford University Press.

Forrester, Duncan B., 1980. *Caste and Christianity: Attitudes and Policies on Caste of Anglo-Saxon Protestant Missions in India*. London: Curzon Press.

Frazer, George James, 1976. *The Golden Bough: A Study in Magic and Religion*, London: Macmillan Press.

Gandhi (Tr.), 1980, *Camutāya varalāṟṟuc curukkam, Part I*, NCBH, Madras.

George, D.S., 1982, *Kumarimāvaṭṭa Peṇṇurimai porāṭṭam*, Madras Maṇi Patippakam.

Gnana Sekaran, Tē., 1987. *Makkal vālvil mantirace caṭankukaḷ*, 1987, Madurai Pārttipan patippakam.

Hall, J.F. (ed.), 1938. *Manual of South Kanara District*, Vol. I.

Hora, S.L., 1921. "On a Peculiar Fishing Implement from the Kangra Valley". *Man in India*, Vol. VII, Nos. 2 and 3.

Hornel J., 1921. "Catamarans and Reed Rafts As Evidence of Former Race Continuity from the Mediterranean Eastward to South America". *Man in Inda*, Vol. I, No. 2.

Innes, 1951. *Madras District Gazetteers: Malabar*, Vol. I, F.B. Evans (ed.). Madras: Government Press.

Iyer, L.K. Anantha Krishna, 1909. *The Cochin Tribes and Castes*, Vol. I. Madras: Higginbotham.

Johnson, Harry, M., 1980. *Sociology: A Systematic Introduction*, New Delhi: Allied Publishers.

Josephine Violet Rani, 1985, Cakuṉaṅkaḷum Nampikkaikaḷum Kīḻappāvūr Urāṭci — Ōr Āyvu M. Phil Āyvēdu (This is not published) Pāḷayaṅkoṭṭai, Tamil Āyvu Maiyam, Tūya Cavēriyār College.

Kesavan, Ko., 1985, *Kataippāṭalkaḷum Camūkamum*, Kumpakōṇam, Tōḻamai Veḷiyīṭu.

Kesavan, Ko., 1986, *Nāṭṭuppuṟaviyal oruviḷakkam*, Tirucci, Putumaip patippakam.

Kodanda Rao, M. 1990. *Cultural and Structural Dimensions of Family: A Study of Jalari Fishermen*. New Delhi: Concept Publishing Company.

Kosambi, D.D. 1975. *An Introduction to the Study of Indian History*, Bombay: Popular Prakashan.

Kosambi, D.D. 1989, *Paṇṭaiya India ataṉ paṇpāṭum nākarikamum paṟṟiya varalāṟu*. New Delhi: Indian Council of Historical Research and Madras: NCBH.

Logan, William, 1951. *Malabar*, Vol. I Madras: Government Press.

Nagam Aiya, V., 1906. *The Travancore State Manual*, Vol. I, Trivandrum: Government Press.

Nambiar, A.K., 1986. "Structure of a Magical Ritual of Kerala", in *The Theatre of the Earth is never Dead*, G. Sankara Pillai (ed.), Trichur School of Drama, pp. 65–72.

Nirmala Bai, J., "*Kumarimāvaṭṭa ampāp pāṭal kāṭṭum 'Pulamai'*, Vol. 6: No. 2, 1980, pp. 44–55.

Peralvar, Ār., 1971. "Irular Tirumaṇam". *'Ārāycci'* Malar 2, Ital 4.

Periyāḻvār, Ār, 'Iruḷappaḷḷar eṉṟa veṭṭakkāṭa iruḷar' *Ārāycci*, Vol. No. 19 (No year) (Pa. 199–210), Pāḷaiyaṅkoṭṭai, Nellai Āyvukkuḻu.

Pushparajan, O., 1976, *Ampā*, Yāḻppāṇam, Alai veḷiyīṭu.

Selvaracu, Yirā, 1983, 'Koṅku nāṭṭil kaṉṉi vaḻipāṭu' *Tolliyal Karuttataṅku* (Tokuti I) Patmāvati, Ā. Nākacāmi (P. Pū.) Madras. Tamiḻaka varalāṟṟup pēravai.

Siva Subramanian, Ā., 1988. *Mantiram caṭāṅkukaḷ*. Madras: New Century Book House.

Siva Subramanian, Ā., *"Vācaṟpaṭimaṟiyal"* *'Ārāycci'* Vol. I, No. 2, Oct. 1969 (page 291–97) Pāḷaiyaṅkōṭṭai, Nellai Āyvukkuḻu.

Siva Subramanian, Ā., '*Pūppuc caṭaṅkukaḷum Nampikkaikaḷum Ārāycci* 26: 1988 (Pa.

45–64), Pāḷaiyaṅkoṭṭai, Nellai Āyvukkuḻu.

Thanancayan, Ā, 1990. "Māṉiṭaviyal Nōkkil Curāmiṉ Valipāṭu" '*Ārāyccī*', 1990: 34 (Page. 23–38).

Thomson, George, 1978. *The Prehistoric Aegean*, London: Lawrence and Wishart.

Thomson, George, 1980. *Aeschyleus and Athens*, London: Lawrence and Wishart.

Thurston, E., 1987. *Castes and Tribes of Southern India*, Vol. V, ed. by K. Rangachari, New Delhi: Asian Educational Service.

Van Gennep, Arnold, 1977. *The Rites of Passage*, London: Routledge and Kegan Paul.

Velluppillai, T.K., 1940. *The Travancore State Manual*, Vol. I. Trivandrum: Government Press.

List of Contributors

Madhav Gadgil
Centre for Ecological Sciences
Indian Institute of Science
BANGALORE

Makhan Jha
Department of Anthropology
Ranchi University
RANCHI (Bihar)

R.S. Negi
29-A, Circular Road
DEHRADUN 240 001

G. John Samuel
Director for Research Programmes
Institute of Asian Studies
377, 10th East Street
Thiruvanmiyur
CHENNAI 600 041

M.D. Subhash Chandran
Reader in Botany
Dr. A.V. Baliga College of
Arts and Science
KUMTA 581 343
(Karnataka)